The
PAUL SIMON
Companion

D1598576

The PAUL SIMON Companion

Four Decades of Commentary

Edited by
STACEY LUFTIG

SCHIRMER BOOKS
An Imprint of
Simon & Schuster Macmillan
New York

Prentice Hall International
London Mexico City New Delhi Singapore Sydney
Toronto

Copyright © 1997 by Schirmer Books

Schirmer Books
An Imprint of Simon & Schuster Macmillan
1633 Broadway
New York, NY 10019

Library of Congress Catalog Card Number: 97-20844

Printed in the United States of America

Printing number
1 2 3 4 5 6 7 8 9 10

Library of Congress Cataloging-in-Publication Data

The Paul Simon companion : four decades of commentary / edited by Stacey
   Luftig.
      p. cm.
   Includes discography (p.   ), filmography (p.   ), bibliographical
references (p.   ), and index.
   ISBN 0-02-864654-1 (alk. paper)
   1. Simon, Paul, 1941– —Criticism and interpretation. I. Luftig, Stacey.
·ML420.S563P38   1997
782.42164'092—dc21   97-20844
                                                                              CIP
                                                                              MN

To Chrissie Donnelley, Paul Simon Fan Extraordinaire, whom I
discovered last year on America Online;

to Michael Benson, who wailed along with me and thousands
of others at the 1991 Paul Simon concert in Central Park;

and to Martha Silano, for the memories of singing harmonies
to "Scarborough Fair," in the summer of '77
on the sunny rooftop of her house in Metuchen, New Jersey,
that are part of my permanent repertoire

Contents

PART TWO: GOING SOLO

PART THREE: GRACELAND

PART FOUR: BRAZIL, BROADWAY, AND BEYOND

Acknowledgments

Grateful thanks to Debra Elfenbein, Steven Goldleaf, and Pat Maniscalco, for providing exactly the help I needed, when I needed it. Thanks also to Ken Blum, Richard Carlin, Kathy Flynn, Heidi Giovine, Lisa Najavits, Jean-Marc Orliaguet, Cindy Strobel, Steven Tabakin, Penny Weingarten, and Paul Zollo.

Introduction

I admit it: I'm a Paul Simon fan. Why else would I spend several months searching library archives, copying endless microfiche, handling yellowing newspaper articles, reading loads of books, and surfing the net, all for details on the man who wrote "Lai la-lai, [crash!], lai la-lai lai lai la-lai"? He moves me with his sounds, with his rhythms. He moves me with his evocative phrases about looking for America and losing love. And odds are good that when I finally get to see his work at the theater (at the time of this writing, Simon is working on a musical), he will move me again with the spectacle he helps to create of sounds, rhythms, phrases, images, and story. I can hardly wait.

All of this is to acknowledge my particular bias in the compilation of this anthology. While I did strive for balance, and occasionally found and included articles that were less than generous, this book on Paul Simon is basically a tribute.

Having said that, however, I want to add that this book is *not* a biography. (For an excellent one, I recommend *Simon and Garfunkel: Old Friends* by Joseph Morella and Patricia Barey, published in 1991 by Carol Publishing Group. I've included my favorite excerpt from that book here in Part One.) Although the book spans the last thirty years or so of Simon's life, and I have tried to represent fairly the main events of his career, what I have amassed is a collection of the most interesting, entertaining, and informative articles, interviews and reviews I could both find and get permission to reprint. To fill in some of the gaps between the articles, I have included a chronology, discography and filmography at the end of this volume.

For the purposes of organizing this book, I divided Simon's career into four periods (thus, the articles are ordered into four parts). The first period is easy to define: it covers the halcyon years of Simon and

Garfunkel. The second period is more arbitrary; it spans the time between the breakup of Simon and Garfunkel and the much-publicized Central Park reunion, plus the writing of *Hearts and Bones*. The reason I call the choice arbitrary is that so many things took place for Simon in those years: experimentation with styles such as reggae, ska, gospel, and Latin rhythms, to name a few; two marriages; writing, scoring, and starring in a film about the music business (*One-Trick Pony*); several television appearances; enormous success; and some failure (though, it's all relative—even *Hearts and Bones,* considered by many to be his least successful album, spent eight weeks on the *Billboard* Top 40).

The main reason, however, that the second period stops where it does is because the third period starts and ends with *Graceland,* the album that revived Simon's career and put him at the center of an international controversy. A decade after the release of this album, it is the issues regarding *Graceland*'s production that still generate the most passion when Simon's name comes up in conversation.

A further comment on *Graceland*: I feel that Simon did South African musicians a great service by helping bring their music to a mass audience, and that he did so in an earnest, honest, and scrupulous attempt to follow his own muse. In trying to present a balanced perspective, however, I searched out articles that would express a tougher stance on Simon's actions. I thought I would find several. Perhaps it's yet another case of bias determining outcome, but what I found, time after time, were criticisms, or referrals to other articles that supposedly contained criticisms, all within articles that, for the most part, came to the same conclusions I did. Well . . . I tried.

The fourth part starts in 1990 with the creation of *The Rhythm of the Saints,* and gives a few glimpses into Simon's current project, *The Capeman.* There is a dearth of published material on this musical-in-progress; however, two interviews conducted by Paul Zollo—excerpted here—do include tantalizing commentary about the show. (For the full interviews with Simon, as well as interviews with other songwriters, see Paul Zollo's book *Songwriters on Songwriting,* forthcoming from Da Capo Books.)

A few other articles I recommend, which I wasn't able to reprint: Ellen Willis's droll review from *The New Yorker* of *Bookends,* including her commentary on the albums that preceded it; Leon Jasper's cutting perspective on *Hearts and Bones* from the *Village Voice*; and the full text of the absorbing *Playboy* interview from 1984, of which I include an excerpt.

As one fan writing to all the rest, I hope you enjoy this book.

Stacey Luftig

Publisher's Note

This book consists of previously published articles, reviews, and interviews, reprinted as they originally appeared. Except for obvious typographical errors, no corrections have been made to them. Lyric citations that originally appeared in some of the articles have been eliminated.

Old

Oddly enough, the music that made Paul Simon famous was not a sort he particularly liked. While Simon considers himself a "rock-'n'-roll kid" whose primary musical influences were '50s R&B, doo-wop groups, Elvis Presley and the Everly Brothers, it was his music with Art Garfunkel, as a "folkie," that first brought him international praise. Part One attempts to provide highlights—and some low points—of that early period of phenomenal success.

In the first article of this collection—a 1967 piece about Simon and Garfunkel from *The New Yorker*—Simon contrasts himself with Bob Dylan. "Our name is honest," says Simon. "If we ever lie, they're going to catch us. I always thought it was a big shock to people when Bob Dylan's name turned out to be Bob Zimmerman. It was so important to people that he should be true."

Simon's critique of Dylan is somewhat ironic in the light of his own recording history. In 1957 Simon recorded his first major hit with Art Garfunkel, "Hey, Schoolgirl," as the second half of the duo "Tom and Jerry." And from 1958 through the early 1960s, he recorded under not one but several fictitious names: True Taylor, Jerry Landis, Tico (of "Tico and the Triumphs"), and in England as Paul Kane. In an excerpt included here from *Simon and Garfunkel: Old Friends,* Joseph Morella and Patricia Barey further expose the story of what, for Paul Simon, is in a name. They also illuminate other inconsistencies between the reality of Simon's life and the image he chose to project.

On the joyous side: Morgan Ames goes into the studio with Simon and Garfunkel in 1967 as they record "Punky's Dilemma," and captures some of the fun, confidence, and camaraderie of that collaboration. Josh Greenfeld, in his article "For Simon and Garfunkel," provides close observations of the duo's career, described through 1968. In her interview for

Rolling Stone, Loraine Alterman draws Simon out on two of the main subjects that subsequent interviewers would plumb: Simon's relationship with Art Garfunkel and Simon's particular process of writing songs. Some reporting from *Rolling Stone* describes the duo's television special that caused considerable controversy in 1970.

Also looking back on the relationship between Simon and Garfunkel is Art Garfunkel himself. In a candid 1990 interview with Paul Zollo, Garfunkel offers his view on what he contributed to Simon and Garfunkel. Record mogul Clive Davis also gives his perspective on the Simon and Garfunkel phenomenon, and how he reacted when the duo split up.

Two reviews conclude Part One: an acerbic critique of Simon's "The Dangling Conversation" from *The 50 Worst Rock 'n' Roll Records of All Times* and Stephen Holden's glowing commentary, best summed up by its title: "Simon and Garfunkel—A Greatest Hits Album That Lives Up to Its Name."

Simon said in a 1973 interview in the *New York Post,* "I like to think of Simon and Garfunkel as the early part of my career." And yes, of course, it was—an early and glorious part. But whether he likes it or not, many fans will continue to remember Paul Simon as the guitar-playing half of the folksinging duo, Simon and Garfunkel.

JAMES STEVENSON
SIMON & GARFUNKEL (1967)

Paul Simon and Art Garfunkel are both twenty-five years old. Paul Simon is short and black-haired. Art Garfunkel is tall and thin and has curly blond hair. When we met them, at a hotel in New Haven late one afternoon not long ago, both were wearing jerseys, Levi's, and low boots. The records of Simon and Garfunkel (including the albums "Parsley, Sage, Rosemary and Thyme" and "Wednesday Morning, 3 A.M.") have sold over six million copies. Their songs—written by Simon, arranged by Garfunkel, and sung by both, with guitar by Simon—form one of the most original and moving bodies of pop music in America. Both Simon and Garfunkel were raised in Kew Gardens Hills and attended Forest Hills High School. Simon graduated from Queens College, and Garfunkel graduated from Columbia, where he is now working toward a Ph.D. in mathematical education.

GARFUNKEL: People who have gone through our kind of experience in pop music are baffled by the role they're in. Only two years earlier, they were fans. The "in" person is not a different cat, but there's a fantastic bombardment of stimuli thrown at you. If you go to work and try to digest them right away, though, the effect will be a kind of growth.

SIMON: Our name is honest. I think if we ever lie, they're going to catch us. I always thought it was a big shock to people when Bob Dylan's name turned out to be Bob Zimmerman. It was so important to people that he should be true. You have to be vulnerable. Then people can see you laid out, and they don't hit, and they know you won't hit them. Every time you drop a defense, you feel so much lighter. There have been times when I've had no defenses, and I felt like I was flying.

GARFUNKEL: I care that what we do is good. A lot of people in pop music are influenced by the fact that you don't have to be good, but I can't do that; I can't help but take it seriously.

SIMON: I think a lot of the praise we've had is really not warranted. If people's standards were higher . . . A lot of the things we've done have been hack. I don't take the title of "poet." It would be a slap in the face of Wallace Stevens to do that. But I see the possibility now that I *could* be one, and that pop music *could* be an art form.

GARFUNKEL: When we were teenagers, we didn't care so much about being good as about being popular. We were real fans of rock 'n' roll. We recorded our first song in one of those booths at Coney Island for twenty-five cents. It was early Alan Freed. We laughed a lot. I used to dig the idea of lists. I'd keep charts of the top forty songs on big sheets of graph paper. Each record was a colored dot on a vertical line. The records became very personal to me; I'd watch a song fall off from No. 2 to No. 7 and then strain to get back up to No. 4. I wish I still had those graphs. I have a real love of facts. Paul and I have different disciplines. I follow the use of logic to an end, rather than the play of ideas. I have very few beliefs. Paul is the opposite—what I call a "divergent thinker." He loves the idea of going off in different directions. The "convergent thinker" takes the facts and thinks the world should make sense. Even as you know it's a dead end, there's a stirring to know: "Is this really right?" The fact that people have so much trouble understanding each other drives me crazy. All I want to do is understand the world. I wonder "How accurately am I reading it?" We had a small hit record in 1956; it was just rock 'n' roll. Then, in 1963, Paul started writing songs—songs that were different. Bob Dylan had opened it up.

I thought Paul's songs were really nice. We made an album for Columbia called "Wednesday Morning, 3 A.M." It had been out for a year, and it wasn't doing anything, so Columbia took one of the cuts, "The Sound of Silence," and overdubbed some background—bass, electric guitar, drums—and released it as a single. In three months, it was an established hit. The music business has taken over now, but teaching is an experience I'd still like to include in my life. Like a trip to Japan. I've been at Columbia for eight years, and I've always been teaching on the side, in my neighborhood. What really excites me is the scientific side of teaching—the lab aspect. Two peoples' brains, and the psychological interaction.

SIMON: After "The Sounds of Silence," the Simon-and-Garfunkel thing just kept going. There was no time to get off. Finally, I said, "This is what I want to do, and I want to do it as well as I possibly can." I'm stimulated to go forward. If I fail, I've got so many ego points I'll never be as paranoid as I was. So—straight ahead, and work! When you find you're in control of your destiny, it's fun. You do things you want to do.

GARFUNKEL: For a long time, I had a real dislike for all aspects of the recording business. The trappings held nothing for me—the fan structure, and that.

SIMON: Interviews are a big danger. An interview is a real ego trip. You have to remember that your opinion is not *important*—it's merely of interest.

GARFUNKEL: I didn't take very well to the stage. To be out, and involved, is not my natural state. When I was in high school, I withdrew a lot. My friends were reduced to one or two. I read a lot, and I played the game of "doing well in school"—maybe by default. My parents never pushed me, or were overly proud, though. I could never accept myself as "one of the gang." Everything I did was cast in the image and perspective of the outsider. I became a sociologist in spirit, an incessant observer. I've got more relaxed onstage, though. It's the impetus of Paul. And singing for large groups increases one's sense of power.

SIMON: I always like to perform, given the proper circumstances—a full house and good sound. I'm in complete control, and I get the pleasure of making music with someone else. When I'm on the stage, I'm up, and happy. I feel like laughing. I'm continually surprised at the response. I never thought we could affect people so much. It's not so much the epiphany for them as the relief. People fear that they're alone. They listen, and they feel what I feel, and they say, "I'm not alone!" The basic approach on the stage is to exaggerate things and make them larger than life. But we're in a time when so much is larger than life. So we take an uncommon approach. I feel you can be effective by being the same size as life, or smaller.

SIMON: Writing is often an excruciating process. I've been working on one song for three months now. In the past, I could go faster, but I wouldn't accept those songs now. Now I say, "No. It's got to be framed right," and I spend months. Every time I pick up the guitar I start on the song. When I go to sleep, I spend half an hour thinking about it. Songs get stagnant, and they turn on me. Lines that were good you begin to discard. I use the guitar. I grab a chord, and then I'm into something. My early songs were derivative. I was influenced by so many people. Elvis Presley influenced me to play the guitar; the Everly Brothers influenced our singing; Bob Dylan . . . Later, these merge with your personality. I use less imagery now, less metaphor. I give you the picture, stretch it, and let you feel it. When your mind is about to turn off, I try and get a word or a line that's different, so you snap back. If I lose the guy, I don't get him back. I want to make the words rich and yet plain—tasteful without being prissy or too delicate. One word can throw it off. It's not poetry. I'm writing sounds that must be sung, and heard sung. I'm conscious of the medium I'm working in. What should be said in a song? What would be better said in an essay? A song is an impression when it's heard only once. Of course, sometimes I make a song purely an impression, like "Feelin' Groovy." I think: Yellow . . . pink . . . blue . . . bubbles . . . gurgle . . . happy. The line "I'm dappled and drowsy"—it doesn't make sense. I just *felt* dappled. Sleepy, contented. The song only runs one minute and twenty-nine seconds, with a long fadeout. When you've made your impression, stop. I don't want the audience to have time to think. It's a happy song, and that's what it was. There's the other kind of song, like "The Dangling Conversation." It's intricately worked out. Every word is picked on purpose. Maybe it's English-major stuff, but if you haven't caught the symbolism, you haven't missed anything, really. You've got to keep people moving. The attention span is very limited. People don't listen carefully. Unless you jolt 'em, it's going to be down the drain. You've got to get the right mixture of sound and words. I write about the things I know and observe. I can look into people and see scars in them. These are the people I grew up with. For the most part, older people. These people are sensitive, and there's a desperate quality to them—everything is beating them down, and they become more aware of it as they become older. I get a sense they're thirty-three, with an awareness that "Here I am thirty-three!" and they probably spend a lot of afternoons wondering how they got there so fast. They're educated, but they're losing, very gradually. Not realizing, except for just an occasional glimpse. They're successful, but not happy, and I feel that pain. They've got me hooked because they are people in pain. I'm drawn to these people, and driven to write about them. In this country, it's painful for people to grow old. When sexual attractiveness is focused on a seventeen-year-old girl, you must feel it slipping away if you're a thirty-three-year-old woman. So you say, "I'm going to stop smoking. I'm going to get a suntan. I'm going on a diet. I'm going to play tennis." What's intriguing is that they are just not *quite* in control of their destiny. Nobody is paying any attention to these people, because they're not crying very loud. I feel a strong affinity with the flower scene. I always think about beautiful people and beautiful fields, and I think about floating through them. People say, "Why don't you split?"—I'm sitting here making a quarter of a million dollars—and "Why live in it?" But I'm really strung out over people. I'm drawn to people; they all know what pain is. I give my money away. I give it in chunks. I'm always trying to run around and patch things up. The ghettos. It's not human to live like that. I met a Puerto Rican acidhead by the Park one day, and he said, "You're Paul Simon," and we talked, and I took him to my apartment. It must have looked like Shea Stadium to him. I said, "I want to lay the Beatles album on him," so I put the earphones on him, and he's flipping out, and I think: Everybody should have what I have. I used to think I was much sharper than everyone else—very aware, perceptive, seeing things. Then, recently, I realized it wasn't true. Everyone's perceptive. Everyone is sensitive and perceptive, and they all know what pain is. I have compassion for that. There's a gentleness and understanding in young people today, and there's only one choice: the human race *must* come to the aid of the human race.

It was now seven o'clock. The evening was cloudy and threatening. Simon and Garfunkel, who were on a concert tour, drove from their New Haven hotel out to the Yale Bowl, where they were scheduled to perform at eight-fifteen. They went out early because Simon wanted to make sure the sound system was right. After parking their car, they walked down a ramp under the Bowl and out onto the football field, near the fifty-yard line. The grass was a brilliant, eerie green under the dark, rainy sky. Carrying Simon's guitars, they walked downfield to one of the end zones, where a stage had been set up. Except for some concert officials and a number of policemen who had gathered at the portals, ready to cope with the huge crowd that was anticipated, the vast stadium was empty. Ten minutes later, Simon climbed onto the stage to test the sound. He stood alone, a slight figure, holding a twelve-string guitar in front of the microphones. He struck the first notes of a song of his called "Homeward Bound," and the sound seemed to leap out and fill the stadium. He began to sing.

He looked up at the rows and rows of empty seats, and then up toward the last row, where Garfunkel, silhouetted against the blustery sky, stood listening.

Then, Garfunkel waved with both arms to Simon, signalling that the sound was fine, and Simon finished the song as Garfunkel came bounding down the concrete steps.

An hour later, the stands had filled with fifteen thousand people, and the concert began.

JOSEPH MORELLA AND PATRICIA BAREY
FROM *SIMON & GARFUNKEL: OLD FRIENDS* (1991)

Tom Wilson, the Columbia Records producer, saw potential in "He Was My Brother." Wilson, who was black, was very moved by the song's message of sympathy for the civil-rights cause. But there was a catch. Wilson was interested in the song for the Pilgrims, a folk group which Columbia was promoting. Paul was disappointed because he didn't want to sell the song for someone else to sing. . . .Simon argued to Wilson that he and his singing partner could do more justice to the material than any other group. Persuaded by the young writer's passion and conviction, Wilson relented and set up a session for Paul and Art to record an audition tape. In what would turn out to be another remarkable stroke of luck, he teamed the boys with recording engineer Roy Halee.

The demo didn't wow the decision-makers at Columbia, but it was good enough for the executives to request a second audition tape. When Simon and Garfunkel returned to the studio the following week, they asked specifically for the engineer in the yellow, oxford-cloth, buttoned-down shirt. They couldn't remember his name, but they had recognized Halee's skill and sensed his enthusiasm for their work. Roy Halee became one of their early champions, and his good opinion helped Wilson convince Columbia to sign the team for an album.

Although it was Paul's song that gained them entry to Columbia, Paul and Art were signed as recording artists, not as songwriters. Columbia was trying to cash in on the folk craze and needed new performers to compete with its rival, Capitol Records. Simon and Garfunkel's album would contain some folk standards, folk songs by other contemporary writers, and a few of Paul's originals.

That was fine with Paul. This was the big time—not a contract for a single on an off-beat label, but a contract for an album to be released by a prestigious and powerful company. Of course, it was also a contract with standard options, and they could be dropped at any time. But for the moment, Paul and Art were euphoric. They would have months to work with top professionals in laying down tracks. Better still, in Paul's view, the album would contain at least four or five original Simon songs.

Paul had recently finished "Bleecker Street," a dark rumination on the hopelessness of skid row, and he showed it to Art. Art found the song's bleak imagery and message "too much," but Paul finally convinced him the song belonged on the album. Together with Wilson, they chose the others, including folk classics like "Peggy-O," "Go Tell It on the Mountain," and "Last Night I Had the Strangest Dream" by Ed McCurdy. Not surprisingly, the trio also chose Bob Dylan's "The Times They Are A-Changin'." Not only were Paul and Art big fans, but Wilson produced Dylan's albums, and Columbia liked to cross-promote its artists and music.

Still, Paul wanted more originals. In November he began struggling with a haunting melody which would become "The Sounds of Silence." Paul had toyed with the idea for this song for years. As a boy, he had played his guitar in the bathroom of his parent's house because he liked the echo effect the tiled room produced. He'd strummed and sung "Hello darkness, my old friend/I've come to talk with you again" a thousand times since then, but that was as far as the song had developed. Simon now focused on that slender thread, and, according to Garfunkel's description, on February 19, 1964, after months of anguish, the rest of the lyric "burst forth." The song "practically wrote itself."

The team needed more original songs for the album, and Paul, always a painfully slow writer, thought a change of scene might accelerate the process. So, in the spring of 1964, he left for Europe, where he was sure he would find inspiration to complete the songs for the album. He knew folk music was popular there, and he planned to support himself singing in clubs, living the life of an itinerant troubadour. In Paris, he met David McLausland who ran a folk club near London. McLausland offered "Paul Kane" a performance date, and he eagerly accepted it.

On the first night he performed at the Brentwood Folk Club, he met a dark-haired girl named Kathy, a secretary from a little town near Essex and a part-time ticket-taker at the club that night. Their attraction for each other was instant. Kathy became his friend, lover, and some say, muse for the next two years.

Shortly after Paul met Kathy, Tom Wilson summoned him back to New York, where pressure was mounting to produce the songs necessary to complete the album. Six months had passed since they'd signed the contract. The change of scene had freed Paul's mental logjam, and he brought back another original song, "Wednesday Morning, 3 A.M." Art contributed "Benedictus," an arrangement of a centuries-old Gregorian chant that he'd researched at libraries in New York. Simon also suggested "The Sun Is Burning," which he'd heard British composer Ian Campbell perform in England, and that gave them the twelve cuts they needed. They laid down the final tracks.

The music complete, they now had to make several other important decisions. For the album title, all quickly agreed on *Wednesday Morning, 3 A.M.* For the cover, they chose a photo of Art and Paul on a gritty New York City subway platform, staring somberly at the camera.

But both Simon and Garfunkel still had reservations about using their real names as performers. They knew enough about the business to realize that being Jewish wouldn't stop them from being recorded, but getting air time, especially in Middle America, might be another matter. Folk music was almost exclusively the domain of all-American types with WASP-sounding names like Woody Guthrie, Pete Seeger, the Kingston Trio, and the New Christy Minstrels. Even Bob Dylan, born Robert Zimmerman, had masked his Jewish heritage by adopting the name of the Welsh poet Dylan Thomas.

Producer Tom Wilson approached the issue from a different perspective. He said, "Why don't we just use Simon and Garfunkel?" Paul reacted strongly. "Hey, man, people might think we're comedians or something!" According to Wilson, Art and Paul feared anti-Semitism would hurt their chances for success. This self-protective attitude outraged the black producer: "What the hell is your music about anyway? You want to be the black man's brother, but you don't want to take any heat." He pointed out that Paul and Art were trying to capitalize on the social and political movements of the day. They wanted to deal with injustice and prejudice—but only in their songs. He was adamant. However, Paul and Art were just as strong-willed. They repeated their concern that people would not buy folk songs sung by two middle-class Jewish men from Queens. The argument raged. "Finally," according to Wilson, "Norman Adler, who was the executive vice president at Columbia Records, slammed his hand down on the table and said, 'Gentlemen, this is 1964. Simon and Garfunkel. Next case.'"

Paul and Art remained uncomfortable about the name change. "He Was My Brother" had been copyrighted under the name of Paul Kane and would be credited to Kane on the album, although all of Paul's other songs were listed as written by P. Simon. The "Benedictus" cut on the album carries the credit: "Arrangement by Simon and Garr."

At the height of Simon and Garfunkel's popularity in the late sixties, Paul commented on the touchy issue: "Our name is honest. I think if we ever lie, they [the fans] are going to catch us. I always thought it was a big shock to people when Bob Dylan's name turned out to be Bob Zimmerman. It was so important to people that he should be true." Coming from a man who employed a series of pseudonyms and would use his own name only because of an executive order by a record company, the criticism seems rather disingenuous.

With the name Simon and Garfunkel finally official, the "new" recording pair was officially launched. All the tracks for their album were completed, and master recording would take place that summer. Meanwhile, "Simon and Garfunkel," the act, was booked into Gerde's [Folk City, a major New York folk club at the time] to gain some exposure for the songs scheduled to be released later that year. Louis Bass, a doorman at the club, remembers the 1964 premiere performance of "The Sounds of Silence." "It was the first time they tested it publicly. At that time, I never thought they would make it. They didn't sounds as good as some of the other acts. But that night at the club was some sort of college reunion, so they went over well because it was their friends."

On the nights audiences were not made up of their friends, Paul's new songs weren't always well received. It wasn't the ethnic sound of their names, but rather their suburban, clean-cut image that was jarring to folk-club audiences. The rather cerebral content of their lyrics, combined with their collegiate appearance, set them apart from traditional folk artists of the mid-sixties.

"Simon and Artie were uptown guys, Queens guys . . . I was struck by a kind of Mickey Mouse, timid contrived side," noted Robert Shelton, who covered the folk scene for the *New York Times*. "And of course through Dylan, [Dave] Van Ronk, all those guys, what was really being venerated was . . . a rough, natural, dirty sound." Shelton knew Simon and Garfunkel from their earliest days as folk performers. According to him, "They sounded very suburban. Simon always struck me as a suburban type of Dylan."

Shelton wasn't the only critic to compare Simon with Dylan and to fault him as a bland imitation of the real thing. Paul was stung by the criticism. He respected Dylan's lyric genius, but in later years he thought critics unfairly ignored his own superior musicianship in the comparison.

With Art busy at school and no major bookings until the album's release, Paul headed back to England. Kathy was waiting there, and he wouldn't have to cope with as many annoying references to Bob Dylan. He took a flat in Hampstead, a London suburb, and continued his solo career as Paul Kane. It was almost summer, and Art had promised to join Paul and Kathy as soon as his semester was over. However, due to his heavy class schedule, he could only manage a brief vacation that summer. Art wrote to Paul about possible bookings but cautioned, "no singing in streets."

While Paul and Art anticipated a summer of fun in Europe, civil-rights workers in America regarded the coming months as a pivotal time in the struggle for human rights. The Student Nonviolent Coordinating Committee (SNCC), an organization made up of black college students, narrowly voted to actively recruit and enlist white, northern college students to aid in their battle against racism. They and the Congress on Racial Equality (CORE) trained thousands of idealistic middle-class students in the techniques of nonviolence and bused them south to begin an intensive voter registration drive.

The movement focused its efforts in Mississippi, a state that epitomized the worst of the nation's racial sins. If SNCC could topple the racist political monopoly in Mississippi by registering black voters, its leaders reasoned the rest of the South would follow suit.

Tensions escalated, and the issue would soon inflame the country. Up to this time Paul and Art were too busy with their careers to take much notice of the ominous developments, but the situation would soon gain Simon's full attention.

In June 1964, Simon's former college classmate Andrew Goodman was one of three men slain near Philadelphia, Mississippi, during a voter registration drive. Paul later described his reaction: "I was in the American Express office in Paris. I had to walk outside. I was going to throw up. I felt dizzy. I was so panicked, so frightened, I couldn't actually believe that anybody I knew was dead."

Paul Simon has led people to believe he wrote "He Was My Brother" after Goodman's death. Regarding Goodman's murder, he has been directly quoted, "It hit me really hard. And that's when I wrote, I guess, my first serious song, 'He Was My Brother.'"

In fact, Paul had already released the song in England on the Oriole label under the name Paul Kane, and it had become a staple of his folk-club repertoire. "He Was My Brother" was also the song which first caught the attention of producer Tom Wilson in the fall of 1963. Paul may have rewritten the lyric later for Goodman. The Columbia album cut, which would not be released until the fall in the States, says, "This town's gonna be your buryin' place," but in later versions of the song the line reads "Mississippi's gonna be your buryin' place."

Paul kept up a busy pace playing folk clubs and appearing at the Edinburgh and Cambridge folk festivals. Between classes, Garfunkel, too, was working as a solo act in New York clubs, singing Paul's songs and other folk ballads. He finally finished the year at Columbia University, and since he was available in New York, he oversaw the album's master recording. He battled with record executives to keep a harmonica accompaniment to "He Was My Brother," but lost the fight. The song was released with a simple guitar background in the classic folk mode.

As soon as school was over, Art met Paul in Paris, and for a while they rented motor scooters and became carefree tourists. It was the fulfillment of every middle-class collegian's dream: to have the time and money to explore Europe with a best friend. They shared expectations for a future brimming with creative endeavors, public recognition, and financial reward. And their personal friendship continued to deepen.

MORGAN AMES
SIMON & GARFUNKEL IN ACTION (1967)

A record date for Simon and Garfunkel's forthcoming album took place recently at Columbia's recording studios on 52nd Street at 11:00 p.m. The moment one enters the building it's apparent why the two prefer recording at this hour. The roaring pressure of daytime activity has left a quiet but animated residual atmosphere for the off-hour minority to enjoy. One is able to hear the neat sound of his own footsteps leading to the sound-proofed door of Studio E. Inside the control booth the air of intimacy continues: a chosen few gathered in an empty place at an unlikely hour with the good intentions of producing something exciting. The booth is lit adequately, but not brightly. Roy Halee, the efficient, loyal, and enthusiastic engineer who has worked with Simon and Garfunkel since their first record date, is talking softly with Lou Waxman, another technician. Producer John Simon is slouched, reading a newspaper. Paul Simon, in jeans (neither tailored, cut to the hip, nor belled at the ankle) and cardigan sweater, and Art Garfunkel, in utilitarian denims and shirt, are conversing with disc jockey Murray the K (dressed in Aging-Boy Mod: pinch-waisted suit, boots, long hair conquered with greasy kid stuff) and his wife Jackie (mini-skirt, sweater, high white boots, and Bardot-styled wig). In a corner are Paul Simon's younger brother Eddie, a disturbingly flawless reproduction of Paul, and his girl friend. Mort Lewis, Simon and Garfunkel's towering, pleasant-mannered manager, arrives a little later. No one else. Though everyone is on time, work starts late. To those familiar with the tension of most pops recording sessions, tonight's mood is remarkable: warm, relaxed, confident.

Finally work begins. The song is called *Punky's Dilemma,* an outpouring of Simon's peculiar brand of whimsey, written for Mike Nichols' forthcoming film, *The Graduate.*

The track is made in layers. First Simon's guitar, then his voice. Later he'll repeat his vocal line, overdubbing it to add body. Simon, who has stopped smoking for the occasion, wants to set his vocal line down before Garfunkel sings, so he can have a cigarette. Garfunkel, who's going through a nonsmoking phase, agrees. They prefer working in that order anyway. The depth of their friendship is evident in the way they work together. Because Garfunkel only sings and does vocal arranging while Simon does the writing, guitar playing, and lead singing, one might think it's primarily Simon's show—until one sees their creative interdependence on a record date.

A glass enclosure and speakers enable Garfunkel to listen from the booth as Simon sings his part in the studio. After the take, Garfunkel flips the intercom switch connected to a speaker in the studio. "Try it again, Paul. I think your feeling was a little better the last time. But your intonation is fine now."

"No, it wasn't," remarks producer John Simon in the booth once the intercom switch is off.

"I know," says Garfunkel. The team's working relationship is built upon listening to each other, asking advice, taking it, building each other's morale. Though it's obvious they enjoy working with John Simon, the last word seems to come from one partner to the other.

"It's no good right now, Art," says Simon after the take. "I'm not into it. Let's work on the other parts and I'll come back to it."

The skeletal guitar track is played over and over. Producer John Simon adds some chords played on a toy piano, the kind sold in variety stores. Whistling is added, then finger-snapping. Between takes, Garfunkel enters the booth from the studio to discuss with the producer the feeling he wants on the finger-snapping. "It has to be light, almost not there."

Work continues slowly. Simon wants more nonmusical sounds dotted into the track, "personality fills." Simon, Garfunkel, John Simon, and Roy Halee go into the studio and the search for usable objects begins. Maraches? No, not right. Coat hangers on vibes? Maybe. Ashtrays? Mmmm. How about a trombone? John Simon, all-purpose producer, sinks onto a bench and plays a trombone as the track is piped into the studio. Sticks on gourd? Yeah, that's nice. Brushes on tambourine head? Maybe . . . yeah. Paul Simon sweeps brushes across the tambourine, which is lying on a handy set of vibes. "We look like we're making mud-pies," he says.

Ideas are tried, accepted, rejected. Time passes. Too much time. Too little headway. "Come on, Paul, " says Garfunkel. "I'm interested in accomplishing something."

"So? I'm not fooling around."

Halee and John Simon return to the booth. In the studio, Garfunkel turns out the lights while Simon puts on headphones. They like to record in the dark. They can see us in the booth. We can't see them. "Where are the candles?" says one voice in the studio.

"I don't know," says the other. "Somebody forgot them."

"What do you want to do?" says John Simon over the intercom.

"Play the track, as much as we've got," says Simon. "Art and I are gonna try something."

"Okay, Lou," John Simon signals the second technician, and the track cuts in. The producer sighs. He's in a peculiar position. On one hand, he's playing foreign ambassador and liaison man for Columbia's brass, who understand little about Simon and Garfunkel except that they're personable and they sell a lot of records. On the other hand, he's working with two artists he enjoys personally and musically, who set their own pace. On a third, impatient hand, he's producing a record—and after nearly four hours, nothing has been accomplished.

Studio time is money. What causes tension on most record dates is the struggle to make maximum use of limited time through intense concentration. Simon and Garfunkel do not subscribe to the economy theory.

The price they are paying for the relaxed atmosphere of this date is, in Maxwell Anderson's words, a plentiful waste of time. *Punky's Dilemma* is not going well. On a previous session, outside musicians were used to supply a background track, over which Simon and Garfunkel would later add vocals and sound effects. Exercising his artistic control, Simon rejected the track on the grounds that there had been a communication problem with the musicians; they hadn't gotten the feeling he wanted. Now, after four hours' work, he realizes that his lone guitar is not enough backing. He'll need an outside rhythm section after all. Success came young and early to Simon and Garfunkel. It is likely that further work and the passing of time will equalize the discrepancy between artistic control and lack of experience. Simon is stubborn, but he's too intelligent to make the same four-hour mistake again in the same way.

Punky's Dilemma is put aside for the moment and Simon begins work on the title song for the new album, "Bookends." John Simon is in the studio playing the piano along with Simon's guitar, forming ideas for an arrangement. There is an instinctive beat of silence after the song, though this is not a take. Suddenly John Simon turns and says, "That could be a smash, Paul, as a single, if only you could expand it another verse. . . ."

Paul Simon sits in surprised silence. Then he sighs. "I know."

Instant laughter everywhere.

"I think," the producer continues, "it's stronger even than *Punky's Dilemma* for a single."

Paul smiles slowly. *"Stronger than Punky's Dilemma?"*

Tension breaks. Everyone is laughing.

At 3:00 a.m., John Simon departs. Simon and Garfunkel stay on, with Roy Halee, to try some new things. There are several hours yet before the regular employees begin to file into the Columbia building.

So it wasn't the most fruitful night in the world. So? They're riding the crest of a fat wave, and they know it. They're more than temporally talented, and they know that too. Success and talent give them great pleasure. It is visible in their composure. As for rock-and-roll, folk-rock, hippie-rock, flower-power, new-pop, all this is best described as the money game of the moment. But when its enormous money-making power fades (as it must, because it's the music of youth; and tomorrow's children will never accept the kicks of their staid, grown-up brothers and sisters), only the best of the period will survive. That's the rule of the game: when a style is in its heat, even its worst progeny sell as well or better than its best. But afterward, when the game has soured, the giftless herd dies. Nothing in life will hold up an outmoded style except an overwhelming talent. Simon and Garfunkel live in a steeple that will remain standing if they want it to stand, when the floods of popular fancy wash over their children's kingdom, down below.

"We'll do something else when we're tired of pop," says Simon. "Art'll teach. I'll be in his class."

Money? "That game is over."

JOSH GREENFELD
FOR SIMON AND GARFUNKEL (1968)

Camera drives along twisting Berkshire road, turns into long gravel-topped driveway leading to manorial estate. Long shot of main house, rolling lawn, gardener's house, marble-lipped swimming pool.

Cut to interior: Huge parlor floor entrance hall. Pan to high-ceilinged sitting rooms, book-lined library, Laotian-silk-screen-hung grand dining room.

Camera enters serving pantry where housekeeper is setting drinks upon tray; follows tray as it is carried out onto long L-shaped screened-in veranda.

Long shots of Tavel-colored sun, of tree-line shadows softly falling across lawn on a lazy late afternoon.

Close-up of tray of drinks framed through legs of departing housekeeper.

Cut to point of view: two young men relaxing harmoniously on white wicker patio furniture.

First young man is short, broad-shouldered, schoolyard-athletic. His hair is combed forward Roman style; he wears a thin neatly trimmed reddish beard. He looks like a reporter for an underground newspaper, a Sorbonne revolutionary, an Israeli N.C.O.

Second young man is taller, thinner, high-holiday-choir-boy ethereal. His thick curly blond hair churns upward, his eyes are a soft grayish blue. There is about him the air of a young and sober Harpo Marx, a boyish Paul O'Dwyer, a Jewish Van Cliburn.

FIRST YOUNG MAN: What do I want to do with myself now? What do I want to do with my life? What's to become of me? (He laughs with self-mockery.) Man, I really don't know.

SECOND YOUNG MAN: I'm more confused than I've ever been. I sense all the infinite alternatives, the endless possibilities. It's all so liberating and terrifying.

They sip their drinks, waiting for the sunset, silently, old friends sharing the same fear. . . .

If Paul Simon and Arthur Garfunkel, the short and the tall of Simon and Garfunkel, seemed hung-up, suffering their generational malaise, recently when I was a camera visiting them at Paul Simon's rented vacation home in Stockbridge, Mass., theirs was indeed a special—and splendid—alienation, attenuated and assuaged by runaway success. In the past three years their five record albums ("Wednesday Morning, 3 A.M.," "Sounds of Silence," "Parsley, Sage, Rosemary and Thyme," "Bookends," and their original sound track for "The Graduate") have sold more than 6,000,000 copies. Their sound—a soft and cool tenor and counter-tenor madrigal-like harmony to the accompaniment of a single rock guitar—has been acclaimed by modern B's as diverse as Leonard Bernstein ("They are inventive and poetic") and the Beatles (Ringo Starr: "We admire them. I play their albums all the time"). Their message—one of literate protest against the pangs of youth, the pathos of old age and the matter-of-fact hypocrisies of the middle-aged and the middle class in between—seems to have transcended the communications breakdown, bridged the generation gap, broken through the usual establishment and anti-establishment lines; *Time* and the *Village Voice, Crawdaddy* and *The New Yorker,* for example, have all issued similar paeans in praise of their smooth articulations. Operating on such a broad basis of appeal it is small wonder they have become one of the two top attractions in the pop-music concert field (Herb Alpert and his Tijuana Brass is the other), earning as much as $50,000 for a single hard night's work. Their joint income for this year—with about two-thirds going to Simon who writes all of their songs and lyrics and thus earns additional royalties—will approach $2-million.

"So you see, I'm 26 years old," Simon said, "and I've already won a game—the money game or success game or whatever you want to call it. I mean I'm fixed for life if that's all I want out of life. But man, I know there are other things than being successful: I just hope I have enough drive to leave *off* being successful."

"Even operating on an over-spend theory in regard to money—which would be like an over-kill theory in regard to weapon stockpiling," agreed Garfunkel, who is also 26 years old, "we've already earned more money than we could possibly need for the rest of our lives. So the money and success races are something we're not only out of, but can stomp upon."

Simon and Garfunkel, cool and detached as philosopher-kings with tenure, represent most of the large changes and small revolutions that have taken place in the white pop music world during the last 20 years. White pop music (pop music, like so much else in America, has long been divided into black and white areas) was always assumed to be the tribal drum upon which white youth could beat out its frustrations and issue forth its major communications. However, the communications traditionally were restricted to those dwelling on love and the frustrations to those dealing with an unrequitedness in that department.

By the late nineteen-forties it became apparent that the prevailing white pop musical monologue had become as artificially sweetened and as unnecessarily overdecorative as a wedding cake for diabetics: almost literally the gooey genre was ready for insults. And in the fifties vitality would be restored by two distinct—but not totally dissimilar—injections. First, the rhythm and blues sound, long a staple of black pop music, was appropriated by white performers and called rock 'n' roll. Second, folk music, long the domain of city radicals and country rubes, was discovered to have a broad mass capability.

Since the guitar was the instrument common to both folk music and rock 'n' roll, it was inevitable that their strains would merge. It was also inevitable that this merger would take place under electronic auspices. For times were changing technologically, too. In the old pop-music world each recording was an attempt to duplicate faithfully the master performer's voice; no one ever dreamed that the medium could be used any more imaginatively, just as early moviemakers seldom thought of trying anything more venturesome than to stimulate renderings of actual stage plays. But then at the end of World War II, with the invention first of recording wire, then tape, the recording medium finally got its own message: it need not only record passively, it could enhance actively; it need not only duplicate, it could create. New effects in sound were produced, tracks were mixed, the engineer became an artistic partner.

Simon and Garfunkel are not without their critics. The veteran jazz-and-bop-music critic Nat Hentoff finds them "a dead end, a cul-de-sac"; the young rock writer, Richard Goldstein, complains of their "Ivy League ennui." *Esquire*'s Robert Christgau dismisses them as "second-hand": "Just as *The Graduate* was a youth movie for people who aren't young,

Simon and Garfunkel are rock 'n' roll for people who don't like rock 'n' roll." And Irwin Silber, former editor of *Sing Out* and currently cultural affairs editor of the *National Guardian,* does not like their "co-opting of protest": "I object to the illusion that anyone can promote revolution on Columbia Records." But these same critics also find Simon and Garfunkel's music "groovy" (Silber), "harmonic and melodic" (Christgau), "delicate" (Goldstein) and "pleasant and refreshing" (Hentoff).

* * *

"This place belongs to a former ambassador," said Simon, showing off his vacation estate. "I was looking for a much smaller place. But when the real-estate agent showed me this, I thought, ridiculous. But then I decided, why not? I'll take it. And man, it's been a ball." He paused before a mantle laden with autographed pictures of Presidents and Secretaries of State: Truman, Eisenhower, Johnson, Kennedy; Acheson, Dulles, Herter, Rusk. "Before I leave here," he said, "I'm going to slip in a picture of Lenny Bruce."

Back in the city Paul Simon lives on the upper East Side, a block away from Mayor Lindsay's Gracie Mansion, in a high-rise apartment overlooking the river. Except for a bright rose-orange carpeting and a giant wooden hobby horse ("I wanted to blow some money on a useless luxury") the two-room apartment is nondescript, antiseptically modern.

"I don't like to waste time on food, clothing, shelter, possessions—I don't even own a car," he explained. "Anyway, I don't have much relationship to my money. Like the first year we hit the bigs I remember writing an income tax check for $125,000. Last year it was over $300,000. This year I'm not even looking. I get an allowance of $75 cash a week from my business manager and I have a stack of credit cards.

"I get all sorts of arguments about marriage, pros and cons, from my accountant and business manager. It seems I can save a lot of money by getting married, but I can blow a lot if I make a marriage that goes wrong. But girls are no problem: *they* don't bug me about marriage. And I don't have to prove anything to myself—or anybody else—anymore."

When Simon is working at song writing he rises at 9 o'clock, "or 10 o'clock if I got to bed real late," breakfasts on toast and coffee, "and I like bacon, but not if I have to make it myself."

"And once I start on a project I never let up: I pace about the living room. I look over the river. I play some licks on the guitar. Or else—I'll just go off to the Cloisters and sit there and think. I always work on the music first because I like to think that I'm stronger in words, that they come easier. But I'm not a poet. And I'm not a musician. I mean like I'm an anachronism as a composer. Pop music is so far behind the rest of music. Like Dylan certainly isn't a musician. And The Beatles technically aren't musicians: they're not virtuosos on their instruments.

"And about being a poet: I've tried poetry but it has nothing to do with my songs. And I resent all the press-agentry. But the lyrics of pop songs are so banal that if you show a spark of intelligence they call you a poet. And if you say you're not a poet then people think you're putting yourself down. But the people who call you a poet are people who never read poetry. Like poetry was something defined by Bob Dylan. They never read, say, Wallace Stevens. That's poetry.

"But poetry is a different bag from writing lyrics. The limitations are different. Like when you write songs you have to throw out your best lines and use instead lines that make it better with the melody. And the compactness of a song appeals to me. I'd certainly rather perform a song than read a poem: I like to feel it all on my fingers.

"But I still spend a lot of time on lyrics. I try to avoid clichés—not always successfully. But I don't try to say anything I think the kids want to hear. You can't do anything real that way. I try to take an emotion or feeling I've had and capture it in one incident. And I don't worry about it entertaining—not boring—an audience; that comes first. Whatever else I get: great. If people see it my way: great. But I don't write for anybody else's feelings, or to convince them of my point of view."

Simon looks upon the success of Simon and Garfunkel as somewhat a natural phenomenon, even though he regards most of the implications as absurd: "I do write good songs, we sing well, we sing in tune—a lot of groups can't sing in tune. But so much of Simon and Garfunkel is fictitious. I mean, Simon and Garfunkel are fictitious characters. For example, how can anyone have a joint identity with anyone else? And there's a big difference between me and the Simon of Simon and Garfunkel. He's a song writer and performer and so am I but otherwise he's a fictitious character.

"I can realize this most clearly when I look at Artie, and I look at this fictitious character called Garfunkel. Can you imagine girls all over the country writing love letters to someone called Garfunkel? Or chicks spending the cold winter nights up in New England towns stitching 'Garfunkel' on a pillow? Man, the whole idea of people accepting Garfunkel as a sex symbol. Can't you picture it? Someone in Hollywood saying, 'Get me a new sex symbol like Garfunkel.' Or people accepting our name; it's like the greatest put-on: Some music publisher or agent gets on the phone and says: 'Bring me something for Simon and Garfunkel.' Man, it's funny.

"Right now it's all kicks and one day it'll stop being kicks and we'll stop. Anyway in pop music if you have five years that's extraordinary. And we've had three already . . . Man, I don't know about the future. Maybe I'll even get married—if that romantic notion doesn't get knocked over."

The contributions of Garfunkel to Simon and Garfunkel are not always clearly apparent. He is the arranger of credit on their albums; he is generally acknowledged to be the better singer of the two—even by Simon's Jewish mother ("Paul has a nice voice, but Artie has a better one"), a judgment with which Simon agrees. But perhaps Garfunkel's most important roles and functions are performed in that vague, gray area in which tenuous creations and interpretations are spawned and nourished. For the close harmony of Simon and Garfunkel derives out of a complete musical interdependence: they listen to each other carefully, then advise and criticize, praise and goad, coach and direct each other.

This is most evident at a recording session where a track is made in layers: for example, first Simon's guitar, next his voice; then his voice might be repeated, overdubbed to add fullness, before Garfunkel is scheduled to set down his vocal line. But all the while, Garfunkel is in the glass-enclosed booth rejecting takes, suggesting changes in intonations, approving or disapproving of Simon's "feeling." Their working relationship at a recording sessions is compared by Eddie, Simon's knowledgeable younger brother, to that of a well-attuned baseball battery: "Paul works a record like a pitcher who's working a batter. And Artie's like the smart catcher who knows just what to call for."

At the end of last summer Simon and Garfunkel gave two concerts back to back at the Forest Hills Music Festival, a few miles from the neighborhood in which they grew up. For their weekend's work they received $100,000. As a chauffeur-driven Cadillac limousine carried them over the

Triborough Bridge to the first concert, Simon reminisced: "A couple of years ago we played Forest Hills. We were the opening act for The Mamas and the Papas. We came in a Volkswagen." Soon the limousine drove past a catering hall: "Imagine, I bet they're playing 'Mrs. Robinson' at bar mitzvahs. It gets me right here," he slapped his heart. "'Mrs. Robinson,'" he laughed, "what kind of name is that for a song, anyway. It's what you call a neighbor, not a song."

The limousine stopped in front of the ticket office. Mort Lewis stepped out for a moment and then returned, happily reporting: "Not a ticket. Scalpers are getting $12 for $6 seats."

A cordon of police waved the limousine by, gates swung open, and it parked behind the Forest Hills Tennis Stadium center court. Across a sea of tennis courts was the Tudor-looking Forest Hills Inn.

Simon with the help of the chauffeur carried three guitars on stage. He tuned them and began to test the sound levels of each of the three microphones that had been set up. He sang and played while Garfunkel roamed through the stands, signaling back when the sound was right, shaking his head vigorously when he thought it was off. When they were both satisfied with the adjustments the technicians made, they went back stage to the trailer that would serve as their dressing room.

Some visitors stepped in: One was Jerry Garfunkel, Artie's 23-year-old brother who is a math teacher. He was asked if Artie had changed with success. "Just got richer," he said quietly. "But that's a lot."

Lou Simon, the moon-faced bespectacled father of Paul, knocked on the trailer door. He had brought a Julian Bream record at Simon's request. Simon gave it to a stage manager to play on the amplifying system. "Let the crowd hear some good music," he said.

Soon it was dark, the stadium was full. Simon changed from one horizontal-barred T shirt into another. Garfunkel took off a white shirt and put on a brightly vertical-striped, open-collared sport shirt. The house lights dimmed and a spot picked out the entrance to the stage, the flaps of a canvas tent-like backdrop.

Simon entered, vamping under the applause. Then came Garfunkel, walking as if he had just gotten off a subway train at the wrong stop. The applause became thunderous. Simon kept vamping under it, and then, as it faded, they began the concert.

After the first song, "Cloudy," Simon leaned into the microphone confidentially: "Let's dedicate this next song to the idiot who's running for Vice President. What's his name? Agnew."

The audience laughed and he and Garfunkel sang "Looking for America."

The audience was young, white and wholesome-looking. During intermission I circulated, asking many of the members of the audience why they had come, why they dug Simon and Garfunkel. The answers: "They have a good sound, nice and peaceful." "They get their points across." "They don't talk down to us." "They show us the way today really is." "They're not afraid to contrast the good things with the bad things."

At the end of the concert, the audience applauded entreatingly for encores. Producer Leonard Ruskin signaled his electrician not to put up the house lights. But after three encores Simon and Garfunkel took their final bows. "I don't understand it. I can't understand these kids," Ruskin mopped his brows. "I've had guys like Sinatra and Sammy Davis Jr. here. They stay on all night when they get a house like this. These guys are getting 50 G's and they go off right away."

In the trailer Garfunkel sat shaking his head: "This was one of our worst shows." Simon shrugged, "It wasn't so bad. It wasn't so good, but it wasn't so bad." And soon they were holding court before the trailer like high school athletes after a football game: there were their parents, neighbors, teachers, a flock of remember-me people. It was a kind of old home week, a reunion, a local-boys-make-good scene and it lasted well over an hour.

Finally the limousine reappeared. A pretty, long-legged, red-headed girl suddenly seemed to materialize, and she sat down alongside of Garfunkel and looked at him. He nodded. And soon the car was Manhattan bound.

I mentioned the rather dramatic absence of blacks in the audience. "Sure," said Simon. "We talk about communicating, they worry about eating. The number of blacks at our concerts is less than one per cent, I'd say. Same with the Beatles. But what do they need us for? They have Aretha Franklin and she's the greatest."

As we reached Manhattan the talk turned to drugs. "I made LSD," said Simon. "But I had one bad trip. Liquor is better for social purposes: it sloshes people together. Drugs lock people apart."

Garfunkel and the red-head were dropped at his house. Then Simon, Lewis and I went to an East Side delicatessen. "I should have planned something," said Simon. "Maybe I should have stayed in Queens. Maybe

I'll drive up to Stockbridge. Maybe I'll go down to the Village. After a concert I always feel so funky and groovy. But, man, I just don't know what I feel like doing now."

LORAINE ALTERMAN
PAUL SIMON (1970)

Paul Simon arrived wearing a blue loden coat with the hood pulled up. Beneath it he had on black trousers and a black shirt. He does not seek attention.

He said he preferred to talk at my apartment, his was on East End Avenue, but, you know . . . he was looking for a brownstone and would be moving shortly anyway. . . . In fact, his other place, a farmhouse in Bucks County, was no longer secluded enough. He was thinking of getting something up in New England, way out in the woods.

Simon spoke slowly, phrasing each answer carefully, almost painfully, repeating points he wanted to emphasize. He normally doesn't talk to the press, he said. He prefers to communicate in his songs. He likes to feel interviewers out, see where *they* are at. Then, if it's OK, he relaxes. It's the same way he likes to work in the studio, going over things again and again, until they are right.

At first he sat hunched up in his coat, looking smaller than he really is. (He is sensitive about his size.) Later, as he talked about his part-time teaching career—he conducts a once-a-week class in songwriting at N.Y.U.—he grew more easy and seemed to begin to actually expand. He goes to the same analyst as his friend, Elliot Gould, he revealed, but he has cut down his visits from four to three times a week. . . .

Why has it been 14 months between 'Bookends' and 'Bridge Over Troubled Water'?

It was a combination of circumstances. In this case Artie went and did the film *Catch-22* and that delayed the album about six months. And then since we're not a band and we produce everything that we do, we have to divide our time. So I write the songs for a certain period of time. Let's say it take me four months or five months to write ten or twelve songs. Then it takes about another four months to record them. We don't have the benefit of rehearsing before we go in because we use studio players. So it takes that long to record. Then it takes another couple of months to mix it. After doing that it takes a couple of months to calm down and then you start all over again. Some people work at a slower pace, that's all.

Did you have a producer in the beginning?

Tom Wilson did *Wednesday Morning* and then Bob Johnston did the *Sounds of Silence* and *Parsley Sage* albums.

So 'Bookends' was the first one you produced yourselves?

Well, *Bookends* was the first one that had our names down as producers, but really most artists know what they're doing and they don't need anybody. I didn't need a producer to say here's a good piece of material to do. And I didn't need someone to say that's the take or somebody to say it's the wrong tempo. Columbia Records just assigned a producer and we just took it, that's all.

At what point does Art enter into how you decide to record a song?

Artie's there from the earliest. We decide generally what the arrangements will be—whether it will be a simple rhythm track or strings or horns, or in the case of "Bridge Over Troubled Water," even though I wrote it on the guitar, I always knew that I wanted it played on the piano. So we had to work with that.

In the studio we usually work with the same musicians each time and we're very friendly with them. I play the song and everybody plays along with me. Artie works with Roy [Halee, their engineer] in the control room or comes outside and says that this isn't making it or this is making it or try to change this or that. He has the ears that are listening inside and we're outside so we have it covered. And then we put a track down and after the track is down, we put a vocal down.

Do you overdub the vocals?

We usually do that because it's very difficult to get a separation when you play an acoustical guitar. When you play an electric guitar and the amp is way across the room, you can sing and the sound of guitar comes from the amp. But if you play and sing the acoustic guitar, it's right there and very difficult to get a separation between the voice and the guitar. Most of the time we record the guitar in stereo. There's three mikes on the guitar and the guitar lays across all the speakers.

On the new album the songs are about different topics and the moods are varied too. There doesn't seem to be one particular thing that you as a writer are trying to get across.

It's fun to do all different kinds of songs. I tend towards always wanting to write slow, simple songs. That comes easiest to me. I like to try writing in other styles just for the fun of it, just to see what will happen when I do that. We didn't set out consciously to do an album of all different songs, but it became apparent somewhere about midway that the songs were very different. Tempos were different, instrumentation was different; I think that's good, I enjoy that.

Did you have all the songs done when you started recording?

No, we had about half of them done. We go from there. In a certain sense I would balance the album, like I'd say I have a lot of uptempo songs. I need a ballad. So working in the studio I would think that when I write I have to do a ballad. Then I wrote "Bridge Over Troubled Water" and that took care of the ballad situation. I'd say now I have a good ballad, it would be nice to have something else.

Many people have noticed a great similarity between "Bridge Over Troubled Water" and the Beatles' "Let It Be." Did you notice this?

That was interesting to me that we both wrote these songs that were very similar. The first time I heard "Let It Be" I couldn't believe that he did that. They are very similar songs, certainly in instrumentation, sort of in their general musical feel, and lyrically. They're sort of both hopeful songs and resting peaceful songs. He must've written it about the same time that I wrote mine and he gave it to Aretha Franklin which is funny because when I first wrote "Bridge," I said boy, I bet Aretha could do a good job on this song. It's one of those weird things and it happened simultaneously.

Do you write a lot of songs that you don't use on your albums?

I have about four songs that I haven't used on this album, but usually I use everything I write.

Does that mean that you write only when you are going to record and do an album or do you also write just for the sake of writing? Do you feel a certain need at times to express yourself and therefore write songs whether you have an album coming up or not?

Well, I write songs up until I have enough for an album, then I record it. Then I wait awhile and that's the way it goes. I'm not writing right now because I have no nails. I broke my nails.

What do your nails have to do with writing?

Well, if I don't have my nails I can't play the guitar.

What if you suddenly get inspired for a song?

I did; just the other night I was suddenly inspired.

What happened without any nails?

I had no nails. I couldn't do it. Someone else got that song that I was meant to write that night.

You could write a song without the guitar.

I'm looking forward to my nails growing in.

Has there been one main preoccupation in your songs?

No, it changes with my mental state.

One theme that ran through some of your songs was the failure of communication between people.

I think that ended about two years ago. You know one of the things that happens with us since we don't put out a lot of albums, the albums tend to last a long time. People listen to them as if they were current. If somebody were to buy *Parsley, Sage, Rosemary & Thyme* today they'd be buying an album that was released three years ago and made almost three and a half years ago. Some of the songs on that were written before that.

What are you concerned with now?

Now I'm concerned with writing nice songs.

What are nice songs?

Just a song that touches something or it's funny or it's sad or it has a nice melody or it has a good line. One of the most important things in popular music for me is songs, not styles. It's not important to me whether I'm writing acid rock, which was the big thing whenever it was. Now the Band is on the cover of Time Magazine and they call it country rock or raga rock. Anything like that is not important; the only thing that matters is the songs. After acid rock has come and gone, offhand I can think of "White Rabbit" which came out of that. That was a pretty good song, just as "Somebody To Love" was a pretty good song. Dino Valente's tune was a pretty good song and that's what's left. If a song lives for a couple of years then that's a pretty good thing.

Is that what you're writing for then, for your songs to live a couple of years?

Well, I would be pleased if something lived longer than a couple of years, but I think if something lasts like three or four years and people still like it or get enjoyment out of hearing it, then you've done a nice thing.

So people should be able to remember the song and hum it?

Right. That would be great if they would. I get no greater pleasure than to walk down the street and hear somebody humming a melody that I wrote. That's really gratifying if you hear that.

On the 'Bookends' album you have that song about going out in search of America, and your TV show examined America, too. Are you concerned with getting a certain message across in certain songs you write? I don't want to use the word protest, but do you feel it necessary to comment about the way things are here?

I don't really think it is necessary to point out what is going on because everybody knows that. You see it on television and you read it in the papers and you see it in the streets and you hear it everywhere you go. So if you live in this society you reflect it naturally when you write. That's what happens and it's not that I'm trying to say, "Hey, look at this. Wake up." Everybody's woken up. We're right in the middle of a nightmare; everybody is wide awake. It's not that message. I'm just writing the way I feel and the way I feel reflects the part of society that I'm in. It's not a teaching thing or I'm not trying to hip somebody to something they don't know because everybody knows that.

Most people think of you more in terms of your lyrics than of melody, but the way you've been talking it seems as if the melody is more important to you.

They're both important because you need them both to make a song. I think that it's easier work to write a melody for me. It's more enjoyable; it happens in an instant. And the lyrics I tend to work over. I say I like that line, now I'm going to go from here and I'm going to see where this line will lead me because I don't know what I'm talking about when I start off. So until I write a few more lines I have no idea what I'm writing about. Then once I realize what I'm writing about then I start to work on the lyric, a change of word here or there. But the melody—that happens. It was as if I were to hear a new Simon & Garfunkel record on the air that I never heard before.

It's like Artie used to say. He used to go into record stores and ask if they had the new Simon & Garfunkel album. He'd just stick his head in. A lot of the time he'd feel so detached he'd be waiting for it to come out even though he'd know that there was no album coming out. He'd just look in just to see maybe it would be there, would be a surprise to him. He wanted to see what the cover looked like. Well that's what happens when you write this melody because it's just such a surprise. It never happened before and here it is.

Does the melody then suggest what your lyrics will say?

Sometimes. Usually I write a melody and a lyric, but it's a line. I write a melody and a lyric line. Now if you're writing a song that's like an A-A-B-A type song, verse-verse-refrain-verse, once you write the melody for the first verse, you know it's the melody for the second verse but the lyrics change. You have to write three different lyrics in an A-A-B-A song on the structure of the verse, but the melody is the same so you get that instantly and you see the whole structure of the song. Now the lyric has to take me probably a lot longer.

You told me that you keep tapes of your songs from the first time you work on them and you can see how the lyrics change.

Melodies change, too. I heard a tape, the first tape I did of "The Only Living Boy In New York" the other day and it was really interesting. There was a lot of things that I forgot, that I left that were better the first time. The first time you sing anything, you're so fresh that every-thing just flows naturally. When you get into a recording studio—if you do a take ten times or 15 times or for a week or a month, depending on your standards, one of the things that you sacrifice is spontaneity. Unfortunately that's one of the things that we have to sacrifice in our music unless we do something very early on that's just a guitar and two voices. Otherwise you have to rehearse it with the band so by the time you rehearse it, the melody is not spontaneous.

I understand you're teaching songwriting and record making at New York University this semester. Can you teach someone how to write a song?

You can teach somebody about writing songs. You can't teach someone how to write a song I don't think. But I am dealing with people who already write songs, so what I can do mainly is tell them what I've learned and go into the studio and say, let's do this, let's cut this song. You see what problems will arise when you go into the studio and cut the song. It sort of prepares you a little bit for going in there. Otherwise you just come in and you're lost. You're just in the record company's hands and you're lost.

That's what happened to most of the San Francisco groups in the early days. Fine live groups, but they didn't know anything about the recording studio and couldn't figure out why their records were bad.

They had to learn the whole thing and they had to learn it while they were putting out an album.

What made you decide to teach?

I wanted to do it for a while. I like talking about songwriting. I like to hear what people are writing and I'd like to spare people some of the grief that I went through by learning by trial and error. Some of the errors can be really costly so maybe I can do somebody a favor.

Nobody teaches anything about popular music. You have to learn it on the street. I'd go to a course if the Beatles would talk about how they made records because I'm sure I could learn something. I was interested in talking to Dylan about how he wrote a song. I wanted to know if he was doing it like I was doing it, but I couldn't find out what he did.

Have you always written the same way?

I write sound and meaning simultaneously now. I used to write meaning. I'd say what it is I want to say and say it in words. Then I set that with the melody. I don't like that so much. That period came to an end with the "Dangling Conversation." You say something specifically. Then I came to realize that you can do it another way. You don't have to do it that way.

Then I went just straight sounds. Now I try to write simultaneously, sounds fit the melody—the right vocal sound, the word as it sounds right with this melody. At the same time you write the meaning. It's just a skill that you learn by practicing. As opposed to writing the melody and then filling in the lyrics or writing the lyrics and then filling in the melody, you do it together immediately at the same time. I sit down with the guitar and I play and sing. I've been working this way for about a year.

What were some of the songs you did just by sounds?

"The Boxer" was an early song that had a lot to do with sound and a lot of people said they couldn't hear the lyrics. I knew that a lot of that came from the fact that the lyrics went just one word into another word so that it was hard to separate the words. The end of one sound went into the beginning of another sound. Now everything I do is sort of like that. Then there are some writers who do that. It's very pleasant for me to hear. Suits my taste. There are other people who cram a lot of words in and they hit you that way. I don't like that way as much.

There's a certain softness in your music which is surprising considering you're from New York.

If you had someone you could sing with like I sing with Artie and you sing together and it goes buzz, you get this sound that's so nice to hear that's all you want to do. When I sing with Artie I'd much rather sing a slow simple song than anything else because it sounds so nice to me. It's such a pleasant soft sound.

Why did you include "Bye Bye Love" on your new album? Was it recorded live?

Yes, that was recorded in Ames, Iowa, mostly because of our fascination with the handclapping. We went out and we said now listen you have to handclap in rhythm; you can't fall behind like every audience falls behind because we want to have the sound of 8000 people handclapping. It's going to be a great backbeat. And it was. We did it twice. We sang and said no, too raggedy, got do it again. And that's why. We sang it in our concerts for a while.

Were the Everly Brothers a strong influence on you in the beginning? Were other groups?

Yes, sure, all the early rock and roll groups. When we were 13 years old, the Clef-Tones and the Heartbeats and all those groups.

Weren't you a rock act too?

When we were 15 we were Tom and Jerry. We had a hit record and went on American Bandstand on Thanksgiving, 1957. We were trying to find the kinescope of that to put on our television show, but it's lost somewhere. They have all those kinescopes, except that month. We were on the same day as Jerry Lee Lewis; he sang "Great Balls of Fire." Our record was "Hey Schoolgirl."

What label were you on?

Big—I think they went out of business on the returns from our second record. It was one of those things where the distributor didn't pay them for the first record and then you put out the second. It wasn't a hit and they got all those returns and went out of business.

How did you get your recording deal?

We were making a demo in Sanders Recording Studio for $2. They didn't even put it on tape; they put it directly onto acetate. You had to do it perfectly because you couldn't wipe it out. We sing the song and this guy came up to us and he said "I'm going to make you guys stars." He bought us clothes and everybody wore the same outfits. In those days you did that—red jackets or white loafers or something plaid. That was it. I bought my first electric guitar and we played at the Hartford State Theater with LaVerne Baker.

After Tom and Jerry flopped what happened?

Nothing happened. I used to do demos. I'd go into studios and work and do demos. At that time Frankie Avalon was very popular, so everybody was making tunes for Frankie Avalon, so I would sing like him. Or if the Fleetwoods had a big hit, I'd sing like the Fleetwoods. I used to work with Carol King for a while. We'd overdub six or seven instruments. She'd play piano and drums and I'd play guitar and bass and you'd put four voices in the background. We'd get like $30 for the recording. That's how we learned about the studio.

Have you ever used a band or electric instruments to back you onstage?

The last tour we used the guys who played on the records: drums, guitar, bass, piano. It worked out badly. First of all we came out on stage with the band, and people would yell: "Get the band off, we just want to hear you!" I would say: "Oh, that riff is so old; you said that about Dylan. Christ that's four years ago that this happened; what are you talking about? Everybody has a band. We're the only ones around without a band." Mostly what happened was that we didn't really rehearse a lot because we were working on the television show then. We didn't rehearse it to the point of real tightness. But they were soft. That's one good thing; they didn't blast out. It was good with "Bridge Over Troubled Water," because we needed a piano for that.

Would you ever try it again?

I'd like to play in a band myself, to play with other musicians. I've never had that and I miss it. I like the thrill of playing with somebody else. I don't know when we will perform again in this country.

What do you mean?

Well, Artie is going to England for the next couple of months, and I'm going to study, relax and do some reading and stay with my friends for awhile. At the end of April we do a short European tour including Moscow. Then Artie starts filming in May for Mike Nichols' next film with Jack Nicholson, *Carnal Knowledge.* So really we're talking about a year.

So whether we go back on the road in a year, I don't know. It's possible. We could easily do it. It would depend on whether we said let's go ahead; let's go out and perform again. You know it gets very hard singing "The Sounds of Silence," as you can imagine. This time we went out and sang mostly new songs and people don't want to hear that. They want to hear the songs that you're famous for. I was talking to Dylan and I said that's my problem with going out on the road. It gets boring for me because of this. They want to hear "The Sounds of Silence." He said, "Well, I'd like to see you and if I came to see you I'd want to see you sing the 'The Sounds of Silence' and 'Scarborough Fair.'"

When I saw the Rolling Stones and they played "Satisfaction," I said, "that's the Rolling Stones playing 'Satisfaction.' That song that I know well by the Rolling Stones, there they are doing it." Knocked me out. I don't care whether they did it good or bad or anything. It's just the Rolling Stones playing "Satisfaction." So I think it's very hard to ever escape from that.

Won't you miss the stimulation you get from live audiences?

Probably I'll come to miss it. It's very emotional. On really good nights I can get very emotional on the stage; what's going on between the audience and us. That's very pleasurable, but on the way to the theater, boy, do I suffer. Oh, no, this again. We always come on late because we're always saying, ten more minutes, have another cup of coffee, have a smoke and then go out. We did a lot of shows—somewhere between 300 and 400 shows in our career and that's a lot of shows.

When you say you may not perform again here, does that mean you'll still be making records?

I don't say that we will never perform again. There are several things that we want to do before we think about that. It may sound strange, but time is running out. You go to do things because once you get a certain point, you've got to ride your energy while you have it. As long as you have energy and curiosity and drive, you use it. And I don't know when that will end. I hope it will never end, but while it's here I want to do it and we know how to perform. It's fun and it's something that you learn and you get good at it and pleasure out of doing anything well, so you enjoy it more. But I just don't know; there are so many things I want to learn.

Someone told me that he thought when he became successful, he'd be happy, but he wasn't. Now that you've achieved success, are you happy?

Yes I am. I'm less confused and more willing to accept things. Maybe it's just because I got older. It takes time to put yourself and your achievements into some kind of perspective and to understand what there is to value in life. I've tried hard and I've had more success than most people and I'm happy. It should be enough. You just go on working then. That was the other thing that Nichols said. Soon as they put you up there and they put the knife in your back, you're getting to the best period of your life. Up until that point people have been saying you were great, when half the time you weren't. And now they'll say that anything you do is bad when it's not true. The pressure is off you and the spotlight is off and you can proceed along with your work. That's the thing new fame does to people—intense pressure, spotlights. So when it gets off you a little bit, it's cooler, just a little bit cooler.

What would you like to be if you weren't a songwriter and singer?

A relief pitcher.

ANONYMOUS

AT&T HANGS UP ON SIMON & GARFUNKEL (1970)

NEW YORK—American Telephone and Telegraph paid out $600,000 for a Simon and Garfunkel TV special. But the company ended up with little more than sounds of silence.

The hour-long program, aired November 30th on CBS-TV, was apparently too political for the phone company, which sold the show at the last minute to Alberto-Culver for minimal time charges of $170,000. An AT&T spokesman explained, simply, "This was not what we contracted for. We bought an entertainment show and they delivered their own personal, social, and political views."

The show was pretty much what a Simon & Garfunkel special *should* have been: Paul Simon and Art Garfunkel not only singing their thoughts in concert but expressing them in the studio, at home, in cars on tour; their song/thoughts not only sung, but illustrated with film footage on grape strikers in Delano; Bobby Kennedy's funeral train; the Poor People's March, and with film clips contrasting Woodstock and Vietnam; country peace and city pollution. Simon & Garfunkel picking out notes and picking out America's discords at the same time.

The show was originally sold to AT&T by producers Pierre Cossette and Burt Sugarman of CoBurt Corporation, who secured the time slot on CBS. Later, Robert Drew Associates, producer of eight previous phone company specials, took over, handing over most production details to Simon & Garfunkel themselves.

AT&T executives, thinking they were getting an hour-long Simon & Garfunkel concert on TV, saw the tape of the show for the first time only days before air time and decided to back off. "We had no right to stop the special from airing," the company man said, "so we sold it off to the highest bidder."

The company was apparently sensitive to the heat generated by Spiro Agnew's well-fanned shit about television news coverage. AT&T uses a rock band called the Yellow Payges in national advertising and featured

Jefferson Airplane and the New York Rock and Roll Ensemble in a previous special.

PAUL ZOLLO, FROM <u>SONGTALK,</u>
THE JOURNAL OF THE NATIONAL ACADEMY OF SONGWRITERS
GARFUNKEL (1990)

PZ: Back in the days of Tom and Jerry, I understand that you and Simon would write the songs together.

AG: That's right.

PZ: Did you write "Hey Schoolgirl" together?

AG: Yes. "Hey Schoolgirl" with its phrase "Woo-bop-a-loo-chi-ba": somewhat taken from "Be Bopa Lula," Gene Vincent's hit, was our attempt to remember an Everly Brothers song that we had both heard one summer.

We were apart, Paul and I, in different places for the summer and at the end of the summer we had both remembered this great record by the Everlys and we were trying to reconstruct it . . . *and we were getting it wrong!* We were, in fact, writing [*laughs*] our own song, "Hey Schoolgirl," in an attempt to remember this Everly Brothers song. When we heard the real Everlys song we realized, "Well, that ain't it, so the thing we were groping towards . . . is ours!"

So we finished writing it and made a demo of it, and signed a contract with a small record company on the strength of it, because the guy was in the waiting room of the demo place, and we actually recorded it. It sold 150,000 copies.

PZ: You actually had a hit at the age of sixteen?

AG: Yeah.

PZ: When that happened to you, did you feel that you had started what would be a long career?

AG: No, I don't remember thinking that. No, I was too realistic. At that age I knew that you can't count on anything, that just because you have a singing voice doesn't mean you have an automatic career. No, your point goes beyond my thinking.

PZ: *How did you learn to be so realistic at such a young age?*

AG: You just look at things. Nobody has automatic follow-up hits. Here I was copying the charts all the time. I didn't see a talented first hit always lead to a follow-up hit. I knew how mercurial the whole thing is. So even though I thought we were good—I thought our harmony and our blend was *real good*—I thought we were competitive and had a shot at making it, but once we did have that first hit, I knew we had a chance of a follow-up hit, but you don't count on anything. You just wing it.

We had a flop and then another one, and then we disbanded the group.

PZ: *Did you write other songs besides "Hey Schoolgirl" back then?*

AG: Yes, we had a whole bunch of them we wrote together. Some were mostly mine with a little Paul on words and music, some vice versa.

PZ: *Is it true that you and Paul used to hang around the Brill Building and walk into offices to play your songs live for people?*

AG: Dozens of them. The Brill Building and 1615 Broadway, two blocks north of the Brill Building. The newer building. We'd knock on the doors, we knew the different companies we liked because we were listening to Alan Freed and we knew the different labels and they were all located there. We'd go up and we'd often sing live for the people. Which was *very* nervous-making, you know? They're busy, so if they don't like you, they cut you off right away. At the end of your first verse they say, "No thanks, we don't need that. Got anything else?" [*Laughs*] You're crushed because wait until they hear the middle part! You haven't even gotten to the good stuff!

So, sometimes you play a demo for them and they pick up the needle about nine seconds in and look for other tunes. Sure, your feelings get kicked around.

PZ: Did the two of you ever have thoughts of being a songwriting team, like Goffin & King or Mann & Weil?

AG: No, because thoughts like that, those are extrapolations beyond what I was doing.

I was just doing it. I wasn't standing back from it thinking what it could lead to, what the name of it is, I didn't have such images. Rodgers and Hammerstein didn't mean anything to me. I just wanted to have a hit. I just wanted to be like those people on the radio. It was all of a case of the present tense with no projecting into the future, particularly.

PZ: Why is it that you and Simon stopped writing songs together?

AG: Well, our whole friendship went into suspension over some thing that happened in those early days. So for about five years we didn't hang out, we weren't each other's friends.

PZ: This started when you were seventeen?

AG: Exactly. And when we next got back together again, we were really on different footing. You know, those are very critical years in your development. So we were more advanced, collegiate types then, and now the world knew of this thing called Bob Dylan. And Joan Baez and all that folky stuff.

So now I just jumped from the late fifties to the early sixties.

PZ: So you're about 21 now?

AG: Yeah, and we became friends again. In those interim five years, Paul had made many a demo and so did I. I had two different label deals and a couple of records out of a folkie nature, but I was basically an architecture student at Columbia.

PZ: You put out albums under the name Artie Garr?

AG: Singles. Artie Garr. G-a-r-r.

One night we [*Paul and I*] hung out. He showed me these things he was writing because, I think it's fair to say, he was so impressed with Dylan.

PZ: Did you share that enthusiasm?

AG: To the extreme. Dylan was the coolest thing in the country. If you were a young person at that age, maybe you don't go for Dylan's gravelly style voice, but who he was and how different and bold his lyrics were, and his look, that was the closest thing the record business had to James Dean. His album covers, if you look at the early Dylan, you see a real charismatic choir boy *star* of a kid.

I remember when *Freewheelin' Bob Dylan* came out, his second CBS album, I was in Berkeley. I was a carpenter. This was my year off from architecture school getting field experience. And I was singing at Berkeley in clubs as well as doing carpentry during the day. And I saw in the record store around early September the new *Freewheelin'* album. And there's Dylan in the village walking in the snow, and the camera's got an upward angle on him and he's with his girlfriend. And I knew I had to try and make another record. [*Laughs*] That was such a great place to be!

So I came back home [*to New York*], ran into Paul, he showed me these new songs he had written, about two or three songs. And they were really wonderful. And I let him know how keen I was to work out harmonies for them.

In my mind I was thinking, "This has got to make it now. Between the commerciality of these folky songs that Paul's writing, and the blend that we had worked on in the past, which will now serve us, we should have a shot at a career."

PZ: Do you recall which songs he played for you?

AG: Yes. "He Was My Brother," that was his first one. A song called "On A Side Of A Hill" which ended up becoming the "Canticle" part of "Scarborough Fair." The third one was probably "Sparrow," The fourth one I know was "Bleecker Street." He was probably up to three songs at that point. So these three did it for me.

And then we started harmonizing them and we were *giddy* with joy over how appealing it was to our own ears. Before the world gets to know something that's neat, *you* get to know it. And you're your own spectator of what's coming out of you. And it's really kind of . . . delirious and happy. It made you want to giggle while you were singing, it was so much fun doing these things.

PZ: Had your voices changed at all by then?

AG: No. . . . Paul seemed to sound a little better and we'd never done these kind of sweet folky things. We were doing rockabilly when we were younger. So the fact that there was kind of an emotional, goose-bump, bittersweet quality was really nice for our voices. So it was a bit of a new blend to soften up this way. I guess that's why there was something new and exciting to our own ears about it.

But we were deeply confident on the inside. I kept thinking, "This has to do it. This is very directly appealing."

We'd go to the fraternity house. It was a good place to practice. But we really wanted the kids to overhear us. And whoever heard us would go nuts over it. [*Laughs*] There was really a *something* going on there.

Paul kept writing these songs. A new one would turn up every three, four weeks. "Bleecker Street" was the fourth, "Wednesday Morning 3 A.M." was the fifth, and "Sounds of Silence" was the sixth.

PZ: You wrote the liner notes to the first Simon and Garfunkel album Wednesday Morning 3 A.M. *and in them you wrote that when you first heard "The Sound of Silence" that it took you by surprise, that level of writing. Do you recall feeling that way?*

AG: No, I don't. I might have been putting on a little bit of gloss for those notes. I was just reading those "Wednesday Morning" notes and they were embarrassing. I was mixing my version of Variety magazine jargonese a little bit there.

I remember thinking "Sound of Silence" was the best of all the songs he had written. It was just a notch above in terms of commercial appeal. But if I could rephrase the way I wrote those notes, I would be happy.

PZ: You also said in those notes that you were not entirely clear about the meaning of the song. Was that true?

AG: Not really. What Paul was doing was touching images that can be taken a lot of different ways. I understood. I knew where he was coming from, what his sensibility was.

PZ: *You put out that album with the original acoustic version of "Sound of Silence" to have it latter overdubbed with electric instruments, which made it a hit—*

AG: A whole year later. In that year, Paul gave up on Simon & Garfunkel, and America. He became a Yankee in London, a street-singer, folk club singer, making twenty, twenty-five pounds a night, which was great money for a college kid.

PZ: *Why did he leave then, after you had released your first album?*

AG: Well, the album, after about a year of doing nothing, looked . . . *defunct.*

* * *

PZ: *So Simon & Garfunkel were essentially broken up when "The Sound of Silence" became a hit?*

AG: Yes. I didn't have a career point of view towards music anymore because our one album with CBS was a flop.

So then I came home at the end of the summer of '65 to find that that year and a quarter-old album had one of its tunes released with overdubbed instruments called "The Sounds of Silence" and it came out in September, '65. And as it slowly climbed the charts, my life changed.

PZ: *How did you feel, from a musical point of view, when you first heard the overdubbed electric version?*

AG: I remember thinking, "Of course it's not a hit. Because I never have hits."

At that point I was very used to how hard it is to really make it, and just because you sing doesn't mean you get anywhere. So I was very well practiced in disenchantment. So when I heard it, I thought, "Well, of course it's not a hit" because a hit is a *one-in-a-million thing.* And I was lucky enough to have such a one. It will probably never happen again.

It was in the electric 12-string style of the Byrds. "Mr. Tambourine Man." Okay, so they did that to us. It's cute. They've drowned out the strength of the lyric and they've made it more of a *fashion* kind of production. And you never know. I was mildly amused and detached with the certainty that it was not a hit. I don't have hits.

PZ: When that did become a hit, did that influence Simon's writing? Did he begin turning them out more frequently?

AG: I would say no. He continued to do just what he was doing. I can't say there was any alteration. He didn't change his style, he didn't change his speed of writing. He came back [*from England*] reluctantly, because he was in love with Kathy and England and his life as a free young Yankee. And he hated to have to relate to a hit record in America. Even though it was the thing we had long wanted, it came at an unfortunate time. It was the winter of '65. And he only knew that it was happening when it broke the Top Ten.

So Paul came home, we met in the basement, we said, "All right, this thing we've been looking for all these years has finally happened. It behooves us to be smart and see if we could have a follow-up hit." We turned all our attention to what would be the single we would put out, to secure this toe-hold we had in the business. To show people it wasn't a fluke and to show people we could make an interesting record in a *whole other vein.* So our goal was to have a hit that was nothing like "The Sounds of Silence." Just to show chart muscle in a different way.

"Homeward Bound" became that second record. I remember cutting it and then thinking, "It's so important that it be commercial. And it's not quite good enough. Let's cut it all over again." And from scratch we redid it. Went to Nashville. We redid it and it came out good. It went to Number 5 in the country.

Paul had just written it. It was one of the latest things he had written in England. He said he wrote it waiting in the train station around Manchester, wanting to get back to London where Kathy was.

PZ: When he would write a new song, would he play it for you on guitar?

AG: Yes. But through *much* of the time, he was writing them as we were touring together or working together. So I knew them very well; it was that thing he kept noodling on.

PZ: Would you ever give him input on a song?

AG: Yes. My head was always listening to these songs as records in the making. So I was always thinking of the structure, the length, the arrangement, where they were headed as the record they'd be.

Records have images. There are wet records and dry records. And big records. . . . "Bridge Over Troubled Water" is a *big* record. There are lighter records. You know, there are *forest-green* records, there's *orange* records. These are the pictures I'm using. These are production thoughts.

So as he was writing the songs, I was thinking of the instrumentation we would use, how thick would the record be, or is it more like a ditty.

I'd put it into a category: this is like the Del Vikings. It's hard to put into words how I was thinking, but I'd look at the song as one of the elements that makes a record. The musicianship, the arrangement, the singing, are the others.

PZ: Would you work on your harmony parts separate or together?

AG: Together. If he was writing the song, I would start seeing, in just the sense I was saying now, the kind of record it was going to be and what the arrangement demands, and what my vocal part should be in the record. This was all emerging as the song was emerging. And we would feed off each other. I would throw back at him what progress I'm making and that would give him a sense of what he's writing.

PZ: "I Am A Rock" was your third hit?

AG: "I Am A Rock" was third. It peaked at number three in the nation. And then we got a manager, Mort Lewis. Mort helped us in the touring area. We branched out to become touring artists. We had a nice show.

Then we tried a fourth single that was really arty.

PZ: "The Dangling Conversation"?

AG: Yeah. We thought, "Can we take the audience where we want to go now and do a ballad?" Because ballads are tougher to have hits on. Something slow and really intellectual and literary. Let's see if they'll go for that, because then we can take them anywhere.

It turned out we couldn't. The record was not a hit.

PZ: Did that surprise you?

AG: A little bit. It informed me that you can't exactly call your shots.

PZ: *Did it change Simon's writing at all? Did he try to steer away from those kinds of songs?*

AG: I would say probably yes, a little bit. At least, you know, you start thinking of songs in two categories: singles and album cuts. An album cut can be as artful as it wants to be. A single should be under five minutes or under four minutes.

There are certain things you think of in singles that you wouldn't necessarily hold yourself to for an album. You look for a more memorable, repeatable chorus in a single, a shorter length. So, certainly for singles, we knew it was best to stay away from the long, intellectual ballad.

After "Dangling Conversation" we began taking albums much more seriously and doing them much more slowly and artfully as we were influenced by the Beatles.

So in '66 we slowed way down for our third album. See, the second album was *Sounds of Silence,* quickly put out because it had a hit single. Made in three weeks. But on the next album, *Parsley, Sage, Rosemary and Thyme,* I think we must have spent nine months making that album, which was sort of unprecedented. But it was such a labor of love and fun, that we thought we were breaking new ground in terms of how creative an album can be. It was something we just learned from what the Beatles were doing.

So when that album came out in late '66, that gave us a certain stature in the business, which helped, because we had obviously spent more time and energy and creative powers on that album. It had that interesting "Silent Night/7 O'Clock News." And it had "Scarborough Fair," which worked great for us.

That was a lot of fun to do.

PZ: *That was the one song in which you and Simon shared writing credit; he said you wrote the "Canticle" section.*

AG: Well, we both wrote it. The lyric, as I said before, came from Paul's second tune which never made any of our albums, called "On The Side Of A Hill." [*Sings softly*] "On the side of a hill in a land called somewhere, a little boy lies asleep in the earth. . . ." It's an anti-war song. "While down in the valley, a cruel war rages, and people forget what a child's life is worth. . . ." A lot of that lyric ended up behind "Scarborough Fair" but the melody [*of the "Canticle" section*] I wrote.

And I wrote it just to be contrapuntal, to weave and swell around the lines of "Scarborough Fair" to increase the flow of the record. So I took the writer's credit.

PZ: It's a beautiful counter-melody.

AG: Thanks. I could write about seven of those things in an hour. Every hour I could write seven more. Supposedly that's an achievement in BMI terms for me. It's like breathing, I don't get it.

PZ: Why didn't you do more of that, then, in other songs?

AG: He wouldn't let me. [Laughs] No, just a joke! I don't know why I didn't do more of that. There wasn't a need to do more of that. It's a specialty thing; it treats a song a little like wall-paper to be weaving in and out between the lines. It makes the song a little less than a proper song. It works in record terms.

I don't remember holding back, it just never came up that that would be the right thing to do on another. Here, for once, we were not starting with a Paul Simon song, we were starting with a traditional folk song, "Scarborough Fair." It's the nature of this flowing song that it could take this countermelody. I can't think of any other Paul Simon songs that could . . . maybe "The Boxer" could do that. No, "The Boxer" is too busy.

PZ: With lyrics?

AG: Yeah.

PZ: On "Scarborough Fair" did you both sing both parts?

AG: Yes. We probably did two-part harmony on the melody and then doubled it. So that gives a kind of tubular, strong, commercial sound to the front. Then on the "Canticle" part, Paul takes some of those lines and I take the others that are higher. And we double that melody. So there's one voice unharmonized in the background but that one voice is doubled.

PZ: How did you learn techniques such as doubling voices, and did Roy Halee have much of an influence in that area?

AG: My guess is yes, that Roy had something to do with that. We did it a lot and once we started doing it, we liked the sound. It's all over our records, doubling your voice.

PZ: *Did you start punching in vocals about at that time?*

AG: I can't remember, but as you know, that's a big phrase we use a lot, punching in. The world's not supposed to know about that. [*Laughs*] It should seem like it's seamless. But sure, we were fixing lines right from the beginning. That's standard recording technique.

As the years go by, you get a little more insecure, so you get more finicky about punching in not a line, but two words. And as years go by, you get more local about the fixes you're making.

PZ: *In "A Simple Desultory Phillipic" Simon wove your name into the song: "I've been . . . Art Garfunkled."*

AG: What about it?

PZ: *I was wondering if you appreciated it.*

AG: I thought it was nice. I did appreciate it. I thought it was cute. Even thought the sentiment is slightly negative. He's implying that he's been *done to* by these people. It's just a touch of a dig.

Paul is like John Lennon. They're feisty. There's a rebellious attitude. You know, that's very acceptable. It's standard rebellious attitude stuff. The public tends to like that stuff. It shows that they're feisty, that they're not busy patronizing the proper sounding, wholesome phrases of the culture.

PZ: *Simon said that in terms of record making, you, he and Roy Halee had a three-way equal partnership. True?*

AG: I don't know. Yeah. I guess. We all respected each other's talents and we all fused what we did. It became, really, a mix.

Roy was very important in that we loved him so much and we pitched ideas to win him over. It was so much fun to turn him on and make him think we were great. So really, he was our audience. We were always throwing ideas with the hope that Roy would fall out of his chair with how neat that was.

He was always surprising us. We'd be out with the musicians in the studio trying to show the drummer what we think he should do. And a half-hour later, we would come back and Roy would say, "Let me show you what I worked out in terms of the sound when you were out there. I went to put a reverb on the attack of the drums, but then. . . ." [*Laughs*] He'd show us what he worked out and you'd go, "What a wonderful contribution! He's just cooking away creatively on the engineering side while we're working on the arrangement." These things put wind in your sails. A lot.

PZ: Was Roy a perfectionist?

AG: Definitely. Roy has brilliant standards. Really a fine artist. There's a difference between a Rolls-Royce and a Toyota, you know. And Roy is really a craftsman, a consummate artist. He's a bit of a misfit in the eighties. They don't do that stuff anymore.

PZ: Do you feel that Roy is out of date?

AG: Well, he's having hits with Paul, so he's not really out of date. But that kind of care and concern is no longer *costworthy*.

Talk to a record company executive and they'll go, "Yeah, well, if he wants to do it, let him turn himself on, but it doesn't *mean anything* commercially anymore."

I'm not saying this right because I do think it means something. Records became much cruder in the last twenty years. Let's put it that way.

PZ: Simon said that he felt Bookends *was the quintessential Simon & Garfunkel album. Would you agree?*

AG: I don't know what you mean exactly by that phrase. I think of *Parsley, Sage* as the first real album in doing what we do. *Bookends* is the one that had a theme running through the whole side one. That makes it literary and particularly interesting in that it has a theme, a theme of youth to middle age to old age.

But *Bridge Over Troubled Water* is the one with the most successful variety. Different songs strike out in different directions with different kinds of production. So it's a kind of a showing off piece in the variety sense. It makes that album, in my mind, kind of the richest, because it goes in so many different directions.

PZ: Bookends features "Voices Of Old People" which is not really a song but a sound painting. Was that your conception?

AG: Yeah. I wanted to set up the song "Old Friends." And I wanted the actual sound of the old people on tape so you can feel what we're talking about before we sing something about old people. I actually wanted to get their coughs, their wheezes, their sighs.

It was really going to be a collage of gutturalisms, real earthy sounds in the back of the throat. Not so much what they were saying but their vocal production, to see if I could capture older people that way.

But we had wonderful quotes from all these interviews I had done. I went to old age homes. . . .

PZ: Did the people there know who you were?

AG: Yes. When they were real elderly, they dimly knew and didn't care. Actually, they didn't know. The lady who ran the place knew who I was and they would accommodate my interest and give me a nice serious treatment. The actual old people I spoke to, they were pretty old, so they didn't know who I was. So it was just a case of cooperating. And I would be the *sophomoric* interviewer asking them about life itself. But they said wonderful stuff. . . .

PZ: Did they know you were recording it?

AG: Yes.

PZ: Did they have any understanding why you were doing it?

AG: Not really. No.

PZ: You said the purpose of the piece was to introduce the song "Old Friends." When you first heard that song, did you have a sense that Simon was writing not only about old age, but above the old friendship between you and he?

AG: Yes. I like that song a lot. I think he wrote a gem there. Sure, I did.

PZ: Also on that album is "Mrs. Robinson." Is it true that you were the one who told Mike Nichols that Simon had a song with that title?

AG: He was writing a song called "Mrs. Roosevelt," Paul was. And it was going nowhere and he was going to chuck it. Paul and I were in this sound stage at Paramount or MGM in Hollywood working with Nichols on the soundtrack of *The Graduate*. And we had sung "Sounds of Silence," we had to resing it to put it in the film. And we had the other thing: "Scarborough Fair" came right off the record into the film.

We still needed one uptempo tune that Paul hadn't written and Mike was struggling. And I said, "There is an uptempo song that Paul is *despairing* of, but it is very commercial. It's called 'Mrs. Roosevelt' but we could change 'Mrs. Roosevelt' to 'Mrs. Robinson.'"

And Mike loved that thought, as if he knew right away this was going to work: "Let's hear this uptempo song." [*Sings*] "And here's to you, Mrs. Roosevelt. . . ." And Mike knew that that was going to work. Changed it to "Robinson." Said, "Let's try to put it down and see if it works against the picture." So you sing it against the screen. And all that existed of the song was the chorus. That's why the verses are "Doo doo doo doo. . . ." There are no lyrics there. And it worked.

PZ: Was he writing about Eleanor Roosevelt?

AG: Yes. The key to me was that he was chucking the song anyway, so we were free to hack it up and do whatever you want with it.

PZ: Then he wrote the rest of the song after the movie was released?

AG: That's right. So by the time our *Bookends* album came out with "Mrs. Robinson" in it, a whole bunch of months later, if not a year later, now, the rest of "Mrs. Robinson" was written.

PZ: Do you have any memory of hearing "The Boxer" for the first time?

AG: Yeah. I knew "The Boxer" was great. For one thing, it's a style that is our strong suit. Paul and Artie could sing most effectively when they were doing a Travis picking, very fluid, running-along-syllable-song like that. Whenever we did those folky, running things, the syllabication is ideal for what we had learned. We were tapping into something that went way back for us, and something we could get a blend on. So I always knew, whenever it was that kind of thing. I had a *particular* feel that I could do really well, and match Paul and make the whole thing *ripple* and articulate it just right.

So just because it was in that category, I had a feeling that I could make it sound good. And the lyric is real nice. And the amount of labor in the studio was just unbelievable. That one took so many days.

PZ: Your harmony part on that one is a classic. Many people have learned how to sing harmony by imitating your part on that song.

AG: I'm doing a bunch of different things: I'm using the classic third above Paul, an interval of a third, and then I do variations, depending on what the lyric asks. [*Sings*] "I'm leaving, I'm leaving. . . ." Yeah.

PZ: Were there any instances of you commenting on the lyric of a song, or making suggestions about the writing, prior to making the record?

AG: Yeah, but there's so many times, who can remember? I wrote some of the lines. Never took a writer's credit because in spirit it was really a small two percent factor. But there's some of my writing in there. In "Punky's Dilemma," which was written for *The Graduate,* I wrote a verse in there.

PZ: Didn't you have any desire to have credit? George Harrison recently said that he felt he should have received credit for lines he wrote in Lennon and McCartney songs.

AG: I'm surprised that he's complaining about it. It does work that way and you don't ask for credit when it's happening because in truth, in spirit, Paul's the writer. Yeah, I wrote a little of that stuff, but that's just *technically* true. In spirit, and in essence of the truth, it doesn't matter. So I don't know, maybe I'm being foolish for not being technical. Yeah, I wrote a certain portion of the things.

PZ: Simon said you wrote the flute solo in "The Boxer."

AG: I wrote a lot of those kinds of things. If you're talking not about the song but the arrangement, now I wrote more than two percent. I wrote a lot of the parts that musicians played, solos and stuff.

PZ: *Do you recall what made those huge crashes in "The Boxer"? I once heard that it was you and Paul dropping drumsticks on a hardwood floor.*

AG: That's Roy's sound effect, which became very much an effect that was used a lot in the seventies and the eighties. It became real popular. We used to call it "the door closing sound." Roy knows about that. It was some trick he did engineering-wise.

We dropped the drumsticks on "Cecelia," which is, if you remember, very treble-y and ticky-tacky and tinker-toys. One of the things that gives that effect is Paul and I, each with about twelve drumsticks, dropping them rather quickly on a parquet wooden floor and then quickly picking them up, bunching them up in our hands and dropping them again. Like twice per second. [*Laughs*] Like, *seriously* dropping and picking, dropping, picking! And we got that down in rhythm. So the bunching, dropping sound, is very woody, ticky-tacky sounding, and runs through "Cecelia."

PZ: *One thing that Simon told me that was hard to believe was that when he first played you "Bridge Over Troubled Water" that you didn't want to sing it, that you thought he should sing it.*

AG: Uh huh, that's right. I thought he should sing it. He sounded real good on it. It was too high for him, so he went into falsetto on the high parts, and he has a really nice flutey falsetto. So I commented on that when he first played it for me, that he had a really nice falsetto and he sounded good up there.

If you want to know the truth, that was one of about six million generous things I tried to say to Paul. I call that simply in the category of a relaxed generosity of creative cooperation. I'm *amazed* that we're talking about this twenty years later to this day as if there's a *thing* or a story, or. . . . When you say that you're shocked, I go, "What are we talking about? Are you shocked that somebody says something that is relaxed and generous to another? Where's the story there?"

PZ: I think he felt that it was his best melody to date and that only you could do it justice.

AG: People do very good work when they write in the spirit of a gift. He *did write* it for me, and because there was a gift-giving attitude in the writing, I think he wrote a little better than he usually writes. And he writes pretty good, usually.

"For Emily, Wherever I May Find Her" is a very romantic ballad and the fact that it was written for me, I don't know, it brought something else out in his writing.

PZ: When you first heard "Bridge," did you consider it to be one of his greatest melodies?

AG: Yeah.

PZ: Was it your idea to hold off the production until the third verse, to make that final verse so huge?

AG: Yes. Now, I wrote a bunch of chords that make up "Bridge Over Troubled Water." The fact that the verses end with a piano part that elaborates the ending and all those chords that give it a turn-around that set up to the next verse. I wrote that stuff with Larry Knechtel on piano. Larry was the player. And I just heard something in my head; this is a producer's moment when you start hearing what the record wants to be, and now you strain toward the musicians: "Give me something, no, it should be a few extra chords, no, give me a different set-up chord, no, that's the wrong chord; something with a more *seventh* feel. Denser. There, that's the chord. Now it should go from that chord to like a ninth. Tilt it just a little." And I remember doing that kind of writing with Larry and a whole bunch of the chords that ended the verses came out of our work.

The song used to only have two verses and that's what Paul wrote. But we knew that these two verses were working beautifully and what we had was not a gem of a record but an almost big record. It wanted to have another verse and the other verse wanted to open up and pull out all the stops, as if the song that Paul wrote is really a set-up for the final verse, which is really something else again.

So, I guess that was my contribution.

PZ: To this day I can recall so clearly where I was and how I felt when I first heard the song. There was a quality in your voice that was so emotional, so beyond anything else we had heard. Did it feel that way to you as well?

AG: Well, the listener gets to hear the whole record from beginning to end in one shot. The maker fusses over it so much that you have to have the concept of the whole record in your head. And as I was just saying before, the concept of the last verse would be a surprise augmentation of power. And a *considerable* augmentation. That concept moved me and so, I knew that the vision was wonderful. And when I recorded it, the fun was to do that last verse first as a vocalist. So peaking out on that last verse was fantastic, knowing where you'd come from and that you'd set it up with two quiet verses. Yeah, I had a great, spiritual time. A pole-vault. You know? You've only done seventeen-foot-six but suddenly you're pole-vaulting *thirty-four feet-nine!* And when you're way up there, it's a great life experience.

The second verse was a lot of fun. I knew how to do that. See, once the third verse is done, now you're going back to do the second verse and you know you haven't released it yet, the world doesn't know it yet. It's all saved up. It's a lot of fun. It helps you do your work to have something so neat up your sleeve.

PZ: Did you record that song in L.A.?

AG: The last verse was done in L.A.; the first two verses were done in New York.

PZ: Do you think that had any effect on it, recording it on two coasts?

AG: No.

PZ: You said that after the release of "The Dangling Conversation," you realized you couldn't put out a ballad as a single. Were you surprised that "Bridge" became such a huge hit?

AG: I thought it was a very strong five-minute tune and record and cut on an album. Real strong. So I had no false modesty that it came out real good.

But I thought it was an album cut. It took Clive Davis to say, "I think it's your first single for this album," for us to say, *"Really? A five-minute single?"* Clive Davis, president of CBS at that point, said, "Yes. Go for it. I hear it."

It is *real* soft. When you hear it on the radio in the context of other records, it's an awfully soft, slow, first verse. It takes a while before it proves that it sounds like a single.

PZ: It sounded so unlike anything else at the time, both the comforting sound of your voice and the healing message of the lyric. Then "Let It Be" was released soon thereafter which had a similar tone—

AG: We thought "Let It Be" was very similar. How did they hear what we were doing?

PZ: McCartney did say, years later, that he heard "Bridge" and wanted to write a song like that—

AG: I see! How interesting. I never knew that.

One day Paul [*Simon*] came in the studio, and I had done the first verse. He said, "Where's the octave leap?" Meaning, "Where's the 'I'll dry them all [*sings up an octave as on the record*].'" You know, you jump up an octave because it wasn't working and I just dispensed with it. Paul said, [*in a high-pitched, upset voice*] "Wait a minute! You can't take the writer's notes and just dispense with them. I wrote that note. I'm the writer and that's what I wrote!" [*In a calm, soft voice*] "All right, Paul, I'll go out there and put the note in." [*Laughs*] I thought that was funny.

PZ: Were there many disagreements over directions you should take?

AG: Oh, there were a lot of points of view. But, I don't know, that's what makes things good. To be unafraid of calling it as your ears hear it, is to have *truth* and *authority* and *identity* and *commitment* and *ears*. Now, of course, it's going to differ with the other all over the place, and the rest is can you be mature and not a pain in the ass about working out different ideas?

See, you get a lot of mileage when you yield. Everytime you say, "I don't hear it that way but let it be your way," you create an emotional catharsis. And that's one of the most *valuable* tools you're dealing with in the studio. To yield is to create, in many ways. I've never heard anybody say this theory but if you know what I'm saying, there's a real truth in there.

So it's mix and match. Hold your line when you really feel something you're saying is wonderful and you really want to get this point across and prove it to your partner by just throwing it into the tape and letting it speak for itself. At times. And then at other times you go, it's a little arbitrary. I hear this but he hears that. Let me see if I can create the *rush of* cooperation by letting it be his way. So I'd play that game a lot.

PZ: You yielded on that octave/jump in "Bridge." In retrospect, do you think that was a good idea?

AG: Yes, although it's somewhat arbitrary. It was a good idea but I don't think it would matter, particularly, if it wasn't there.

PZ: On that same album, there are two songs that Simon wrote to you, as opposed to for you, "So Long, Frank Lloyd Wright" and "The Only Living Boy In New York."

AG: That's right. That is correct.

PZ: He wrote those after you went to Mexico to work on Catch-22. *When you went there, did you have any feeling that it might break up the team?*

AG: No, there wasn't at all on my part. And at first there wasn't on *Paul's* part. I went off to *Catch-22* thinking I'd be gone two months, possibly three at the most. Because I had a small cameo role in the movie, and that's the *maximum* it should take. Usually those kind of things can be done in three weeks.

So I was gone, at first, for what I thought was just a little interruption. See, our way of working was for Paul to write while we recorded. So we'd be in the studio for the better part of two months working on the three or four songs that Paul had written, recording them, and when they were done, we'd knock off for a couple of months while Paul was working on the next group of three or four songs. Then we'd book time and be in the studio again for three or four months, recording those.

So my thought was, rather than *wait* for Paul to write the next bunch of songs, I went off and did this movie. When Paul's songs were ready, he was ready to be in the studio before I was finished with *Catch-22*.

And here, Mike [*Nichols*] held me in Mexico for like four and a half, five months. And I should have really said to him, "You don't need me this long. I've got work in New York. You know? Call Paul Simon. Call Roy. What am I doing down here?" I should have said that. But I was many miles away. And you don't realize what you're missing when you're out there.

The fact that it turned out to be that many months was frustrating. And that's probably what Paul meant that it's going to be tough to continue this way.

PZ: Was it ever your intention to pursue acting as much as music?

AG: No, not at all. No. I thought. . . .

Here's what it was about: When we were making *Bridge Over Troubled Water,* and I forget how much of it had been already recorded when I went to Mexico. Maybe two thirds of the album was done.

When I went to Mexico, the feeling was that we weren't having a good time. We weren't enjoying ourselves. We were *tired* of working together. We wanted a break from each other. We were not getting along particularly well and there were a lot of *conflicts* that were unpleasant conflicts. They all took the form of music and what kind of record are you making, but whereas in the past, differences of musical ideas, it was pleasant enough to work them out and get the maximum result. Here, on *Bridge Over Troubled Water,* it was not particularly pleasant at all.

I remember thinking, "When this record's over, I want to rest from Paul Simon." And I would *swear* that he was feeling the same thing, like "I don't want to know from Artie for a year or so." We've *toured* together, we've done so many things together for a whole bunch of years, we've had a great run in front of the world, let us privately now *renew* ourselves and get a reappreciation of the other one by *cooling it* for a while.

So my feeling was, "*Surely* Paul agrees that when this album is over, we don't want to work together for a while. I'm *sure* he agrees. If he doesn't, he's crazy. This is *not fun.*"

Oddly enough, the results were coming out fine on tape. Because when you put on the earphones and go to work, I guess your commitment to art is greater than your lack of commitment to each other. So you always get responsible and serious toward doing your best work from the heart with all the beauty you have within you when it's tape time.

So I went off to Guaymas thinking, "This is the right thing to do, this is fine. For Art Garfunkel to be a little bit of a movie actor in addition to my role in Simon & Garfunkel is very nice for the identity of the group." After all, Paul plays the guitar on stage; Arthur just has his hands. Paul writes all the songs. So it beefs up my side of the group.

I thought it was excellent. It's almost as if George Harrison suddenly did an acting role to balance out the McCartney-Lennon contribution. My sense of show-business told me it was the perfect balance. And I thought I was going to help give my side of the group a little more interest to the public, and I'd be bringing it back to the duo after we had our rest from each other, and we'd go on and make more albums.

I was in love with Simon & Garfunkel. I thought we were a neat act. I didn't want to tip that over, I just wanted to take a rest from it. And here, with the help of Mike's offer, I wanted to enrich my side of the group with this acting role.

Well, Paul couldn't abide by these things. They were evidently threatening. So, in his mind, waiting for Artie is something he couldn't do. Now, I was waiting for Paul to write the tunes all the time, before we'd go in the studio.

PZ: When you heard "The Only Living Boy In New York" or "Frank Lloyd Wright," how did they strike you?

AG: "Only Living Boy" has a very tender thing about it. There's something really musical and from the heart about that song.

I don't know what it is, but it's undescribably sweet. The attitude of the lyric.

"So Long, Frank Lloyd Wright" is another kind of song. The chords don't have quite that *emotionalism*. It's more about cleverness. I think I go to the chords first to give you the answer, because chords are feelings, and that's where the answer lies.

PZ: I always thought the beginning of "Only Living Boy" was so touching, the way he refers to you as Tom, the name from your first childhood team.

AG: It's sweet. That's Paul saying, "How's it going down there in Guaymas?" I have a letter he wrote in those days that was *really* affectionate. You can see they missed me. I blew it by letting Mike Nichols hold me down there for so many months. That was a mistake on his part.

PZ: *Those are two of his most moving songs, and they were both written to you—*

AG: There's a lot of depth of feeling between Paul Simon and Art Garfunkel mutually. A lot of depth of feeling. Our lives are *amazingly* intertwined. You don't know the beginning of it. It's extraordinary the way these two lives wrap around each other.

CLIVE DAVIS WITH JAMES WILLWERTH

FROM *CLIVE: INSIDE THE RECORD BUSINESS* (1975)

Clive Davis rose from being an accountant at CBS Records to heading the label. Flamboyant, and prone to exaggerating his own importance, Davis nonetheless had an ear for a hit—and the knowledge of how to promote an act. He left Columbia in disgrace after a scandal involving his alleged misuse of corporate funds, but quickly bounced back, establishing the Arista label and eventually promoting new acts, such as Whitney Houston, with great success. In this excerpt from his autobiography, Davis traces Simon and Garfunkel's rise to fame and the duo's breakup—S.L.

Among Columbia artists, the two who came closest to being personal friends of mine were Paul Simon and Arthur Garfunkel. They were already on the label when I took over, and our friendship developed slowly, sometimes with difficulty.

Producer Tom Wilson had signed them in 1964. They had recorded an album, *Wednesday Morning, 3 A.M.,* which got little or no attention, but a year after the album's release, one of its cuts, "The Sound of Silence," was programmed out of the blue by a Boston disc jockey who loved it and wanted to test public reaction. Students at campuses such as Harvard,

Tufts and Boston University immediately began requesting it. Our local promotion man picked this up and reported it to New York. After repeated listening we decided that the record required some instrumental backing to be a real hit. So Wilson went into the studio and did the necessary overdubbing. Neither Artie nor Paul was available: Paul was in England and Artie was studying for a master's degree at Columbia.

The record was then re-released as a single—and it resoundingly launched the extraordinary careers of Simon & Garfunkel. By this time I had A&R reporting to me and I took particular interest in the fatalistic nature of all this. If that disc jockey hadn't experimented with a song from an unknown, year-old album, Simon & Garfunkel probably would not exist today in music. They had already separated. But when the news reached Paul in England that the single was exploding across the country, he came back and, in December, 1965, he and Artie rushed into the studio to record the album *The Sound of Silence,* which included the overdubbed hit version of the title song. There followed a succession of hits, including "Homeward Bound," "I Am A Rock" and "Scarborough Fair," and by 1967 they were established artists selling several hundred thousand copies of each album.

We related easily at first. They had both gone through public schools in Queens and were bright and articulate. I always had the feeling that we could be close—quite apart from our business relationships. But business always managed to get in the way. One example involved the film score for *The Graduate.* Paul had been asked by Mike Nichols, the film's director, to write the motion picture score. When I heard about the project I felt that there was real potential for a best-selling soundtrack album. Soundtracks do not always do well; their success often depends more on the extent of the movie's appeal than on the quality of the music itself. Still, when Embassy Motion Pictures asked if we wanted the soundtrack rights, I grabbed them; the movie had all the ingredients of a big box-office hit.

Then Mike Nichols decided to use little or nothing of Paul's new material. Apart from about a minute of a new song, "Mrs. Robinson"—named after the character played by Anne Bancroft—he chose four cuts from the earlier Simon & Garfunkel albums, the two best-known being "The Sound of Silence" and "Scarborough Fair." When I asked Paul if he thought there was enough material in the movie for an album, he said no. I was extremely disappointed, for I felt the movie would do very well.

When it came out the reviews, of course, were superb. I called Paul again—"Are you sure there's not enough material?" I asked. "This could be an absolutely giant album."

No, Paul said again.

But I couldn't get it off my mind. I sent Ed Kleban, an A&R man in charge of soundtrack and Broadway show albums, to see the movie. "There just isn't enough music," he said afterward. "You can't come out with an album that has only fifteen or eighteen minutes of songs from older albums on it."

"Well, it's a damn shame," I said, and brooded further about it. Columbia's profits were then shaky. I needed a blockbuster album to replace Mitch Miller and the Broadway show albums. This was no passing academic question: one good album that year could make or break the year's bottom line. A simple hit-movie theme—the theme from *Exodus* or *Never On Sunday*, for example—can take an album of routine background music to the top of the charts, where it will stay for months.

The problem continued to gnaw at me, and one day, right in the middle of an afternoon's work, I left to see the film myself. Inside the theater, I suddenly realized that all I had been told about was the fifteen minutes of Paul Simon music. No one had mentioned that composer Dave Grusin had written background music for the film as well. There was *plenty* of music to fill out the album. Grusin's music was standard background material, the kind of music in every other soundtrack album. So why not this one? Besides, people who buy soundtrack albums are entirely different from regular record consumers. Mostly, they want to reidentify with a film they really liked. It was already clear to me that *The Graduate* would be one of the major box-office films of all time; it made obvious sense to release an album.

I called Mort Lewis, Paul and Artie's manager, and argued my case. He said that Paul did *not* want the album released; Artie agreed. They felt that a Simon & Garfunkel album should have eleven strong cuts on it; anything less would insult their fans. Besides, they were working on the *Bookends* album, and they didn't want any soundtrack album to interfere with its sales. I argued that the soundtrack album would reach a vast number of moviegoers rather than just Simon & Garfunkel fans; many wouldn't have even *heard* of them. A whole new audience would open up to them, far larger than the half million or so who had bought each of their previous three albums.

I asked to speak to Paul. I told him my reasons and assured him that the album would be packaged as a movie soundtrack. I said that the album's cover would use a scene from the film, that the album title would clearly state this was the official motion picture *soundtrack* rather than a specific Simon & Garfunkel album. Something like: "Mike Nichols directs . . . starring Anne Bancroft and Dustin Hoffman . . ." with a credit saying

"Songs by Paul Simon, performed by Simon & Garfunkel." I added that the album's hoped-for success would *not* cause me to push back the release of *Bookends,* which was to contain the complete version of what looked to be a smash single, "Mrs. Robinson."

Paul felt very strongly about this. "We've been working on the *Bookends* album a long time, we love it, and we think it's a major creative breakthrough," he said. "We don't want to wait six months to release it just because of your commercial problems."

I repeated that *Bookends* would be released right on top of the *Graduate* soundtrack album. I loved the idea of this from a career point of view. "These albums together," I said, "could really make you superstars. If *both* hit the top of the charts, you'll have undreamed-of commercial success, a breakthrough that will firmly establish you."

The rest, of course, is history. Paul and Artie agreed reluctantly to its release in the spring of 1968, and sales of the soundtrack album, coupled with *Bookends,* took them over the top of five million units. Simon and Garfunkel became household names all over the world.

Unfortunately, Paul and Arthur were fairly indifferent to *The Graduate* album's smash success; they harbored negative feelings about Columbia that lasted almost two years. Disputes kept cropping up. We charged an extra dollar for *Bookends,* for example; it had a large poster inside and I was trying to establish further the concept of variable pricing. They opposed this. They were concerned about the consumers, which was laudable. I was concerned about the increasing cost of recording and a shrinking margin of profits, which cast me in the villain's role. Soon after, the renegotiation of their contract put us on opposite sides of the fence again. They were now on top of the rock world and felt that they deserved a much better royalty deal than when they signed as total unknowns.

I didn't disagree but I was smarting from their coolness. I had pushed for the *Graduate* album and it had paid off handsomely; when that album and *Bookends* went to the top of the trade charts, my predictions of their superstardom came true. An album that reaches Number One creates a star. For two albums to reach the top at the same time creates a superstar. For all the usual human reasons, I felt that I deserved their thanks; nothing happened.

So feelings on *both* sides clouded the negotiations, delaying them longer than was really necessary. The matter was finally resolved by giving them the higher royalty and giving us an extension of the contract.

My relationship with the two of them still needed improvement. I began to try harder. I related to both of them on emotional as well as music levels, and I knew that the barriers could be broken down. What's more, I loved their music; at home I played their albums more than any others for pure enjoyment. I started inviting Paul to lunch and he began to open up slowly, partly because some difficulties were developing in the Simon and Garfunkel relationship as a result of Artie's extended stay in Mexico making the Mike Nichols movie *Catch-22*.

The *Bridge Over Troubled Water* album, which was well over a year in the making, was finally completed in 1970, and Paul and Artie asked me to come to the studio to listen to the tapes. Paul's parents and his brother were there and it was a very special moment; the album was absolutely breathtaking. After we listened, and I told them how beautiful it was, they asked what I thought the single should be. "It just *has* to be 'Bridge Over Troubled Water,'" I said; they were surprised. It was not a typical single; they had assumed that I would suggest "Cecilia," a more up-tempo cut (which later became a hit also).

"We love 'Bridge,'" Artie said, "and we planned to make it the album's title song—but do you *really* think it could be the album's hit single?"

"I can't be absolutely positive," I said, "but this is one time to go for a home run. It is the age of rock and this is a ballad—and a long one at that—but *if* it hits, it could become a classic." I wanted to release it as a single simultaneously with the album and avoid even the slightest chance of another record breaking out first. The market response might have dictated "Cecilia" or "El Condor Pasa," but they would be just hits, not a shot at an all-time standard. The rest, again, is history. The *Bridge* album had the biggest worldwide sales of all time, selling about nine million copies—approached only in recent years by Carole King's *Tapestry* album. It won more Grammys than any other album had ever received, and Simon & Garfunkel were carried still further along on a wave of huge success.

Our relationship had settled down by now and we had become friends. Artie was traveling a lot at the time, but when he was in town we would talk and I'd bring him up to date on what was happening in music. Paul and I had lunch often, and once he touchingly said, "I think our lives are going to be interwoven at some point. I may not always be a recording artist. I just know we will be more closely involved in some way."

Then trouble developed between Paul and Artie. It began, as I've noted, when Artie's role in *Catch-22* unavoidably held up the recording of *Bridge Over Troubled Water*. Paul becomes very impatient once he finishes writing all the songs for an album. He wants to go into the studio immediately. Artie had taken the *Catch-22* role as much to kill time as for any other reason—but without realizing that Mike Nichols would take a year to finish the picture. The original Nichols estimate was a few months, but once you commit yourself to a film, you can't leave. Money was hardly the question. Artie made around seventy-five thousand dollars for his role in *Catch-22;* he made about a million dollars from *Bridge.* But he couldn't leave the set in Mexico, and Paul felt quite burdened. Then, too, their approach to album production was painfully slow, requiring enormous teamwork—laying down one track at a time, then deciding *together* whether they were happy with it. For this to work, you have to be perfectly compatible in taste, and this was becoming an increasing problem with them. So somewhere between his impatience with Artie's movie-making, and a feeling that he wanted more exclusive control over the songs he'd written, Paul decided they should part company.

One day he called and asked to see me. "Before others find out," he said, "I want you to know I've decided to split with Artie. I don't think we'll be recording together again." I was *very* much taken aback. I knew that there were problems, but I didn't think *this* was the solution. Simon & Garfunkel were an institution; they were among the two or three top artists in the world. And now, once again, a winning group at the absolute peak of its success wanted to split! But, as usual, there was really nothing I could do. You can't legislate love between a married couple, and you can't make two artists stay together.

It is a theme I can't help but repeat: an *institution* is far more important commercially than its component parts. I remember thinking how stupid it seemed for The Mamas and the Papas to break up at the height of their career. Each member thought that he or she could be bigger than the group, a misguided idea. This always seemed so obvious—I couldn't understand why Paul felt forced to take this risk. I had hoped it would be different with him and Artie; they'd grown up together, they seemed to me like brothers.

I warned Paul that he would have to work for a long time even to attempt to reach the level of success that Simon & Garfunkel enjoyed. No matter how well each of the Beatles has done individually—and they have done exceptionally well—no one of them has achieved the kind of success the group did. I believed that Paul's individual career would have the same problem. This upset him a great deal, though I didn't realize it at the time; a year later I read an interview in *Rolling Stone* in which he said that he'd wanted *total* support from me—and that my theories about individuals and institutions disappointed him. I can understand his feelings; yet for my part, I could not have feigned enthusiasm. I didn't want Simon & Garfunkel to break up.

It is to the enormous credit of both men that their careers have continued to prosper and grow. Paul's subsequent albums have received tremendous critical praise. His *There Goes Rhymin' Simon* album was nominated for the Grammy Award for best album of 1973 and sold over a million units. Artie was at first hesitant to record. He felt pressure to do something, but for a while he didn't know which direction to take. We stayed in touch, and I kept encouraging him to do an album of other people's material. He resisted this, misconstruing it to mean that I wanted him to "cover" hit songs, like Johnny Mathis or Andy Williams. That wasn't my thinking at all; I wanted him to sift through the best of current writing—and also have songs written for him—to put together a very personal album. Composers and music publishers will go great distances for you because of your name, I argued; you'll have the pick, if you want, of writers like James Taylor, Carole King, Paul Williams and Jimmy Webb.

Artie continued to equivocate. For a while he wanted to combine classical and contemporary music; next he talked of church music, and then of Greek music. At each turn, I tried to push him as far as possible in the direction of contemporary writers. The others were fine concepts, but they were very eclectic and unlikely to reach any sizable audience. Finally he came around and went to San Francisco to record the album with Roy Halee, the brilliant engineer-producer who had worked on all the other Simon & Garfunkel albums, making an invaluable contribution to each of them. I listened to a few cuts at one point, and I thought the album was shaping up beautifully. But, as I expected, Artie's perfectionist tendencies had emerged strongly; he took more than a year to record the album. At one point he even called to hold *my* hand.

"Look," he said, "I just want you to know that I haven't lost my perspective. The album is taking a long time, but I'm fully in control." Rather than directly bring up the cost of studio time, he backed into it. "How many copies will I have to sell for Columbia to recoup its investment?" he asked. I figured about two hundred to two hundred and fifty thousand, and he said: "Don't worry about a thing. It's in the bag." That was like Artie. He knew that I must have been very concerned about the wildly mounting studio costs, but in view of his past contributions and our relationship, I wasn't bringing it up. He appreciated that; so he dealt with it in his own way.

His prediction was correct. The costs of *Angel Clare*—more than two hundred thousand dollars—were recouped. In fact, sales of the album were close to the million-unit mark by the spring of 1974, a major winner for him.

Paul finished his first album in 1972, and, as usual, I met him at the studio—this time with a few of his good friends: Charles Grodin, the actor who starred in the *The Heartbreak Kid;* Zohra Lampert, the actress; and Michael Tannen, his lawyer, business advisor and closest friend—to hear the tracks. Paul and I spoke afterward and decided that the first single should be "Mother and Child Reunion" and the second, "Me and Julio Down By The Schoolyard."

This would be the follow-up album to *Bridge,* and we realized that it would attract a great deal of attention; we wanted everything to go smoothly. Paul felt more comfortable about doing the initial press interviews in England and then the rest of Europe. He was a giant star there— the *Bridge Over Trouble Water* album had sold more than a million copies in England alone—and we knew that the coverage would be tremendous. I planned to be there at the same time to make it easier. Obviously, questions would be asked about the split-up, and I knew that Paul would be candid; that's his style. But I didn't want him to be so blunt that he and Artie would never be able to get back together again.

For I believed—and still believe—that they will record together again. They will undoubtedly continue to pursue their own individual careers, but every so often the special magic they create will be heard again. It happened in 1972 at a special fund-raising concert for McGovern at Madison Square Garden. Three great "groups" were reunited for a cause they strongly supported: the brilliant comedy team of Elaine May and Mike Nichols; the group that crossed all barriers of folk and rock music, Peter, Paul & Mary; and Simon & Garfunkel. Nichols and May started the evening off. Although they were a little rusty in their timing, they showed the eighteen thousand people who jammed the Garden—most of whom were young and had never seen them before—how their comedy had created a whole new dimension in humor. They were devastatingly funny. Peter, Paul & Mary came next. I was moved listening to them breathe their special meaning into Dylan's "Blowin' In The Wind" and seeing them charm the audience with "Puff (The Magic Dragon)" and then bring them to their feet with "This Land Is Your Land." Then, after Dionne Warwick had showed everyone why she is a such a unique interpreter of the great Bacharach and David hits, Simon & Garfunkel came onstage.

I loved watching them amble on, Garfunkel striking that awkward, boyish stance at the microphone and Simon shuffling back and forth and then from side to side, grinning and waving to the crowd, which was standing up shouting greetings to these two troubadors who had brought so much good music to them. And then they started to sing—"Mrs. Robinson," "Emily Whenever I May Find Her," "The Boxer," "The 59th Street Bridge Song (Feelin' Groovy)," "America," "The Sound of Silence," "Cecilia," "Mother and Child Reunion," "Me and Julio," "Homeward Bound" and, of course, "Bridge Over Troubled Water." It was staggering. The audience responded with wave after wave of applause. All in all, a beautiful evening, ending with a party I arranged for them in the glass-enclosed penthouse of the New York Hilton Hotel.

But things didn't change. Paul still planned to record his next album alone, and we met one day to discuss it. His first album had sold a million—great for anyone else . . . but not satisfactory to Paul. With typical self-appraisal, he asked where he had gone wrong. I assured him that the album was a smashing success. The only way it could have done better would have been if he had toured, giving performances in major cities behind the album's release, or if the single had become a major copyright in the "Bridge Over Troubled Water" or "The Sound of Silence" tradition. "Me and Julio" and "Mother and Child Reunion" were big hits, but they weren't the ballad kind of hit which is recorded by many *other* artists, thereby providing an extra kick to album sales.

Paul agreed to tour behind the *Rhymin' Simon* album. For a long time he had been against giving any more concerts—saying how wearing it was to tour. We had discussed the subject when his first solo album was coming out, but he was adamantly against it. When we were in England for the press interviews, however, he began to change his mind. We went to a Cat Stevens concert with Michael Tannen, who was in England helping Paul coordinate his affairs, and Barry Krost, Cat Stevens's manager, had reserved the Royal Box for us; we were joined there by Prince Rupert Loewenstein, the business advisor to The Rolling Stones; Penelope Tree, the famed society model; and her beau, photographer David Bailey. Paul and I sat in the first row and I watched him reacting to the stares from the audience down below. I could see his adrenalin rise during the concert as the performance built in intensity. He was getting excited. I had an idea; I debated with myself whether to ask Barry to have Cat Stevens introduce Paul from the audience—maybe he'd even play a number or two. I thought that it would be great for Paul to be on a stage again after such a long absence. The publicity would be tremendous. But would he mind? He had said that his performing days were over. Did I dare encourage it? Would Cat Stevens mind sharing the spotlight? I decided against it.

After the concert, I asked Barry what he thought of the idea. Would he have been upset? "Hell, no," he said. "It would have provided great electricity and made the evening even more of an event." Then I asked Paul, "Suppose Cat had introduced you to the audience and then asked you to join him onstage. What would you have done?" His answer: "I had three numbers all picked out." It was clear that Paul would tour again.

The question of which single to release first from *Rhymin' Simon* was discussed at length. Paul said that he thought "American Tune" would be the best single. I disagreed. I didn't think it would take off that easily and I suggested "Kodachrome." "My God," said Paul, "*you're* the one who talks so often about the importance of a ballad hit! This is a quality song with strong lyrics. It could be another 'Bridge Over Troubled Water.'" The lyrics *were* strong; but I didn't hear a strong enough melody line. "If it's going to be a hit," I said, "it will break out of the album anyway. But up front it's a questionable choice. Since you haven't really toured yet, your solo image still isn't fully established; it's better for you to release a safer and more obvious single."

"Kodachrome" was a much surer thing. I urged him to pick it first.

He said he'd think about it. By the next day, he agreed. As a result, *There Goes Rhymin' Simon* got off to a tremendous start. It picked up further steam when a second single, "Love Me Like a Rock," was released after AM stations had begun to request it heavily. That single went gold, selling over a million copies. Paul toured fairly extensively, building a great show around his awesome list of classic standards. Then *Rolling Stone* delighted Paul by choosing "American Tune" as the song of the year. Its quality was finally recognized.

JIMMY GUTERMAN AND OWEN O'DONNELL
"THE DANGLING CONVERSATION"
FROM *THE 50 WORST ROCK 'N' ROLL RECORDS OF ALL TIME* (1991)

NUMBER THIRTY-NINE

Simon and Garfunkel

"The Dangling Conversation," *Columbia, 1966*

Highest chart position: number twenty-five

Lots of overeducated guys say they're poets to pick up girls, and many of them eventually think they are. Paul Simon is no exception. How many got the feeling while watching *Annie Hall* that Simon wasn't acting?

Throughout their tempestuous career, Simon and Garfunkel were always thought of as the one folk group who could bridge the generation gap: they were pseudohip enough for the younger set and pseudointellectual enough for the older. Many have credited Bob Dylan with starting the singer-songwriter genre, but it was actually Simon who made hypersensitivity an inescapable hallmark of the form. "The Dangling Conversation" is the exemplar of Simon's writing during the heyday of Simon and Garfunkel.

Using his best professorial tone (one he still reserves for folks who don't understand he was right to bust a United Nations cultural boycott), Simon relates the story of lovers who can relate to their choices in literature better than to each other. Using the standard clichés of people who tend to overintellectualize everything (the same people who thought Simon and Garfunkel were so wonderful to begin with), Simon falls into his own trap. He's supposedly asking us to feel pity for these people, which makes sense: virtually all Simon and Garfunkel songs—including such dubious classics as "The Boxer" and "I Am a Rock"—are soft requests for pity.

But the only ones you pity after hearing "The Dangling Conversation" are the inner-city kids deprived of a good education who would certainly have gotten more out of the opportunity than the narrator and the woman he's dangling with. The whole point of "The Dangling Conversation" is for Simon to sound smart and poetic, so he drops names and hopes he accumulates some of the power of those whose names he uses for rhymes. He lists poets who happened to be hip at the time (Emily Dickinson, Robert Frost), but the only thing those names do is fill out the meter: he's not singing about them, just listing them. He could just as easily mention Wallace Stevens or Rod McKuen. In "The Dangling Conversation," it makes no difference.

As if the conversation isn't enough to make you want to dangle Simon out of a high-floor apartment window, his description are even more appalling. His point is to sound smart, sensitive: i.e., a good catch. But his overenunciated delivery (augmented by strings that seem to have wandered in from a different studio) also says, "Look how cool I am that I live this life of the mind. I am so, so smart." Simon didn't invent folk rock, as some have claimed: he invented elitist rock, and he carries its standard to this day.

SIMON AND GARFUNKEL—A GREATEST HITS ALBUM THAT LIVES UP TO ITS NAME (1972)

Here is a greatest hits album that lives up to its name—a generous collection of 14 Simon and Garfunkel classics, from "The Sound of Silence" to "Bridge Over Troubled Water." The only single hits not included are "A Hazy Shade of Winter," "At the Zoo," and "Fakin' It." In their place are a couple of earlier album cuts, plus excellent live versions of "For Emily, Wherever I May Find Her," "Kathy's Song," "The 59th Street Bridge Song (Feelin' Groovy)," and "Homeward Bound."

Why bother to review an anthology of such familiar material? In this case, it seems to me that Simon and Garfunkel deserve particular homage for their quiet but extraordinary accomplishment during the late Sixties— especially since there was a definite reaction against them. Perhaps it was simply that they became too popular, embraced by the middle class, praised by The New Yorker, and apotheosized by *The Graduate*. At a time when it was hip to drop out and blow your mind, when the rhetoric of protest escalated into the rhetoric of revolution, when the communal idea began to spread, Simon and Garfunkel suddenly seemed old hat, even reactionary, to many people. Simon's songs were intellectual and meditative, hardly the right background music for manning barricades.

There was no cryptic psychedelia buried in their records. Nor did Simon and Garfunkel ever invoke sensuality. Indeed it was probably their image of chastity in an atmosphere of aggressive sexual ostentation that most set them apart from the vanguard counterculture. There they were, crooning to the dream figures "Kathy" and "Emily"—ideals that didn't so much stand for a type of woman or relationship as for virginal adolescent romanticism itself. The poignancy of unconsummated longing, so very *un*hip, was made all the more acute by the purity of Garfunkel's voice and his angelic face. I recall reading sarcastic remarks about Paul Simon's "bridge fixation." Well, Hart Crane liked bridges too. And besides, the musical-cultural role of Simon and Garfunkel was precisely that of bridging gaps between styles.

I'm a little sorry that the cuts on this collection aren't arranged in chronological order so that we could trace directly Paul Simon's development as a songwriter. Unlike Dylan, who executed a series of dramatic stylistic changes, Simon's evolution has been subtle, but in the long run almost as significant. Though the distance he has traveled is far more apparent on his solo album than it is here, it is still very evident after close listening. Compare, for instance, "The Sounds of Silence" and "I Am a Rock," with "America" and "The Boxer." The difference represents a triumphant movement away from folk rock formalism and an academic poetic style toward a more relaxed, more assured narrative style with greater depth and range of expression.

The first Simon and Garfunkel hit, "The Sounds of Silence," appeared late in '64, a couple of months after *Another Side of Bob Dylan,* but it didn't become popular until the end of '65, with a newly-dubbed electric backing. By that time the first two Dylan electric albums were out. Listening to the song today, it sounds even better than it did then, its statement as powerful and provocative as Dylan's "Mr. Tambourine Man," which at the time I preferred infinitely. "The Sounds of Silence" has a strong melody, simple harmony, and knock-out words—an outpouring of beautiful imagery flawed only by the predictable excesses of a gifted but still-young poet intoxicated with language and a little uneasy working with close rhymes in a tight structure. There was stilted poeticism and pontification ("'Fools!' said I. . . . ") but these faults scarcely detracted from the lyrics' cumulative impact.

Toward the end of '66, *Parsley, Sage, Rosemary and Thyme* was released. Two cuts from it, "The Dangling Conversation" and "Scarborough Fair/Canticle," are included in this collection, plus the new live versions of three other cuts. Listening to *Parsley* today is almost as staggering an experience as it was nearly six years ago. One glorious melody follows another, each brilliantly arranged and impeccably sung. "The Dangling Conversation," for all its literary self-consciousness, expresses better than any song before or since the pervasive *angst* of the affluent collegiate. *Parsley* also contained "The 59th Street Bridge Song (Feelin' Groovy)," Simon's most relaxed, least "poetic" song up to that time. As a whole, *Parsley* was a kaleidoscope of moods and ideas communicated with unprecedented tenderness and intimacy.

"America," from the *Bookends* album, was Simon's next major step forward. It is three and a half
minutes of sheer brilliance, whose unforced narrative, alternating precise detail with sweeping observation, evokes the panorama of restless, paved America, and simultaneously illuminates a drama of shared loneliness on a bus trip with cosmic implications. I don't think a song could be more compact and fluid at the same time. Also from *Bookends* are the title

cut and "Mrs. Robinson." The latter, as deft a putdown as any, goes to express with humor and pathos a general loss of faith and innocence, skillfully equating the national sport with the American dream.

Songs taken from Simon and Garfunkel's last album, *Bridge Over Troubled Water*, are "Cecilia," "El Condor Pasa," the title cut and "The Boxer." In some ways "The Boxer" is even more ambitious than "America." Both songs are essentially dramatic monologues with commentary. But "The Boxer" is more daring, since it is the autobiography of a loser in the big city and risks sounding false. In "America," Simon was able to call upon a stereotypical middle class ethos, familiar since *The Catcher In the Rye*. The saga of the boxer goes beyond that ethos into social tragedy. The reason it works so well is that Simon does not literally enter his character. The impersonality of the monologue is accentuated by the cut's excellent streamlined arrangement which keeps the singing partly submerged and provides just the right amount of telling sound effect.

"Bridge Over Troubled Water" is of course the ultimate Simon and Garfunkel hit. Though I think the cut suffers from too much echo and syrupy strings, it contains Garfunkel's finest inspirational singing. In recent years, only one other song has so thoroughly saturated the national psyche—Carole King's "You've Got a Friend." Both songs are basically pop spirituals that can be done by everyone from Aretha Franklin to Andy Williams. To discuss them in depth would be almost meaningless, since they transcend categories of popular music and are already so much a part of our cultural lifeblood. It is enough to say that "Bridge Over Troubled Water" has one of Simon's greatest melodies—a long soaring arch that perfectly carries forward the spirit of the lyrics, whose sentiments of hope and promise of comfort are universal.

Goi

In the 1972 *Rolling Stone* interview included here, Simon says that putting Simon and Garfunkel behind him left him "free to do what I want. I want to sing other types of songs that Simon and Garfunkel wouldn't do. . . . It was a chance to back out and gamble a little bit."

Part Two: Going Solo is about some of the experiments Simon tried and the gambles he took after breaking up with Art Garfunkel. It's about Simon's depression, reoccurring in good times and in bad. And it's about the way Simon and Garfunkel's lives remained, in Garfunkel's words, "amazingly intertwined."

One of the ways in which Simon "did what he wanted" was by experimenting with musicians from a variety of cultures, something that brought him praise as well as criticism—especially in later years for the creation of *Graceland.* By 1975, according to Timothy White in *Rock Lives:*

> [Simon had] been instrumental in introducing to mass audiences the talents of such artists as reggae guitarist Hux Brown, the Dixie Hummingbirds [gospel], South American folk instrumentalists Urubamba [also known as Los Incas], bottleneck guitarist Stefan Grossman, the Jessy Dixon Singers [gospel], Brazilian singer-accordianist Sivuca, and jazz greats like [french] violinist Stephane Grappelli.

According to Bruce Pollock, whose 1976 article from *Stereo Review* is reprinted here, these gambles paid off big: "He's produced three fine albums, each one revealing a variety of influences, each one musically rich as well as emotionally complex."

In his article from *Harper's,* George W. S. Trow also roots for Simon, in his fashion. While he claims that Simon is one of the few pop musicians "worth following," he also indicates that Simon doesn't experiment as much as he might. The work on "Still Crazy," he says, shows "that unsuc-cessful encounters with adulthood can give a man a mean tongue. This would be all right," he continues, "if Simon's mean tongue took any risks or drew any blood."

Simon may not be "mean" enough for Trow in regard to his lyrics, but he certainly has no trouble being mean to himself. In "The Odysseus of Urban Melancholy" by Paul Cowan, Simon discusses his struggles with depression. Sounding like a draft of "You Can Call Me Al," the voice in Simon's head says, "Maybe I can't write anymore; maybe what I did wasn't very good anyway; maybe I'm not generally attractive to people; my life is unstructured; what am I doing here?"

The depressions that lingered while albums went gold and Grammys were garnered became worse when projects were ill-received. Such was the case after the release of the movie and soundtrack of *One-Trick Pony* in 1980. As Simon told Tony Schwartz in an interview for *Playboy,* excerpted at the end of this section, "The movie came out to mixed reviews—and the sound-track album didn't do nearly as well as I'd hoped. It was a period of great depression for me. I was immobilized." Yet despite bad reviews and their repercussions, the process of writing, scoring, and starring in a film about the music business was, for Simon, another source of growth. Included here is Dave Marsh's piece, "What Do You Do When You're Not a Kid Anymore and You Still Want to Rock & Roll?", which describes the creation of *One-Trick Pony.*

Less than a year after the film was released, Simon and Garfunkel reunited for a concert in Manhattan's Central Park. The event received a lot of press. Over the years, both had made guest appearances at the other's concerts; in 1977 they did a television special together; in 1975 they recorded "My Little Town" and included it on two albums, one of Paul's and one of Artie's; and in 1972 they reunited on behalf of George McGovern. Yet the 1981 performance was their first full concert together in eleven years. Perhaps because it came at a time when neither career was at a peak, there was speculation, as Stephen Holden puts it, that the reunion "looks like a lasting thing." In an article for *Rolling Stone,* Holden said:

> You can almost hear cynics snorting about this particular reunion—a shrewd, desperate move to sock some life back into two sagging solo careers, *n'est-ce pas?* But Simon and Garfunkel insist that's not the case. . . . "I don't think we'd get together if the potential for a joyous reunion weren't there," [said Simon]. "We'd never decide to grit our teeth just to make a couple of million dollars."

Or would they? These two men and their famous collaboration are revisited here, in "It's 'Simon & Garfunkel' Again" by Tony Schwartz.

What was "safe" for Simon in the early 1970s—working with Art Garfunkel—was now, in the 1980s, another "experiment," and not his most fruitful one. But risks like the ones described here were to set the stage for even bigger collaborative gambles yet to come.

JON LANDAU
THE <u>ROLLING STONE</u> INTERVIEW WITH PAUL SIMON (1972)

The interview with Paul Simon took place on three days during late May and early June. It produced 13 hours of tape for some poor soul to transcribe, a task made more difficult by the similarity between mine and Paul's New York accents.

Paul divides his time between a farm in Pennsylvania and a triplex, once owned by guitarist Andre Segovia, in New York's Upper East Side, where the interview was taped. Peggy, Paul's wife, was present only briefly. She and Paul are expecting their first child in September.

Paul had just completed production on the first album of his friends Los Incas, whom he used for the background track on "El Condor Pasa." In September and October he plans to produce his second solo album and in November will embark on a national tour.

We had not met before and so found ourselves getting to know each other while doing the job. I found him open on virtually every subject, but always deliberate and intent on saying exactly what he meant. At times, as his voice and pace would become more measured when the subject became more important, I realized he really did approach this interview the same way he approaches writing, recording, performing—as a perfectionist.—*J.L.*

How would you describe your current relationship with Art Garfunkel?

Cautious. We get along by observing certain rules.

You're aware of what irritates each other?

We're aware. We try not to do that.

Was there a specific confrontation or meeting or decision that finalized the breakup?

No, I don't think there was. During the making of *Bridge Over Troubled Water* there were a lot of times when it just wasn't fun to work together. It was very hard work and it was complex, and both of us thought—I think Artie said that he felt that he didn't want to record—and I know I said I felt that if I had to go through these kind of personality abrasions, I didn't want to continue to do it. Then when the album was finished Artie was going to do *Carnal Knowledge* and I went to do an album by myself. We didn't say that's the end. We didn't know if it was the end or not. But it became apparent by the time the movie was out and by the time my album was out that it was over.

What were the immediate feelings brought on after the split?

Having a track record to live up to and the history of successes had become a hindrance. It becomes harder to break out of what people expect you to do. From that point of view, I'm delighted that I didn't have to write a Simon and Garfunkel follow-up to "Bridge Over Troubled Water," which I think would have been an inevitable let-down for people. It would have been hard on me, hard on both of us. But more hard on the writer, because he takes the responsibility. If an album stiffs, I think to myself it stiffed because I didn't come up with the big songs.

So dissolving Simon and Garfunkel was a way of unburdening yourself of a lot of pressure.

Yes. And it left me free to do what I want. I wanted to sing other types of songs, that Simon and Garfunkel wouldn't do. "Mother and Child Reunion," for example, is not a song that you would have normally thought that Simon and Garfunkel would have done. It's possible that they might have. But it wouldn't have been the same, and I don't know whether I would have been so inclined in that direction. So for me it was a chance to back out, and gamble a bit; it's been so long since it was a gamble.

When Simon and Garfunkel was most active doing concerts—around '68—what was the day-to-day relationship like between the two of you? How did you function on the road?

On the road I remember things were pretty pleasant from the point of view of us getting along. It was hard and boring to travel so much. But at the end, during the concerts in 1970, I would go with Peggy and everyone would bring whoever they wanted and it was more like festivals, because we didn't go out too much, and when we did go out, we went to places we wanted to play, Paris, or London . . .

How did you feel on the road?

I always felt weird on the road. I was in a state of semi-hypnosis. I went into a daze, and I did things by rote. You got to the place, you went to the hall, you tested out the microphones, changed your guitar strings, read the telegrams, found out who was coming to the concert that you knew and planned out what you were going to do after the show and usually tried to find a decent restaurant in the town and that was it. Just sort of hung out with friends, assuming that there were friends in a place.

Anything on the road contribute to the breakup?

I don't think the road had much to do in exacerbating our relationship because, first of all, we weren't on the road that much in the end. The breakup had to do with a natural drifting apart as we got older and the separate lives that were more individual. We weren't so consumed with recording and performing. We had other activities. I had different people and different interests, and Artie's interest in film led him to other people. His acting took him away, and that led him into other areas. The only strain was to maintain a partnership.

Because it was unnatural?

You gotta work at a partnership. You have to work at it, you got to . . .

But at this point it was not a natural one.

At this point there was no great pressure to stay together, other than money, which exerted really very little influence upon us. We certainly weren't going to stay together to make a lot of money. We didn't need the money. And musically, it was not a creative team, too much, because Artie is a singer and I'm a writer and player and a singer. We didn't work together on a creative level and prepare the songs. I did that. When we came into the studio it became more and more me, in the studio, making the tracks and choosing the musicians, partly because a great deal of the time during *Bridge,* Artie wasn't there. I was doing things myself with Roy Halee, our engineer and co-producer. We were planning tracks out and to a great degree, that responsibility fell to me.

Artie and I shared responsibility but not creativity. For example, we always said Artie does the arranging. Anybody who knows anything would know that that was a fabrication—how can one guy write the songs and the other guy do the arranging? How does that happen? If a guy writes the song, he obviously has a concept. But when it came to making decisions it had always been Roy, Artie and me. And this later became difficult for me.

I viewed Simon and Garfunkel as basically a three-way partnership. Each person had a relatively equal say. So, in other words, if Roy and Artie said, "Let's do a long ending on 'The Boxer,'" I said, "Two out of three," and did it their way. I didn't say, "Hey, this is my song, I don't want it to be like that." Never did it occur to me to say that. "Fine," I'd say.

It wasn't until my own album that I ever started to think to myself, "What do I really like?" Roy would say, "That's a great vocal, listen to that." And I would listen, and I wouldn't think it was great but he said it was great, so I believed it was great. I just suspended my judgment. I let him do it. On my own album I learned every aspect of it has to be your own judgment. You have to say, "Now wait a minute, is that the right tempo? Is that the right take?" It's your decision. Nobody else can do it.

You said that more and more on 'Bridge' you were exercising the judgment and making the plans. Is it that Artie wasn't that interested?

It's hard to say, but I guess that's true—no, I can't say that. He had other interests that were very strong. But he certainly was interested in making the record. From the point of view of creativity, I didn't have any other interests than the music, I had no other distractions. On several tracks on *Bridge* there's no Artie on it at all. "The Only Living Boy in New York," he sang a little on the background. "Baby Driver," he wasn't there. He was doing *Catch-22* in Mexico at that time. It's a Simon and Garfunkel record, but not really. And it became easier to work by separating. On *Bridge Over Troubled Water* there are many songs where you don't hear Simon and Garfunkel singing together. Because of that the separation became easier.

Was he there most of the time?

He was there most of the time. This would be an example of how it worked: Artie would be away for maybe three months. He'd come back and I'd say, "I wrote the lyrics to 'El Condor Pasa.' We'll do this. Here, 'The Only Living Boy in New York,' OK? 'Baby Driver"s finished. Me and Roy mixed 'The Boxer.'" So, to a degree, there was a separation without there being a lessening of musical quality.

What was his reaction when he'd come back and you'd show him all this stuff?

"Bridge Over Troubled Water" was written while he was away. He'd come back and I'd say, "Here's a song I just wrote, 'Bridge Over Troubled Water.' I think you should sing it."

It seems like his absences would tend to make you more resentful if he were to reject any of your ideas. Did they?

That's true. If I'd say, "We'll do this with a gospel piano and it's written in your key, so you have the song," it was his right in the partnership to say, "I don't want to do that song," as he said with "Bridge Over Troubled Water."

He said that?

Yes.

He didn't want to do the song?

No, he didn't want to do it.

He didn't want to do it altogether, or he didn't want to sing it himself?

He didn't want to sing it himself. He couldn't hear it for himself. He felt I should have done it. And many times I think I'm sorry I didn't do it.

Would you ever record it?

No. I think it's too late to record. Many times on stage, though, when I'd be sitting off the to the side and Larry Knechtel would be playing the piano and Artie would be singing "Bridge," people would stomp and cheer when it was over, and I would think, "That's my song, man. Thank you very much. I wrote that song." I must say this, in the earlier days when things were smoother I never would have thought that, but towards the end when things were strained I did. It's not a very generous thing to think, but I did think that. I resented it, and I must say that I was aware of the fact that I resented it, and I knew that this wouldn't have been the case two years earlier.

Do you mark the strain from Catch-22 *or does it go back before that?*

I think it started before that.

When did you become aware of it?

There was always some kind of strain, but it was workable. The bigger you get, the more of a strain it is, because in your everyday life, you're less used to compromising. As you get bigger, you have your own way. But in a partnership you always have to compromise. So all day long I might be out telling this lawyer to do that or this architect to build a house in a certain way and you expect everything. You're the boss. When you get into a partnership, you're not the boss. There's no boss. That makes it hard.

There's 11 songs on *Bridge Over Troubled Water* but there were supposed to be 12. I had written a song called "Cuba Si, Nixon No." And Artie didn't want to do it. We even cut the track for it. Artie wouldn't sing on it. And Artie wanted to do a Bach chorale thing, which I didn't want to do. We were fightin' over which was gonna be the twelfth song, and then I said, "Fuck it, put it out with 11 songs, if that's the way it is." We were at the end of our energies over that.

We had just finished working on this television special, which really wiped us out because of all the fighting that went on, not amongst ourselves, but with the Bell Telephone people. We were very tired. It was all happening in the fall. We did a tour in October. We filmed the television special from September until October. We then had to postpone working on the album until the TV special and the tour were over. And then we went into December and we had to stop for Christmas and we didn't finish the album until like the first week in January. We were really exhausted, and we fought over that. Well, at that point, I just wanted out, I just wanted to take a vacation. So did he, I guess. So we stopped at 11 songs.

You didn't know when you finished that album . . .

I thought that was the end. In my mind I said, "That's the end. It's good because we had all our strength for this album, and we did a hard amount of work on it," and now we've finished it, and we'd just about cleaned ourselves out. We had no songs left except for "Cuba Si, Nixon No," which eventually got lost. It wasn't that great a song anyway. So my ideas were wiped out. I'd used up all my ideas on this album that I'd stored up, and it was time for a resting and a time for thinking up new things, and it was an ideal time to start on something new and less auspicious than a new Simon and Garfunkel album. That's when I knew that I was gonna do my own album and do it simpler and do it, I hoped, faster.

The obvious question is why didn't it split up earlier?

That is a really good question. The answer has to go back to me. I always look for partnership, because I probably felt I couldn't do it myself. I would have been afraid or embarrassed. So I looked to work with a bunch of people. "We'll all do this. Actually I'll do it all, but we'll all take the credit or take the blame." Peggy brought me out of that and made me feel like I should do it myself and take the responsibility. If it's good, it's yours, and if it's bad, it's yours too. Go out and do your thing and say, "This is my thing."

One of the things that upset me was some of the criticism leveled at Simon and Garfunkel. I always took exception to it, but actually I agree with a lot of it, but I didn't feel it was me. Like that it was very sweet. I didn't particularly like sweet soft music. I did like sweet soft music, but not exclusively.

You thought Artie was contributing a lot to that?

That is Artie's taste. Artie's taste is much more to the sweet and so is Roy's. Sweet and big and lush. More than me. There's nothing wrong with that, there's a place for lushness. It's not generally the way I go. This is what I've said on the new album to Roy. I want the tempo to be right, I want it to be a good tempo. I want to get like the basic rhythm section and one coloring instrument maybe, like in "Duncan," the flutes and "Peace Like The River." That has its own coloring . . .

Simon and Garfunkel were known for their fastidiousness in recording. You seem to be looser on your own.

It was all three of us, but particularly Artie and Roy. Many times I had arguments where I wanted to leave in something that was poorly recorded, because it had the right feel, and they would always end up doing it again. They'd say, "It's bad, I didn't like it, I didn't mike it right, it was the first take and I didn't really/didn't get the balance," and I'd say, "I don't care, leave it. Leave it." That was the three-way partnership coming back to haunt me. Everybody has a voice and everybody's voice is equal. But actually not, there's an order of importance. The song and the performance. Those are both equally important, and next is the arrangement and next is the sound. That's the way it goes.

Was 'Bridge' your best album?

Yes. *Bridge* has better songs. And it has better singing. It is freer, in its own way. "Cecelia," for example, was made in a living room on a Sony. We were all pounding away and playing things. That was all it was. *Tick a tong tick a tick a tong tuck a tuck a toong tuck a . . .* on a Sony, and I said, "That's a great rhythm set, I love it." Everyday I'd come back from the studio, working on whatever we were working on, and I'd play this pounding thing. So then I said, "Let's make a record out of that." So we copied it over and extended it double the amount, so now we have three minutes of track, and the track is great. So now I pick up the guitar and I start to go, "Well, this will be like the guitar part"— *dung chicka dung chicka dung* and the lyrics were virtually the first lines I said. They're not lines at all, but it was right for that song, and I like that. It was like a little piece of magical fluff, but it works.

"El Condor Pasa" I like. That track was originally a record. The track is originally a recording on Phillips, a Los Incas record that I love. I said, "I love this melody. I'm going to write lyrics to it. I just love it, and we'll just sing it right over the track."

That's what it is and that works pretty different. "Bridge" is a very strong melodic song.

How was "Bridge Over Troubled Water" recorded?

We were in California. We were all renting this house. Me and Artie and Peggy were living in this house with a bunch of other people throughout the summer. It was a house on Bluejay Way, the one George Harrison wrote "Bluejay Way" about. We had this Sony machine and Artie, and a piano, and I'd finished working on a song, and we went into the studio. I had it written on guitar, so we had to transpose the song. I had it written in the key of G, and I think Artie sang it in E. E flat. We were with Larry Knechtel and I said, "Here's a song, it's in G, but I want it in E flat. I want it to have a gospel piano." So, first we had to transpose the chords and there was an arranger who used to do some work with me, Jimmie Haskell, who, as a favor, he said, "I'll write the chords, you call off the chord in G and I'll write it in E flat." And he did that. That was the extent of what he did. He later won a Grammy for that. We'd put his name down as one of the arrangers.

Then it took us about four days to get the piano part. Each night we'd work on the piano part until Larry really honed it into a good part.

Now, the song was originally two verses, and in the studio, as Larry was playing it, we decided—I believe it was Artie's idea, I can't remember, but I think it was Artie's idea to add another verse, because Larry was sort of elongating the piano part, so I said, "Play the piano part for a third verse again, even though I don't have it, and I'll write it," which I eventually did after the fact. I always felt that you could clearly see that it was written afterwards. It just doesn't sound like the first two verses.

Then the piano part was finished. Then we added bass—two basses, one way up high, the high bass notes. Joe Osborn did that. Then we added vibes in the second verse just to make the thing ring a bit. Then we put the drum on, and we recorded the drum in an echo chamber, and we did it with a tape-reverb that made the drum part sound different from what it actually was, because of that afterbeat effect. Then we gave it out to have a string part written. I gave the song to—I can't remember now who it is. But the arrangers wrote the title down as "Like a Pitcher of Water."

What!

I had it framed. The whole string part—instead of having "Bridge Over Troubled Water" on it—the way the guy heard it on this demo tape was "Like a Pitcher of Water." So that's what's written down. And he spelled Garfunkel wrong. So we did the string part, and I couldn't stand it. I thought they were terrible. I was very disappointed. It had to be completely rewritten. This was all in L.A. And then we came back to New York and did the vocals. Artie spent several days on the vocals.

Punching in a lot. [Recording in small segments to achieve greater control and accuracy.]

Yes. I'd say altogether that song took somewhere around ten days to two weeks to record, and then it had to be mixed.

Were you finally happy with the concluding string arrangement of the third verse?

I would say I was happy. It was changed around quite a lot, and there was a lot of engineering added to it. I think it served its purpose. I don't think it bears a lot of scrutiny. If you listen to just the string part, it's not really great, but it did do the job that it was supposed to do, which was to expand the record tremendously, and it feels like one of those string parts that makes things big, and that's what it's supposed to do and it did. I was happy. The last note was too long.

"Bridge" was gospel, "El Condor" was South American, "Mother and Child" was reggae—you seem to be incredibly eclectic.

I like the other kinds of music. The amazing thing is that this country is so provincial. Americans know American music. You go to France: They know a lot of kinds of music. You go to Japan, and they know a lot of indigenous popular music. But Americans never get into the South American music, I fell into Los Incas, I loved it. It's got nothing to do with our music, but I liked it anyway. The Jamaican thing, there's nobody getting into a Jamaican thing. Jamaicans have a lot of good music, an awful lot.

That one you really pulled off—"Mother and Child Reunion."

I got that by making a mistake. Because "Why Don't You Write Me?" was supposed to sound like that but it came out a bad imitation. So I said, "I'm not going to get it out of the regular guys. I gotta get it out of the guys who know it." And I gotta go down there willing to change for them. I started to play with them. I started to show them the song and play, and we started to work it out, and they were playing, and I would play, but, I couldn't play with it. Couldn't fit.

Did you sing it with them when they were recording it?

No, I played the track. I'd sing the song, we'd write down the chords. Now we know the song. Now, I start to play the guitar, a rhythm guitar part. Like I do on almost all the stuff. But it was bad. So I sat down and said, "You play it. Play what you want." That's the key thing. Let them play whatever they want, and then you change. You go their way. That's how you get that.

You didn't have the words to that song written when you recorded the track?

I didn't.

That's amazing.

Know where the words came from on that? You never would have guessed. I was eating in a Chinese restaurant downtown. There was a dish called "Mother and Child Reunion." It's chicken and eggs. And I said, "Oh, I love that title. I gotta use that one."

I read a lot into that one.

Well, that's alright. What you read in was damn accurate, because what happened was this: last summer we had a dog that was run over and killed, and we loved this dog. It was the first death I had ever experienced personally. Nobody in my family died that I felt that. But I felt this loss—one minute there, next minute gone, and then my first thought was, "Oh, man, what if that was Peggy? What if somebody like that died? Death, what is it, I can't get it." And there were lyrics straight out forward like that. The chorus for "Mother and Child Reunion"—well, that's out of the title. Somehow there was a connection between this death and Peggy and it was like Heaven, I don't know what the connection was. Some emotional connection. It didn't matter to me what it was. I just knew it was there.

I still don't see why you would do the track, before you had written the words. Why did you do that?

I had no words. The words I had I never intended to use. But sometimes you get a very good record that way because you fit the words right to the track. You play with the feel of the track and the words. What happens then is when you go to sing the song without the words, like when I go to sing "Mother and Child Reunion," for example, I go back and play it the way I originally played it in Jamaica, which is not Reggae, it's Ska. There's a difference in rhythm. But they said Ska's old. They're always doing Reggae, so I said, "Well, what's the difference between Reggae and Ska?" I thought it was the same thing. So then they started to play. "This is Reggae. This is Ska. This is bluebeat." Each was a different style.

What were these guys like?

They were nice guys. They were Jamaican guys.

Did they get into it?

They got into it. At first it was awkward I was the only white guy there and I was American—American, white guy, famous, coming to them . . .

They knew who you were.

And the funny thing is like they do sessions down there. They get paid like $7 or $10 per tune. That's how they do it. And I worked all day and the next day. So I had to say to them, "Look, just assume I'm doing three tunes a day, OK? So I'll pay you like three tunes a day," 'cause otherwise they get dregged. "Forget about that," I said. "Let's get it right." And even then I had changes to do. I had to put the piano on later, I had to put the voices on later, that was done in New York, and the vocal was done later.

The humor on Paul Simon *is elusive.*

Yes. For example, at the beginning at "Papa Hobo," it opens light because it's stylized. It's an obviously constructed line. It's not a cry of anguish. It's too thought out. It's carbon monoxide and the old Detroit perfume. It's satirical. The "basketball town" line. It's got a little bit of bitterness, but it's also, it's in its own way, an element of humor and a putdown of a place, a basketball town. It reminds me of a Midwest thing. The "Gatorade" line . . .

I hate that word "gatorade" . . .

That's why I use it. That word doesn't belong in a song. It comes out, and there it is. It's the whole thing. It's where that guy came from.

You have said that "Run Your Body Down" had a comic intent. But the title line is a very real thing to many people.

It is true. I don't mean it to be any less serious by the fact that I feel that there's humor in it. I think that that's a delicate combination. If you can get humor and seriousness at the same time, you've created a special little thing, and that's what I'm looking for, because if you get pompous, you lose everything. If I should write a preachy song about "for God's sake take care of your health" it would sound like a Nichols and May bit: "My God, your mother and I are sick with worry." You can't do it in a song. Even "Me and Julio," it's pure confection.

What is it that the mama saw? The whole world wants to know.

I have no idea what it is.

Four people said that was the first thing I would ask you.

Something sexual is what I imagine, but when I say "something," I never bothered to figure out what it was. Didn't make any difference to me. First of all, I think it's funny to sing—"Me and Julio." It's very funny to me. And when I started to sing "Me and Julio," I started to laugh and that's when I decided to make the song called "Me and Julio," otherwise I wouldn't have made it that. I like the line about the radical priest. I think that's funny to have in a song. "Peace Like a River" is a serious song. It's a serious song, although it's not as down as you think. The last verse is sort of nothing, it sort of puts the thing back up in the air, which is where it should be. You end up, you think about these things that are, something to do with a riot, or something in my mind in the city.

The middle part was very surreal.

Part of the reason the thing sounds surreal by the way, is that there's a sound effect in that record which I don't think you can hear, but it's there, and it creates a very real effect. What I did was to take a piano, hit the bottom notes of the piano with a hand, like with my fist, like that, played it at half speed backwards, and took a middle section out, which sounds something like *Rrrrrrrr*. It's just a low level rumble, but it creates a tension, and that thing is just in there. It's in the track. You can't hear it. The only time you can hear it is in the last verse where it's out. It's just a dark color. It creates tension in that song. Also the track was a loop.

What do you mean? The whole track?

That whole bass, the whole drum thing. I recorded a whole thing and I didn't use it, and a guy while he was standing there with a conga drum was talking and he was playing *doom dakka doonka doonk doom dakka doonka doonk*. I just did things like that for three minutes and made a loop out of it and then recorded over it.

The music is pretty but the words are very frightening.

That's just a thing with me, to do something that sounds pretty or light to have a nastiness in it. That's just a style, I don't do it consciously, it just comes out naturally with me.

What was Simon and Garfunkel's vocal style? Is there any, what was it? Did it change? Was there a progression?

S&G's vocal sound was very often closely worked out harmony, doubled, using four voices, but doubled right on, so that you couldn't a lot of times tell it was four voices.

Not four-part harmony?

No. Four voices. Like "The Boxer" is four voices.

You're each singing your part twice—doubled back?

Singing it twice. "Mrs. Robinson" was four voices.

Harmonically, was there a lot of progression?

There wasn't a lot of harmony on it. The thing that I learned at the end of S&G, was how to make an interesting album, was to let Artie do his thing, and let me do my thing, and come together for a thing. All of the other albums up until then, they're almost all harmony on every song. How much can you do with two voices? You can sing thirds or you can sing fifths or you can do a background harmony. Something like "The Only Living Boy in New York," where we create that big voice, all those voices in the background. That's my favorite one on that whole album, actually. The first time those background voices come in.

You recorded the album 'Sounds of Silence' in New York, Los Angeles and where else?

We tried a few cuts in Nashville. We did "Flowers Never Bend with the Rainfall." Was that on that album? [It was on *Parsley, Sage, Rosemary and Thyme*.] We tried to cut "I Am a Rock" in Nashville, and it didn't work. At that time, we had an asset that we didn't know about, which was our engineer in New York—Roy Halee.

We really didn't know Roy too well. We did "Wednesday Morning" with him, but we didn't have any sort of relationship with him. He was a young engineer at Columbia who was coming up, and nice to get along with, but we didn't pay much attention to him; we looked to the producer for direction. It took a while to realize that the people who were getting what we wanted was the three of us, Arthur and me and Roy. So at that time Roy was the engineer, and he was making things good, but we weren't saying, "This is the engineer who's really doing a good job."

'Sounds of Silence' is a morbid album. It has suicides and . . .

That's right. I tend to think of that period as a very late adolescence.
Those kind of things have a big impact on an adolescent mind, suicides
and people who are very sad or very lonely and you tend to dramatize
those things.

It depends on the song. "A Most Peculiar Man," which dealt with a
suicide—that was written in England, because I saw a newspaper article
about a guy who committed suicide. In those days it was easier to write,
because I wasn't known and it didn't matter if I wrote a bad song. I'd
write a song in a night, and play it around in the clubs, and people were
very open then. No attention and so, no criticism.

Now I have standards. Then I didn't have standards. I was a beginning writer then, so I wrote anything I saw. Now I sift. Now I say,
"Well, that's not really a subject that I want to write a song about."

Have you been bootlegged a lot?

I think Columbia estimated that over the world, there's something like a
million bootlegs on Simon and Garfunkel. I get letters every day from
bootleggers. They send in the license to the publisher. That's their sort
of loophole. I have them upstairs. I get them every day. Every day I can
see what's being bootlegged. It's pretty annoying, because it's stealing.
Now, what justification do they have for that?

Does a bootlegger ever send you money, publishing money?

Yeah, they send you $4.25, you know, $13.00.

I think it's slowed down now.

I'm still getting the same amount of letters.

*You can't buy them anymore. You used to be able to. The stores won't
take them anymore. For a while, a lot of head shops would take them,
but now if you sell them most of the big companies won't sell you any
records.*

Right. Bootleg records, but tapes. How about tapes? They say something like between 1/3 and 1/2 of the tape sales are bootlegs.

That's the counterfeit approach. They pretend it's the original, which is easier to do with tape.

My brother wanted to bootleg me once. He asked if it was alright with me.

Younger brother?

He teaches guitar. He drifts around. My brother's had a rough time, because of me. It's hard. I wouldn't want that burden. If he walked in here, he's younger than me and he's about 20 pounds thinner than me, but he looks a lot like me. On the street people very often mistake him for me. He's about the same height and it's been hard sometimes for him.

You mentioned before, referring to the second side of 'Bookends,' that the lean period for Simon and Garfunkel was . . .

"The Dangling Conversation," "Hazy Shade of Winter," "At the Zoo," and "Fakin' It."

You didn't like any of those?

"Fakin' It" was interesting. Autobiographically it was interesting. But we never really got it on the records.

I'm surprised because I like "Fakin' It" so much.

That's because you are thinking of "Fakin' It" on the album. And "Fakin' It" on the album is vastly improved over "Fakin' It" as a single. For one thing, I think it's speeded up. For two, it was re-mixed and greatly improved in stereo. It was a jumble, it was a record that was jumbled, sloppy. When you hear the original mono, it's slower and it's sloppier. It was improved on the LP, but by then it was already poisoned in my mind.

. . . What was the Simon and Garfunkel groupie scene like?

Simon and Garfunkel had a peculiar type of groupie. We had the poetic groupies. The girls that followed us around weren't necessarily looking to sleep with us as much as they were looking to read their poetry or discuss literature or play their own songs.

How did you feel about that?

I think that maybe that was the best thing for me, because to a great degree it embarrassed me to pick up somebody on the road, because it was so obvious that you weren't interested in them. I felt it was insulting. You obviously didn't care anything about the person if you were just picking them up to take them back to a Holiday Inn with you and it required pretense. You had to pretend that there was something more to it. Or else you had to pretend that you didn't care at all what they thought, or you didn't care at all about other people. And I couldn't make either pretense. I wasn't terribly involved with them as people, but on the other hand, I couldn't do something that I thought was insulting.

Ultimately how did you cope with the situation?

Ultimately I wound up going back to the room and smoking a joint and going to sleep by myself. Most of the time, sometimes not.

But toward the end I always avoided any contact with people after the show. I never encouraged it. There were always exceptions, but in general, compared to what I've read about most rock groups or pop groups, for me (I can't speak for Artie), I wasn't into picking up girls on the road. Couldn't do it. Too embarrassing to me. I wasn't interested in their poetry either.

What was "Armistice Day" saying to you about politics?

Well, "Armistice Day," which I consider to be the weakest song on the album, is an old song, written in 1968—the first part of it was. That song mainly meant, let's have a truce. I chose the title "Armistice Day," because it's not even called Armistice Day anymore, it's called Veteran's Day. Armistice Day is like an old name, and I didn't really mean it to be specifically about the war. I just meant that I'm worn out from all this fighting, from all the abuse that people are giving each other and creating for each other. And I like the opening line on "Armistice Day"— "Armistice Day, the Philharmonic will play"—from strictly a songwriter's point of view, like rhyme and the way it sings.

What do you think of George McGovern?

I think McGovern is the best candidate that has a chance of winning.

Do you think there are other good candidates?

There are some other candidates I'm interested in. Shirley Chisholm. I don't hear too much about Shirley Chisholm. The media is obviously not as interested in Shirley Chisholm. I think George McGovern is a very principled man, and I think that the other candidates are more political in the sense that they represent special interest groups to a greater degree than McGovern appears to.

In several interviews after your Shea Stadium appearance for peace candidates in 1968, you indicated that because of the clumsy, sloppy way you were presented you had a general distaste for that kind of thing at that time. Now you seem to be more willing to give freely of your time. Why is that?

First of all you have to realize that if you do a concert and it comes out lousy, when you come off the stage you're mad. It doesn't matter who you do it for. Now that concert at Shea Stadium was done on too short notice, and it was not sufficiently publicized. So instead of getting a maximum of 50,000 people, which they could have had considering the bill, which was Janis, Creedence Clearwater, Johnny Winter, the Rascals, John Sebastian and others. It should have been a big show, should have done really well. But only about 20,000 people showed up. They took in $100,000. For peace candidates. I never found out where that $100,000 went . . .

Did you pursue it?

I did, but I couldn't find out. Because before the concert you get a lot of high pressure calls all the time—"You gotta do it. It's really important. You gotta have faith that it will work, either you're gonna trash the system or you're gonna work for it," and I said, "Well, OK, right, I'll do my thing. I don't think this concert is well-planned, but I'll do it." And then the concert comes out to be a relative stiff, and now they say, no money was made. It cost $100,000. Where? Where was it spent? I certainly didn't make any money out of it. Nobody I knew made any money. Creedence Clearwater Revival paid their own airfare to come from California to do it, and all their equipment. They lost money on it.

So, naturally you're left with a feeling of having been taken. Nobody benefits. The peace candidates—whoever they are—didn't benefit. And I'll never play Shea Stadium. It's ridiculous. Airplanes were comin' over, and you couldn't hear me. I'm embarrassed, because everything's bad and so I'm sluggin' through it because, shit, it's a worthwhile cause, and it's all over. It's all for nothin'. You can't find the people who organized it and the promoters.

The thing about McGovern is that he seems to have elevated the idea of benefit concerts to one of the staples of his fundraising.

I feel that the concert I did in Cleveland was done in a poor hall. It wasn't a good hall for music. But there was a feeling of event that surrounded this Cleveland show. And McGovern was there, unlike the show they did for Gene McCarthy, or the peace candidates or something. The man showed up, and you could talk to him, and he's impressive. He's honest. He's not an eloquent guy, but he's straightforward. You ask a question, he gives you an answer. So how could you not feel that you'd do anything to help, if you care about your country? I care about the country. I care about the world.

McCarthy made a direct appeal to youth, or rather youth intuitively supported McCarthy right away. But McCarthy never progressed the way McGovern has in pursuing the nomination. And McGovern is the first candidate that is really directing himself to youth as a group, making statements about it.

I don't see that McGovern has made a lot of statements that are directed particularly to youth. I know that he has a very strong appeal to youth, but . . .

Like the rock concerts vehicle is . . .

Yes, that's true. But that doesn't say anything about his position. Show business people have always gotten behind certain candidates. Lorne Green is out there working for Humphrey. And Sinatra is pals with Agnew. The important thing, I think, about youth to these candidates is, there's a group on which you can rely for volunteer help, because it costs so much money to run a candidacy that if you can get volunteers to do a lot of work for you, I think you have a chance against a very well-funded Republican party. Otherwise the Democratic party would be in debt. It still is in debt.

I think it's impressive that people are willing to put aside the cynicism that has been nurtured for six or seven years and come out for a candidate again. A lot of people felt after 1968, "I'm not gonna get duped into this system again, this crap." And yet now they're doing it again. I think that's hopeful.

But I'm not going that idealization route again for these people. Politicians as a group have dirtied their names to the point they have to *earn* our respect again. It's like I used to say to Warren Beatty: "A lot of my friends, they're not crazy about McGovern. Politicians have fucked around for so long that we all have the right to say, 'You prove it. You prove that you're a super guy, that I should go out and look at you sittin' there asking us to go and do this kinda stuff.'"

But in the end I'm not indifferent. When Nixon was elected, I cried. I actually cried. I remember puttin' on the TV set in the morning, and I saw he was coming down to make his acceptance speech. Tears started rolling down my eyes. I didn't know what was going to happen in the next four years. Humphrey sold himself out. He does not deserve to get it again. It's too late, so like, what's the choice?

How do you feel about the rock liberation front, that kind of thing? Their notion, put in its most extreme form, is that rock musicians have an obligation to be actively bound and committed to radical movements, that they have some sort of political obligation, that there's something wrong with the notion "I earn a living, I write songs, I get paid for them, whatever else I do is my business."

I think they are very illogical. I don't agree with that at all. First of all I think, if a musician is serious about his music, his obligation should be to become as fine a musician as he could. This country has a tremendous lack of people who are good in what they do, including musicians. This country places a tremendous priority on being successful, being famous or infamous, but it doesn't give you a great reward for being good.

So, for a musician to be involved in politics (and of course, it's up to the musician), I don't see that one should be involved in radical politics any more than conservative politics, if that's their inclination. I don't see what one thing has to do with another. The fact of the matter is that popular music is one of the industries of this country. It's all completely tied up with capitalism. It's stupid to separate it. That's an illusory separation.

If one has strong political beliefs one should do whatever they think is right about them.

So you don't recognize any specific obligations inherent in your particular situation?

Not because I'm a musician, no. Certainly no. Why should a musician have any more obligation than anybody else? I don't know what radical politics necessarily is. A million things come under the term radical.

What's your reaction to the kind of involvement that Lennon has shown?

I have reactions to it. First reaction, he strikes me as being very interested in being seen or heard. Then I have to think, "What is he doing? What is the purpose of it? Is his purpose to get publicity for himself? Is his purpose to advance a certain political thought?" I don't know what his motivations are. Many things he's done, I think, have been pointless. Some have been in bad taste. Others have been courageous. I think he's generally a well-intentioned guy. I don't know, it's not my style.

What do you think of a record like "Power to the People"?

It's a poor record, a condescending record. Like all of these cliche phrases. They're dangerous. What does that mean—"Power to the People"? And who is he saying it to? Is he saying it to people who have any idea what it means? Isn't it really a manipulative phrase? And since he's picking it up, consciously aware that this is going to be broadcast over the air waves, my question is, who is he manipulating and for what purpose? That's even putting aside the question of whether he has the qualifications to manipulate, because obviously you don't even need any qualification to manipulate in this country. Anybody who wants to manipulate can. Not necessarily for the general good.

Did you hear the other record of "Power to the People"? There were two records called that. There was one record called "For God's Sake Give More Power to the People." It was a good record though. It really was a good record. I think it was the Chi-Lites. I like that record much better than Lennon's record.

How about "George Jackson"? Do you like that record?

Not too much. Mildly catchy tune, that's all.

You're taking those two examples, and I'm giving my reactions. I'm not saying that there is no place for a politically stirring song. "La Marseillaise" swings pretty good, actually. And there's nothing wrong with "We Shall Overcome," right? So it can work. "Give Ireland Back to the Irish"—that's garbage. I don't say that someone can't write a social song, or even a song that's a political song, and have it work, as a song and as a political statement. But mass manufacturing of tunes, sort of "let's knock off 'Power to the People,'" I find it in bad taste. It offends me. I don't feel it talking to me at all. John Lennon's not interested in me when he makes that statement.

You as a listener?

As a listener. I'm outside that record. It's not affecting me. It's not that I'm not interested in what Lennon has to say. I am. He usually has my ear. When he makes a record or makes a statement, I'll read it or listen to it. I am a potential audience for him. But I find that he seldom says anything that's interesting or innovative to me, and yet, I listen, based on a long-standing respect. Based on his musicianship, based on the fact that he was involved in some great music over the years, and so I keep listening to stuff that's no longer great.

Expecting something?

Yes. Out of respect for what he once did, out of respect for what once moved me. Now how long will that keep up, I don't know. I find I'm less and less inclined to hear what he has to say. What do you think about that?

I agree. There are several artists whose work is in decline, no matter however else they may conceive of it. In particular in rock, when you look at rock as a whole, as a body of music. Let's say, rock in the Sixties, since '63–'64, what do you think of it as a music? You're involved in studying classical music now. Your work has always included different ways, different elements from different kinds of music. Where do you think rock fits as music?

Well, rock is the staple. Rock is the main part of the meal for me. It's the music that I not only grew up in, but I participated in, so I like rock and I like rock and roll. I like a lot of different kinds of music. I think that there have been very talented people come up in the last decade, people who have done really good work, and there have been great performers. I think Aretha is a really fine performer. I think Otis Redding was really great. Sam Cooke was great. The Beatles were great. Dylan was great, I gotta say he was great. I don't feel that at the moment, but I feel that he was great. Although now we're into another category, because I wanted to save that, I think he'll come in more as a writer, those other people are performers. Except the Beatles are both.

This is what will survive . . .

If you go for what has a chance of surviving, then you have to go for songs. You can go for artists, but to what degree has Bessie Smith survived today, by her recordings?

I think to a great degree.

I think not a great degree. I think Grand Funk Railroad is much more well-known today by most people than Bessie Smith, and yet, I'll tell you this, a lot more people know "St. Louis Blues" than know Bessie Smith. In other words, her work is preserved on records, and that record remains a part of history. A song is capable of having several life spans.

What songs for the Sixties do you think will have additional life span?

It's hard to remember. There's so many, so many.

Start off with the Beatles.

I would pick "Yesterday." I would pick "Strawberry Fields"—although there is your example of a total record. A very important record to me, I like it a lot. You can't even sing the song. It's really hard to sing the song.

Yes, but many of their songs have dated.

It may take a song instead of being dated after three years, maybe some songs won't be dated for five years. Eventually all records are dated, but the song comes back. "Eleanor Rigby" was a really fine song. There's no way of picking out the best songs. There's the whole group of Smokey Robinson songs that mean something. There's a couple old Steve Cropper tunes that mean something. I think there are some of my songs that are, that will last.

Which ones?

Judging from the amount of recordings and the amount of airplay and the amount of that kind of measuring device, the most popular songs of mine are "Sound of Silence," "Mrs. Robinson," "Bridge Over Troubled Water," "Feeling Groovy," and a song that's not mine, but is associated with us, "Scarborough Fair." That song's alive still. You hear it still, and those songs are, if not quite standards, almost standards. In other words, when I say standards, I think they'll live at least ten years. Now "The Sound of Silence" has already lived about six years, and it's still played and it's alive.

It's primarily played in your version.

No, I think it's played all over the place. There must be 100 recordings of it.

S&G must be a hard thing to let go of.

I don't find it hard. I find it a relief. It took me to a nice place. I can't say it took me where I wanted to go, because I had no idea where I wanted to go, but I found myself at the point of leaving S&G in a very nice place. I've done a lot of satisfying work, we were ready to move out, and I could go and do what I wanted without being tense about succeeding or not succeeding. I'd already been successful. I mean, I knew I never could top the success of "Bridge." I'm not going to sell more than eight million records, so it's kind of a nice place to be. So you start again, but actually you have nothing to lose. I'm also older than I was, so I don't have that drive, I already had a few years of being successful.

You had advisors and so forth, but nobody told you for the sake of your career you were going to do, for example, a Coke commercial, and you said, "Well, if you say it's best, I'll do it"?

No. Nobody ever did that. And the people that we did have were right in line with our thinking. Mort Lewis would say, "They offered us $25,000 for a Coke commercial, I think you could go more if you wanted to do it." "How much more?" I would say, "Well, maybe we could get $50,000." "Well, let's see if they'll go 50." Then they'd say 50, and we'd say, "Nah, but we wanted to know, would they pay 50?" We wanted to know.

And ultimately, with the TV special, we were at the point of them not allowing the show to go on the air unless we changed, and we said, "Fuck you, that doesn't go on the air. That's all. This is the show we made, this is what we believe in, don't put it on then." Well, they didn't put it on, but CBS got another sponsor to put it on for us, AT&T, they backed down. They lost a lot of money on that, because they didn't want to be associated with that show. They were bad people.

The people you dealt with at AT&T?

Bad. Stupid people and bad people.

At that time it had become an album every two years for Simon & Garfunkel . . .

Right. Where can you go as a group when you actually think about it? You can keep putting out an album every once in a while. You can go on tour. That was over. I didn't want to go on tour. I didn't want to sing "Scarborough Fair" again. I didn't want to sing all of those S&G songs every night. When you've developed, it's harder. Two people can go so far and then they're locked to each other. There are just so many combinations of two. So that was over. As it should have been. It lasted a long time. I've known Artie since I was 12 years old, and we were friends all that time.

I'm 30 now, so that's a long time for that partnership. It's over. We grew up. From the musical point of view, in the time that he was off in the movies, Artie didn't do anything musically. I was doing things musically, but to Artie it would have to go back to the old practicing a song, have to learn the harmony.

I wouldn't say that my ideas were bigger than S&G, but I would say that my ideas were different than S&G, and I didn't want to go in that direction of a duo. First of all I wanted to sing. I always felt restricted as a singer, partly because there always had to be harmony, and it had to be sung in the same phrasing, and then you had to double it. You couldn't get free and loose with your singing, and in this album, I am pretty free.

What was the record company's attitude toward the split?

Oh, tremendously discouraging. They didn't want that split at all. They still don't want it. The first form it took was self-delusion: "Paul has to get this out of his system." Then they would ask, "When do you think you'll do the next S&G album?" Which would bring me down. I'd be working on this album. It was important to me. And they would want to know when I was going to put aside this little . . . toy.

How about Clive Davis?

He didn't encourage me at all to do this. It became obvious that I was going to do it, and it was stupid to get in the way, but nobody encouraged me to do it. Sort of a predictably conservative attitude. I was dragged. I shouldn't have been, but I was. Everybody said, "What the hell's wrong? Why don't they stay together?" And everybody said, "Gee I always like S&G, boy, that's too bad." It was too bad, but that was it. It was over. For the sake of me personally, it was great that I was doing this by myself, but for the sake of the world it wasn't great. Nobody said, "Oh, boy, can't wait to hear it."

George Harrison said to me, "I'm really curious to hear your album, because now you hear sort of what we are like individually, since the group broke up, and I know what you were like together, and I'd like to hear what you're like individually." And all the while in my head I thought, this breakup is not really comparable to that Beatles breakup, because there was a tremendous interaction in that group that came from the sound, and I said to myself, "I write better songs now than I used to write years ago, so I'm going to make a better album, but nobody knows that. They won't know it till it comes out." That was my fantasy.

In fact, many critics said that. But the public didn't in terms of buying the record, and that's unsettling. I'm getting used to it now, I'm getting used to the fact. At first I said, "Look, when it breaks up you're going to have to start all over again. It may take you a couple of albums before people will even listen." But actually, emotionally I was ready to be welcomed into the public's arms, as I had been in the past. And not that I'm not now, because it's a successful album, this just goes to show you my perspective.

You sold 700,000, right?

About 850,000.

That's more records than any single Rolling Stones album except for Sticky Fingers.

Yeah, but, permit me my arrogance, I never compare myself with the Rolling Stones. I never considered that the Rolling Stones were at the same level. I always was well aware of the fact that S&G was a much bigger phenomenon in general, to the general public, than the Rolling Stones. The Rolling Stones might be bigger with a certain segment, but the general public, S&G really penetrated, really got down to many many levels of people—people and really young kids. That was really gratifying.

Wednesday Morning *ended up being a good-sized selling album.*

Wednesday Morning sold somewhere around 5–600,000. No other album that we made has sold less than two million. *Parsley, Sage* is around three million and *Bridge,* of course, is bigger. They all sold.

When people who are 40 years old buy your albums, and they like your music, I liked that. That turns me on that they did that. That's very fine to me. That's what it's about—that's music. I don't say, "Don't you listen to this music, you, this isn't for you." I want everybody to listen to it. I hope everybody likes it. That's where S&G had got me. And I wanted to be the same thing. Now I'm at the start and building slowly, and maybe I'll never get there.

Clive once said to me, "S&G is a household word. No matter, however successful you'll be, you'll never be as successful as S&G."

So I said, "Yeah, like Dean Martin and Jerry Lewis. Don't tell me that. Don't tell me that statement, that I'll never be bigger than. How do you know what I'll do? I don't even know what I'm gonna do in the next decade of my life. It could be maybe my greatest time of work. Maybe I'm finished. Maybe I'm not gonna do my thing until I'm 50. People will say then, funny thing was, in his youth he sang with a group. He sang popular songs in the Sixties." Fans of "rock and roll," in quotes, may remember the duo Simon & Garfunkel. That's how I figure it.

PAUL COWAN (1976)

PAUL SIMON: THE ODYSSEUS OF URBAN MELANCHOLY

Paul Simon has a recurring nightmare. Before most performances he dreams about microphones that are so tall he can't reach them or that are facing away from the audience and fastened so tightly he can't budge them, or that he's singing inside a glass booth and people can't hear him. Simon is a tough, competitive man, whose emotional security depends on his ability to maintain control over his career, his business affairs, his personal life. But the nightmare is about problems that are beyond his control, that make him look foolish, that isolate him from others.

Sometimes you could hear those fears in his conversation as we talked in the austerely elegant living room of his Central Park West duplex, in the conversation area overlooking the springtime greenery of the park.

I sat on an Italian canvas couch, while Paul was in a Bauhaus chair. In the sweeping blond expanse behind him were a Deco Steinway piano built especially for the man who taught George Gershwin and a graceful potted tree standing near a huge pale blue and orange Helen Frankenthaler painting. When he first made his money, Paul said, "My tastes weren't educated so I didn't know what to buy. Of course, I knew about music. I bought this piano effortlessly. But I didn't go out and buy paintings because I didn't know anything about paintings. Then, gradually, my taste was shaped— usually by women."

Across the room, above the long, black cabinet which contains his stereo equipment and records, are photographs that document the upward arc of his career—a black and white publicity still of his first hit record (a Fifties rock 'n' roll single he and Garfunkel made as the crew-cut duo Tom and Jerry); a picture of Artie, his hair grown wavy; another of Paul Simon throwing out the first ball of the 1969 baseball season in Yankee Stadium with CBS board chairman William Paley looking on; an autographed photo of Cesar Chavez who appeared on a Simon and

Garfunkel TV special in 1969; a photo of Simon hosting NBC's *Saturday Night* last fall.

Now his career is at the highest point it has been since he and Garfunkel broke up five years ago. And yet the magic is still there for him. His speaking voice is rich with the words and rhythms of New York in the Fifties—of a kid who assumed "that the nation's economy was pegged to the price of egg creams," who spent gentle spring days in his room learning how to flip baseball cards so that they fell at the base of the nearest wall; of the ambitious, withdrawn stickball champ who seethed with resentment at his failure to grow tall, who dreamed he was Elvis Presley walking the cautious, middle-class streets of Forest Hills.

A decade ago Simon wrote, "The words of the prophet are written on the subway walls." But now, at 34, he rides through New York in a black Cadillac, which he rents from a limousine service (his regular driver said that Simon and Leonard Bernstein are his two favorite passengers). When Paul talked about the car his voice filled with wonder, like a boy describing a set of Lionel trains he got for his birthday. "You pull up in front of a place, just like in the movies," he said. "When you get out, the driver is there waiting for you. It's the New York dream come true."

But he's often morose, though he's grown accustomed to those moods. "I can get pretty depressed at times," he said, "though it was much worse before, especially when I was into dope some years ago. Then I could get very, very moody. Now it comes and it goes. It's very cyclical.

"I develop a generally pessimistic attitude. I get lethargic and physically tired. I tend to construe news in a negative light even when it's very positive. For instance, I'd be thinking I'm depressed because so-and-so hasn't phoned me for a week. Then she phones me and I find I'm still depressed. Or else I'm depressed because I'm not writing anything. Then I write something and I'm still depressed. Somebody from Columbia Records will send me a note saying they're going to release 'Still Crazy after All These Years' as a single [which could be the fourth hit single from that Grammy-winning album] because some big radio station picked it, which would normally put me in a good mood, but that news doesn't have an effect. Still, whatever my depression is, I'll come out of it."

But what, I asked him, is the voice inside your head saying when you become depressed? Why do you get so pessimistic?

"My voice is saying to me, 'Maybe I can't write anymore; maybe what I did wasn't very good anyway; maybe I'm not generally attractive to people; my life is unstructured; what am I doing here?' Just typical depression bullshit. I don't really pay great attention to it. I don't take it seriously. It's just there. I've been through it enough to know it's just depression; it's not necessarily accurate."

Then he began to talk about the moodiness and sorrow that pervade his music. "The songs tend to emphasize that aspect of me because it's easier to exorcise those things in a song. To write about them is a relief. If you're jubilant there's no need to do anything. You're happy, you're content. So I tend to write about the serious things that happen to me or the sadder things. I don't write too much about the positive things because then I'm feeling too good to sit down and write." In a way, he added, the songs are "a false representation of me."

Simon usually referred to the decade after his first hit, "The Sounds of Silence," as "the success"—as if his celebrity constitutes a geological age. When he talked business he referred to himself and his closest boyhood friend, Artie, as Simon and Garfunkel. It's as if he can retain mastery over that unexpected cascade of good fortune only by shrinking back from it, studying it, emphasizing how difficult it has all been. Sometimes his reminiscences sounded like a series of barely soluble problems. Hearing them, you sometimes had the bizarre experience of forgetting that you were listening to one of this generation's most consistently triumphant popular artists, whose talent has spanned two eras. . . .

His life has become more orderly. He lives in a wonderworld of friendly aides: a Czech housekeeper who cooks, shops, gets his clothes from the cleaners, takes care of [his son] Harper when he's working; a limousine service; an agent; a lawyer; a business manager who looks after his money and weighs all requests for his time. He is very close to his family and a few friends, like the playwright Israel Horovitz and the NBC *Saturday Night* crowd, but he consciously tries to limit his availability to other people. "That's partly my nature and partly protective coloration," he said—he doesn't want a large cast of characters traipsing through his life.

Paul is equally careful about his body. Drugs are out—he believes, quite passionately, that they've damaged some of the best talents of his generation—and he tries to keep in shape by running a few miles every day. Right now, he's confronted with a practical physical problem. He has a calcium deposit on one of the fingers of his left hand—it frequently swells up and gets discolored. He can't take cortisone anymore, so he treats it with another drug "which tears my stomach apart." In five years, he may be unable to play guitar. So he's learning to compose on the piano.

He's very thoughtful about the pace of his production. "I write and record at the same time. But in recent years, especially after Simon and Garfunkel broke up, I felt I had to spend a lot of time on tour, gaining acceptance, selling my records. And when I start to move to the performing stage, which I don't particularly like, I stop writing.

"Like now, I haven't written anything since early September. And I stopped performing in January. It took me two months to calm down from stopping performing. And now it's taken me another month to get back up to write. So it'll be a while before I can write something.

"I don't like this period. It doesn't scare me now, but right before it ends I'll panic. I always panic. Invariably, the first song will come because I lower my standards, which are always too high. I'll write a blues."

Yet Simon, the Odysseus of urban melancholy, seems to know the geography of his despair quite thoroughly. He's not likely to get lost in its thickets. In fact, he's made something of an aesthetic of privacy and self-preservation.

There was an intensity of feeling when he talked about Dylan Thomas and Saul Bellow. "I think Dylan Thomas's life became the symbol of such fascination that it overshadowed his work," he said. "If Thomas hadn't gone and killed himself publicly, if he'd just become a great poet, maybe John Berryman wouldn't have jumped off that bridge. Anne Sexton. Sylvia Plath. Why did they have to do it? The public hungers to see talented young people kill themselves. I love it that Saul Bellow just does his job, out there in Chicago. His talent didn't stop when he aged."

Simon prays that, like Bellow, "my talent will keep growing until I die." He works very hard to improve his craft. When his finger was so swollen he couldn't play guitar, he decided to take voice lessons to lengthen the time he could sing in the studio and to make the top range of his voice fuller. Now he is studying musical theory, pursuing whatever problems interest him. For example, the music in his last album starts with the question, "What is a diminished chord?" He's also studying the nature of musical scales. "I don't think it matters what question you start with," he said. "As long as you start off with a question, it's going to lead to something interesting." He finds that the quest itself gives him energy. "When I've finished an album, I can't begin to work again unless I get some new input of information. Otherwise, I wind up doing exactly what I did before."

He also has a theory about lyrics—that listeners can't absorb line after line of rich poetry, that songs should consist of simple spoken English backed by a single powerful image that makes them magic. He's reading poets like W. S. Merwin, Edwin Muir and Ted Hughes to learn what he can from their art.

Simon's work, like that of many other popular artists of the Sixties, was too rich and complicated to be classified as either folk or rock & roll. His music began to reflect his interest in other forms like reggae and gospel (the title line for "Bridge over Troubled Water" was suggested by a gospel song). His urbanity and his interest in musical techniques led him to identify as well with the tradition represented by George Gershwin. Still, critics usually lumped him with contemporaries like the Beatles and Bob Dylan and he himself felt a sense of "terrific competition" with them.

"Dylan was the standard against which American songwriters were measured," he recalled. "I liked a lot of his songs, particularly the early songs, but I don't have a clear perspective on that because I'm so entangled in it. I wasn't able to just like the music. If I liked it a lot, it would make me feel bad at the same time. So jealousy was a factor. I didn't have a perspective on the Beatles either. I thought they were great but I never enjoyed them the way the world enjoyed them. I always felt bad. I would listen to them and the question would be, 'How did they do that?' Not, 'Wow, isn't that great!'"

Then, a couple of years ago, his sense of competition with his contemporaries began to ebb. He realized that there were a lot of people who knew a great deal more than he did but were less popular. "So I started to follow musical examples, not sociological examples. I realized that how you dressed or how you looked or what you said wasn't as important as whether you had the musical goods.

"I could certainly see George Gershwin as somebody to measure against. Leonard Bernstein is somebody to measure against. Which is not to say that I aspire to write songs like Leonard Bernstein or like George Gershwin. But there was an excellence they achieved that was right for their time. I wouldn't do that. It wouldn't come out that way.

"But I don't feel that it is truly significant that my record goes to Number One or that I win a Grammy. Those things are pleasant rewards. It's nice to get that popularity. But I understand there's a higher standard that can be applied to the work. And then"—he laughed self-deprecatingly—"there's a higher standard even than that. When you get to be Gershwin that doesn't make you Bartók."

He seems to be on the verge of searching for his place in the tradition represented by Bernstein and Gershwin. Though he won't talk about it much, his next major project is not another album but a movie musical.

Throughout the music industry, he has a reputation as an especially shrewd, tough businessman. His royalty rates are among the highest in the field, over $1.25 an album. He thinks that his background gave him an edge over other performers. "I'd been hanging around record companies and the record business since I was 14. And I made records when I was 15 or 16. So by the time Simon and Garfunkel hit, I'd been around for eight years and I knew something about the business—more than the Beatles, say, who seem to have made some really egregious business mistakes. For example, I knew I could keep the publishing rights to my songs if I wanted to. That was enormously beneficial to me.

"Still, in the first few years of the success I didn't want to sit around business meetings. Just straight hippie dope scene was all I was into—and 'fuck capitalism.' That was what we all thought at the time. Then I explained to my lawyer Michael Tannen that I didn't want to know about corporate minutes. But he said, 'You are entitled to whatever you earn. You don't have to go out and build an empire, but whatever money accrues to you because of your work, you should get it all.' He put me in a business frame of mind that I could accept as fair and right."

Paul talked about the record business—about techniques for bargaining or the idea of buying a property like Frank Loesser's music publishing company—like a very good Monopoly player, except that his dollars are real. But, he said, "Outside my own field, business interests are an unnecessary diversion. Nor is my self-image being very wealthy, even though I am." When I asked Simon how he sets a limit for the money he spends, he answered wryly, "It's like the national budget. There's no real limit. I'm not living even near the true economic level I can afford. I could buy whatever I feel like buying, but I don't. My values are still what I grew up with, tempered with my nouveau riche experience."

It took him years on the analyst's couch to get over his guilt about the money he's earned. His analyst had to keep telling him that he didn't exploit anyone to make the fortune, that his songs brought people pleasure, not pain. "He told me, 'Sure, the system's unfair, but that's beside the realistic point. It's not going to change unless you go out and change it.'" Simon contributes to causes like the Farmworkers' efforts and gives money to little-known performers whose work he respects, but he is not an activist. He finally decided that "either by luck or natural ability I've done well by the rules. I didn't make them up. They were in existence a long time before I got here.

"This is perhaps not an admirable thing to say but, practically speaking, I'm on the side of the capitalists. It's a rare person who gives his money away. And those who do usually trade it for power. Christ, Gandhi, they were the best. But I'm not such a lofty character."

Forest Hills, when Simon was raised, had no traditions. The place had been farmland until the end of the Depression. In the years when he was growing up, you could still see patches of swampland just beyond the apartment buildings and hastily constructed houses that were springing up everywhere. Everyone came from the Lower East Side or Pitkin Avenue or the Grand Concourse. They were eager to escape the embarrassing traces of their parents' greenhorn generation, to live like Yankees at last—and to give their kids an education that would enable them to move on to the greater luxuries of Scarsdale or Great Neck. For the assimilationist Jews who lived there, it was an entrance to the sterile paradise, America's utopia of the Fifties: it was a way station for the upwardly mobile.

Now Paul is actively trying to retrieve his heritage. "It just came over me that I wanted to know about being Jewish," he said. "Peggy, my wife, comes from Tennessee, and her family, the Harpers, the Thomases and the Mathiases, had been there for hundreds of years. And they all still live there. If someone came across the border from North Carolina, that was a big move. If there's anyone named Harper down there, they're related. But the thought came over me, I had no idea what I was, or even what my family's original name was. It's like being cut off at your roots." To his parents' surprise, he hired someone to investigate his genealogy, learned his European name and plans to spend some time next year in the Rumanian town where his ancestors were born. He is proud that his grandfather was a cantor in a synagogue. Unlike earlier generations of American celebrities who Americanized their names to broaden their appeal—indeed, unlike Bob Dylan—he has always been openly, freely Jewish.

On a bright Friday afternoon I took him down to the Lower East Side—once Jerusalem for millions of Eastern European Jews. His grandparents had been married there, at a synagogue across the street from the Fillmore, but he'd never spent time in the neighborhood.

I am an assimilated Jew of Paul Simon's generation. The neighborhood has done a great deal to ease my loneliness. It has taught me that, secularized and Americanized as I insist on being, I—like the people who came here from Italy or Ireland or Africa—do have a home in a culture. By the time of our trip there, I had grown quite fond of Paul. I wanted to introduce him to the Lower East Side.

It's a legend now, as a result of movies like *Hester Street,* books like Irving Howe's *World of Our Fathers,* but its present condition is more complex. Puerto Ricans and Chinese form a majority of the population. Most of the Jews who remain are old people, living on fixed incomes of $4000 or $5000 a year, Orthodox people who fear they'll be mugged if they go to synagogue but who could never move to Forest Hills or Great Neck, never live with children who don't keep kosher, with grandchildren who celebrate Christmas, who marry gentiles. Yet the place is still alive with reminders of the old culture—the small Orthodox synagogues where landsmen from the same Eastern European towns still gather to pray, the kosher cafeterias where anarchists, socialists and communists drank hot tea from water glasses and argued politics for hours, the Yiddish language shops and stalls where bargaining is more fun than buying, the Yeshiva students with their sidelocks and the older Orthodox men with their caftans who still walk on East Broadway as if it were an extension of pre-Hitler Vilna.

We got out of our taxi near the Garden Cafeteria, once the thriving center of political debate on the Lower East Side. Paul blended into the neighborhood perfectly, unobtrusively. With his beard, his windbreaker, his white hat pulled over his eyes, no one on the street recognized him. Most of the old people had never heard of Paul Simon anyway. Two friends of mine, Eddie and Mischa from Project Ezra, an organization of young people who serve as surrogate grandchildren for the elderly, had agreed to take us around the neighborhood.

Farber, the jokesmith, is a blind old Orthodox man, one of the few Jews who remain in the low-income Lillian Wald housing project—the scene of frequent muggings. The elevator had broken that day so we had to walk up the two flights to his apartment. As soon as we entered, Farber offered us a piece of cheesecake, complained about his spreading paunch and then sat us down for a session of jokes and riddles.

Simon sat on the tattered seat next to Farber's chair. Soon he began to watch the lively old man with the fond composure of an affectionate grandson who is enchanted with the sheer joy of wordplay.

Farber—who'd never heard of Simon—had practiced his routines as thoroughly as any comic in the Catskills. "In the South they say 'I is' all the time," he began. " 'I is coming,' 'I is here.' Smart fellows like you tease them for that. But I wonder whether you're smart enough to tell me whether 'I is' is ever grammatical."

As we sat there silently, the old man kidded us, rather proudly, about our slowness.

Paul answered first, "I is the second letter in 'big.'"

"Hey, that's close to my answer," Farber said, surprised. "I say, 'I is the ninth letter of the alphabet.'" Soon he quickened his delivery and, throwing us off pace, mixed jokes in with his riddles.

"Who does a rabbi take his hat off to?" Farber asked.

"The barber," Paul said. Mischa, a Bulgarian Jew and a refugee from the communists, laughed with delight. His leftist consciousness had been strongly influenced by the lyrics of "The Sound of Silence." "Simon and Farber," he said. "What a vaudeville team."

Then Mischa remembered that the old man was an accomplished accordianist and asked him to play. Simon urged him even more eagerly. But he couldn't. Orthodox Jews are forbidden to play musical instruments in the weeks that follow Passover. "What's the matter?" he chided. "You aren't Jews? I know. Jews, but not Jews."

Soon we had to leave. It was nearly sundown, the beginning of Shabbos. But Farber had a more intimate, urgent message he wanted to convey. As we were parting he asked his social worker, Ed, to give him his hand. Then he pulled the younger man close. "I want to tell you this where your friends can hear," he said. "I love you. You're wonderful to keep visiting an old man like me. You give me strength."

Paul must have been moved by the tribute. Anyway, as we were leaving he touched Mr. Farber fondly, said goodbye, and then added, "I'll get you a half-hour on network TV." It was probably a joke—the old man had no reason to construe it as anything else—but it suddenly reminded me of the magic powers of Paul Simon's celebrity. Or at least the power such celebrity seemed to promise.

What a potent, American gift! If Isaac Bashevis Singer had conferred such capacities on someone who lived in the pre–World War II shtetls, that character would have had to dwell in the realm of the supernatural. In the Old World, there was no way to account for the incredible blessings that an ordinary person like Paul Simon could summon.

It was a languid spring afternoon when Simon held his final rehearsal for the Madison Square Garden concert he was organizing to benefit the New York public libraries. The hall was on one of those tattered, postindustrial blocks that dot New York's West Side. Some Spanish kids playing stick-ball on the street provided a lively contrast to the antiseptic room where the musicians had gathered. But Paul was happier than I'd ever seen him. His liquid, joyous ease affected everyone who was around.

The musicians were good friends of his, though he hadn't gotten together with them since they toured Europe last fall. In fact, Paul hadn't played with any musicians at all for the past five months. He was at a loss to explain why. He loves to practice with bands, so it seemed like an incomprehensible form of self-punishment. Anyway, it was over for now. The rehearsal was a release from his self-imposed isolation.

He was clearly in charge, but he exercised his control in a loose, good-humored way. That afternoon, the almost compulsively verbal man communicated most of his emotions, most of his ideas, through gestures, smiles, phrases. At one point during a short break between songs, he rested his guitar on a chair and, exercising his fingers to prevent cramps, mentioned the "melismatic" quality of the music they'd all been playing. He drew that formal word out so that he seemed to be making gentle fun of his own studies in that huge living room overlooking Central Park, assuring his fellow musicians that he could still get down and boogie, that he was still part of their fraternity.

Toward the middle of the rehearsal Phoebe Snow came in to practice the version of "Gone at Last" that she and Paul would perform with the Jessy Dixon singers. With Paul standing by, fooling with two tambourines, Phoebe and Ethel Holloway, a black gospel singer, got into a riff where they exchanged high and low shrieks for nearly a minute. Paul was delighted. The exchange brought out the director in him. With a craftsman's satisfyingly intense concentration, he had them rehearse it six separate times, until they were able to syncopate their parts perfectly and still stay loose enough to incorporate the audience's response which, Paul realized, was both unpredictable and certain to occur.

At most benefits, the featured performers are somewhat casual about the amount of time their sets will take, about the precision of their own work. But Simon was afraid of ragged edges—afraid of looking bad. That was one reason he'd spent so much time giving newspaper and television interviews to promote the concert—he didn't want to be shamed by a half-empty house. He was intent on assuring himself that the music in his set would last exactly 46 minutes. So, while he sang and played guitar, while he nodded encouragement to anybody whose work pleased him, he kept glancing at the clock on the studio wall with the studied care of a Walt Frazier in the fourth period of a Knicks game. Sure enough, the set lasted as long as he'd planned.

As Paul began to rehearse his encore, "American Tune," Harper, wearing a bright red Superman T-shirt and a red and yellow cape, began to dart back and forth in front of the sound system. When the song was over he asked, eagerly, "Did you see me?" and his dad answered, "I saw a shape, but it was going so fast I couldn't figure out what it was. Was it you?" The boy ran up to hug him.

Moments later, after the musicians had gone, Harper, his cape flowing behind him, hurried to the mike in front of the room and, standing among the maze of wires, began to sing in a strong voice, "Still crazy after all these years, still crazy after all these years."

Peggy was there, too. Going down in the freight elevator she said, in a slightly amused voice, "A star is born."

"No," Paul replied. "A star is duplicated."

Before the Garden concert, Paul kept telling me how much he hates to perform. He never gets nervous, except for those dreams. . . . But before a show he gets very sleepy and wonders why he's there at all. For days before he goes onstage, his suppressed fears add to his woes.

But that night, alone and tiny on that distant stage, he seemed more personal, more tender, than in any of the more intimate settings where I'd interviewed him. Though his songs were full of the adult melancholy of "Still Crazy," he seemed to reach the child, the Harper, in most of the audience of 15,000. And the applause was majestic—a tribute that was as heartfelt as the one Mr. Farber paid his social worker, Ed. The audience clapped and waved matches with such fond intensity that Paul was forced to depart from his plan and make a completely unexpected second encore: to sing "Me and Julio Down by the Schoolyard" and "Bridge Over Troubled Water" even though he hadn't rehearsed them.

It seemed to me that the applause wasn't for the performance alone. It was for all the songs that had poured forth from him for the past ten years: for all the experiences he'd helped shape. He was one of us. More important, his music was part of us. That was why, even after the second encore, the applause was relentless.

He was touched by it. He even applauded back. But he decided to end the concert after the second encore, with a few words about how more music would mean paying triple overtime to the Garden's workers, how that would cut into the money that had been raised for the libraries. Then he shrugged gratefully, uncomfortably, and hurried off stage.

Later he told me he'd been worried that if he kept singing, the audience might begin to feel "bloated"—it sounded as if he was afraid that, in the midst of his triumph, he might still be a disappointment, as if that recurrent nightmare about losing control, looking foolish, had echoed faintly in his brain.

He also discussed the evening in astringent, competitive terms—as a vindication of his decision to leave Artie. He'd "redeemed" songs like "Bridge over Troubled Water" and "The Sounds of Silence," he told me. Now people knew he wrote them. "It's been a long time since I've heard those cries of 'where's Artie?' from the audience. . . . It took me five years to get there."

Now he's there. He won the stickball championship. But that unceasing dissatisfaction with himself, that reflexive need to remain in control by keeping his distance—by staying behind the glass control booth, however much he might want to get out—still persists.

One day, in the cool elegance of his apartment, I mentioned a contemporary of his at Forest Hills High School who told me she loved "The 59th Street Bridge Song (Feelin' Groovy)" because it captured her buoyant mood whenever she came into Manhattan. He changed the subject very quickly, but that casual remark must have left a much stronger impression than I'd imagined. For he mentioned it again an hour later. He doesn't like the song anymore, he said. Anyway, it makes him uncomfortable when anyone—even friends—try to analyze his work. He'd appeared a little uncomfortable when the Garden audience applauded him so long. Now he seemed to feel invaded. "What I like," he said, "is a quick compliment, and then goodbye."

GEORGE W. S. TROW
GROWING UP IS HARD TO DO:
THE SUCCESSFUL SOPHOMORE AND OTHERS (1976)

It is a contention of people who don't like popular music that popular music is sophomoric, and, of course, they are right—but the sophomoric state is more complex and more interesting than they suppose, and non-black rock-and-roll stars are usually happy when they achieve it. Sophomores, after all, are one step ahead of freshmen. Freshmen (like the Bay City Rollers—whose youthful appeal is so determinedly preliterate that when they spell out S-a-t-u-r-d-a-y, as they do on their recent single, you half expect them to get it wrong) bash ahead, amplify their mistakes and make up any deficit by writing large checks against their energy.

The Successful Sophomore (like Paul Simon) is different. The Successful Sophomore is potent: he has *completed* freshman year with the other guys and then had an Experience over the summer.

He is still a member of the group, but his Experience (with women, cars, crime, or the writing camp at Banff) has given him an edge. His position is tricky. If he has been too deeply moved by his woman or his car or his crime or his writing camp—if he has begun, in fact, to pursue any important excellence—his edge is lost, and his group will desert him. To maintain his position, the successful sophomore must continue to have Experiences just beyond the experience of his group, but only *just* beyond their experience, and he must learn how to refer these experiences back to his group in a way that will allow his followers, without great effort, to appropriate them for their own strange use.

An important mode of the successful sophomore on television is the talk show. Johnny Carson is the most successful sophomore in America: he has refined and modulated mediocrity to a degree that is not to be despised, since it represents the maximum achievement consistent with maximum popularity. An important mode of the successful sophomore in popular music is the Personal Statement. (*Question:* What happens to rock and roll after adolescence? *Answer:* Postadolescent rock and roll, and in one mood, at least, the Personal Statement.)

The Personal Statement covers the old emotional ground, but at a more leisurely pace; it allows itself some irony and some distance, and it pays attention to interesting wounds and accidents. Carole King, an important early proprietor of this form, has slacked off, and so has James Taylor. (Taylor recently applied his listless talent to "How Sweet It Is," the great Marvin Gaye song, and one which had not cried out for his interpretation.) This seems to be because the energy at the center of the movement (which drew its strength from its break with the group orthodoxies of the Sixties) has run out. Although Joni Mitchell still gives good value in this department, only Paul Simon is really worth following, and he's turned mean.

On Simon's first two solo albums, the most forceful energy emerges from autobiographical songs that expose the oppressive mediocrity of some situation or other. On *Paul Simon*, the forceful song was "Me and Julio Down By the Schoolyard." On *There Goes Rhymin' Simon*, the song was "Kodachrome." On his latest album, *Still Crazy After All These Years*, the forceful, mediocrity-mocking tone is in almost every song. The gentleness that surfaced from time to time, in "Julio," for instance, has been excised. "Fifty Ways to Leave Your Lover," "You're Kind," and the title song seem to reflect a professional dilemma as well as an Experience, and an obvious truth: that unsuccessful encounters with adulthood can give a man a mean tongue. This would be all right if Simon's mean tongue took any risks or drew any blood. But there is a smugness in these songs that betrays Simon's years as a Successful Sophomore. He is used to having all his thoughts admired by an uncritical audience. And his thoughts, this time around, are not so interesting as he seems to think.

Simon has run straight into the stone wall that divides postadolescent rock and roll from the real world, but he hasn't jumped over it yet. Simon must understand, intuitively at least, that if he goes one step farther away from his pleasant second-rate origins the boys in the home room are going to realize that he isn't their friend any more, and he must be bothered by this. He wouldn't be bothered, of course, if he were a genius, but he isn't a genius or anything close, and he has spent much of his life in the warmth of his peer group's adulation. If only Paul Simon had been a Mouseketeer, we could have spent our *whole lives* growing up with him! In the Fifties, he and Art Garfunkel (as Tom and Jerry) recorded a pleasantly crass rock-and-roll song called "Hey, Schoolgirl in the Second Row," and had a hit. Later, he wrote bad poetry and had a hit with "The Sound of Silence." He wrote a pseudo-folk song ("Scarborough Fair/Canticle") and contrived the most awful protest song ever conceived ("Silent Night," sung over, or under, the seven o'clock news) without ever straining the capacities of his constituency. He has been consistently successful because he has moved along at just the right speed for the people who buy his records. But now he's sick of it. Sick of his own twenty-year adolescence, and left without any interesting means of access to adulthood. (*Question:* What happens to rock and roll after postadolescence? *Answer: Adult* rock and roll? What could it possibly be? We all know what serious talk shows are like and, well, we prefer Johnny Carson.)

Simon now is like the talk-show host who, contemplating the awful consequences of first-rate work, has decided to renew his contract with the network and take out his frustrations on his guests.

PAUL SIMON: SURVIVOR FROM THE SIXTIES (1976)

The Sixties was a time during which my generation regarded its songwriters as previous generations had viewed Pound and Eliot, Fitzgerald and Hemingway. We attended concerts as if they were poetry readings, looking for passion and commitment; we devoured the latest albums like epic novels, finding in them direction and identity. To the exclusion of nearly every other form, the sung word provided the generation with its most potent art, its most enduring fantasies.

The songwriters who produced these works were not only artists and leaders but peers of our realm; all of their consciousnesses had been raised in the frantic heyday of our mutual burning adolescence. At every turning point of the Sixties, we found—in the words of our sundry street-corner poets—a path to follow, a code to live by. That our poets spoke for us proved beyond a doubt there *was* an us. It made the world more bearable.

While Bob Dylan stands as the central figure, the one who woke this sleeping giant of a generation determined not to go silent, none of the other poet laureates of the era addressed himself to all of us middle-class cowboys as directly as Paul Simon. We were the ones who rode through the Sixties on Schwinns rather than Harleys, who dropped out, grew our hair, then cut it again (and are now losing it), moved through dope and the draft, into and out of "meaningful relationships," while at the same time proving too brainy (or repressed) to follow the freak-out route of the kids in San Francisco.

Dylan and Simon, of course, were not the only pop poets to gain prominence in the mid-to-late Sixties. Working the same side of the street were John Lennon and Paul McCartney, Laura Nyro, and, later on, Joni Mitchell. Just down the block were lesser laureates like John Sebastian, Tim Hardin, Phil Ochs, Tom Paxton, Pat Sky, Buffy Sainte-Marie, and Eric Andersen. But Simon, like Lennon and McCartney and Sebastian, used the three-minute form of the single to its full potential, and thus—through AM radio—reached a far wider audience than many of his more prolix contemporaries who depended on the long-play format.

Paul Simon's recording career began in the late Fifties when he and partner Art Garfunkel had a hefty New York hit called "Hey Schoolgirl," which managed to nudge its way onto the national charts while the two were still in high school. In 1965, after a hiatus for college, the duo were back in action with "The Sounds of Silence," a song that helped to usher in the age of folk/rock.

On the eve of a recent benefit concert in Madison Square Garden for the New York Public Library, Simon recalled those beginnings. "What separated us from the rest of the folkies, and a fact that was completely ignored, was that we had had experience in the recording studio. I had been writing rock-'n'-roll songs since the age of 15—they were all flops, but we knew about the studio, we knew about sounds, textures, voices, overdubbing. We really came out of the rock 'n' roll of the Fifties, although the music we were singing was the folk/rock of the early Sixties. But I think that's why we had the hits."

From "Homeward Bound" to "Dangling Conversations" to "Mrs. Robinson," Simon's songs mirrored the alienation, malaise, and despair of the era, but did so melodiously, with a good beat, so you could dance to them. Meanwhile, on the streets, the dancing turned to fighting as the decade churned toward its climax. "Actually," Simon admitted, "I wasn't involved in anything at the time, I was just by myself. I was crazy most of the time, high, and relatively depressed throughout those years—quite alone. I lived on the East Side, by the river, uptown. So even where I lived was not connected to anything—it was largely unaffected by the youth culture."

After the election of 1968 there seemed to be a general dimming of the creative lights on the part of our principal songwriter/poets. The blackout took shape in these grim tableaux:

• Simon in 1970 abdicated his seat atop the singles empire he had built with Garfunkel to seek a singular identity. He got married and settled down, withdrawing as 30 approached.
• Dylan, after the explosive, tortured heights of *Blond on Blond* (1968), suffered a nearly fatal motorcycle accident and emerged from it a country singer, his caustic edge and poetry gone, praising the simple virtues of family and religion in a succession of banal works.
• Laura Nyro, the candy-store madonna and battered child of pop, was creatively stilled after the extremes of *Christmas & the Beads of Sweat* (1970). She released a collection of old rhythm-and-blues tunes in 1971 before escaping to an austere life with her husband deep in the woods of Massachusetts.
• Joni Mitchell seemed to hit a simultaneous artistic top and personal bottom with the trenchant and evocative *Blue* (1971), and disappeared into seclusion for several years after it, releasing during the interim only the melancholy and self-critical *For the Roses*.

There was the passing of Jim Morrison and Jimi Hendrix and Janis Joplin, all before they'd truly realized their potential, and the schizophrenic crack-up of the Beatles into four separate nonentities, so soon after the glory that was *Sergeant Pepper*. Sebastian, Hardin, Ochs, Andersen, Tim Buckley, Buffy Sainte-Marie, were all stifled on the brink of major works—voices from our past that seemingly could not break through into the present. With the deteriorating politics and depleted economy of the Seventies full upon us, the dissipation of these inspirational figures could only bode ill for the creative future of the generation. Many among us packed up our old records and traded in our stereos for color TV sets.

"My feeling is it bottomed out about 1971," said Simon. "People were so angry by 1971 that the ones who still had their wits about them and had talent and had enough energy and drive to do something, started working. Don't forget, involved in that hippie ethic was a very strong anti-work thing. It was all 'Get out there and do it, feel it, just let it happen.'

"For me the significant change, as far as songwriting goes, was around 1969, after I wrote 'The Boxer.' At that point I stopped smoking grass, and I never went back. I told a friend of mine, a really fine musician, that I had a writer's block. And he said, 'When are you going to stop playing this folkie stuff, all the time the same G-to-C chord? You could be a really good songwriter, but you don't know enough, you don't have enough tools. Forget about having hits; go learn your ax.' So I started to study guitar, classical guitar, and I started to study theory. I began listening to other kinds of music—gospel, Jamaican ska, Antonio Carlos Jobim. Gospel music was very easy for me to feel at home with because it sounded like the rock 'n' roll of the early Fifties which I grew up with.

"'Bridge Over Troubled Waters' was a gospel-influenced song. Paradoxically, it was the end of Simon and Garfunkel, but it was our most intense success. As the relationship was disintegrating the album was selling 10 million copies. And by the time I decided I'm going to go out on my own, you can imagine how difficult it was telling the record company there's not going to be any follow-up to this album that sold 10 million. But for me it really saved my ass, because I don't think we could have followed it up. And it allowed me to just naturally drop down a couple of rungs on the ladder, because there was less attention. I could go and learn what I had to learn again about writing and singing and making records. It was like stepping back into the shadows for a while. It was good; it gave me a chance to think."

The years in the shadows have been fruitful ones for Simon. Combining further study with a less frenetic performing pace, he's produced three fine albums—*Paul Simon* (1971), *There Goes Rhymin' Simon* (1973), and *Still Crazy After All These Years* (1975)—each one revealing a variety of influences, each one musically rich as well as emotionally complex. In the meantime, his miraculously consistent singles output has continued virtually unabated. From "Kodachrome" to "Mother and Child Reunion" to "American Tune" to "My Little Town" to "Fifty Ways to Leave Your Lover," Simon tells us as much as we need to know about the 10 years he's been out there on the edges of his sensibility. Not only is he producing songs of quality, but he's reminding us who we are, as he sadly reflects on the past, slyly flirts with affairs, and fears (but secretly hopes) he might still someday let go.

"I write about the past a lot," he said, "my childhood and—the last couple of years—my marriage. Not intentionally, though. I didn't set out to write about the disintegration of a marriage. It's just that that's what was happening at the time. I guess I have an easier time expressing myself in a song than in real life. It's a structure that works for me. I can say things in a song that I would never say otherwise. It's a way of telling the truth—but again, not intentionally. It just turns out that way.

"Most of the time, though, what I'm writing is about music, not about lyrics, and critics pay scant attention to the music. I mean, if you're saying something with music *and* words—if you're saying one thing with words and the opposite with music and you're creating a sense of irony . . . that's lost. Or if the idea of the song is a musical idea, how to write a song in 7/4 time and make it feel natural, let's say . . . it's beyond them. I never heard anybody say, 'Now, that was a clever way of doing 7/4 time.' Instead, most critics are basically analyzing words—it's English Lit all over again."

Like the rest of us, Paul Simon has finally passed through adolescence, long considered a terminal condition not only of rock 'n' roll but also of the generation that came to majority in the Sixties. That generation became hooked on rock music as a way of receiving its essential data. And today these same listeners, older and somewhat wiser, continue to respond to Simon and to those other artists who have arrived at a more mature perspective and are able to mirror in their works something beyond pop platitudes.

For Simon's ability to survive the hectic Sixties and grow up in the Seventies has been mirrored by the era's other major song/poets as well. Bob Dylan ended his long siege of passivity in 1974, regaining his voice in a couple of momentous cross-country tours. His latest albums, *Blood on the Tracks* (1974) and *Desire* (1976), have the feel, if not all of the poetry, of his early raging creations. Joni Mitchell came back to the stage in 1974, too, with a jazz band behind her; and though the songs on *Court and Spark* (1974) and *The Hissing of Summer Lawns* (1976) are just as candid and jarring as those of her past, the mood is that much more uplifting and positive because of the vital music now in them. And Laura Nyro broke her five-year silence to record and perform again. She is, at 28, a screamer no more; the songs on her new album, *Smile,* convey an unexpected sense of inner peace. I believe she speaks for many of her peers in "Stormy Love" when she says, "I'm gonna love again, but I won't be the same."

Not everyone was as successful in passing the great divide—Sixties into Seventies, twenties into thirties. We lost Tim Buckley some time ago. And Phil Ochs's recent suicide was all the more tragic in the light of the positive energy in the air. It was as if he could sense this resurgence and couldn't bear to face being absent at the creative front lines of his generation. We have not heard from Tim Hardin in a long while, nor from Tom Paxton or Pat Sky. And that long-awaited "one time only" closed-circuit-televised intergalactic billion-dollar coming together of the Beatles has once again failed to materialize.

Nevertheless, we now have many songwriters able to speak to those of us in our thirties who draw on experiences beyond the ken of the average teeny-bopper. With any luck, these survivors from the Sixties (and there are others, like Leonard Cohen, Randy Newman, Dore Previn, and Jackson Browne) will be with us for a long time, writing songs that will help our generation define itself through adulthood; as well as providing a literature upon which future generations will build. And we will need them as we retrench in the Seventies for the long work that remains ahead.

Something like that is very much on Paul Simon's mind as he looks to the future. "Today," he says, "I'm functioning on a value system that is relatively well defined in my head, and it doesn't matter what somebody says about my work. I feel I know how far away I am from what I could potentially be. It's nice to be praised, but my eye is on a place farther down the line. It will require more work, and either I'll get there or I won't—check back in 10 years and see if I've done anything." Meanwhile, we'll all be listening.

DAVE MARSH

WHAT DO YOU DO WHEN YOU'RE NOT A KID ANYMORE
AND YOU STILL WANT TO ROCK AND ROLL? (1980)

There's nothing chic about the block of West Fifty-fourth Street between Seventh and Eighth avenues. Studio 54 used to be there, but it's been shuttered, and the block's film-cutting rooms, rehearsal studios and the like are on high floors of faceless buildings. Out in the street, there's only traffic and loose trash blowing around. But on one night last August, there was light and bustle till all hours as Paul Simon completed the last details of his first feature movie, *One-Trick Pony.* A couple of floors below him, Phil Ramone was finishing synching the soundtrack.

Perched on a stool before a Moviola, a beer in one hand, Paul Simon looked like a refugee from a Woody Allen film, improbably younger than his thirty-nine years and not a little bleak. He is clearly concerned about the fate of *One-Trick Pony*—which he wrote, scored and stars in, and which his business manager produced—but he is definitely collected. Awkwardness and vulnerability belong to his public persona, not his private one.

The movie was brought in several weeks later, at about $1 million over budget (which was in the $6 million to $7 million range), but still close enough to the mark that Simon retained control of the final cut, a privilege few filmmakers are ever granted.

Additionally, "Late in the Evening," the first single from his new album and, not coincidentally, the song that plays over the movie's title sequence, jumped onto a record number of Top Forty radio stations in its first week. Despite the five years that have elapsed since *Still Crazy after All These Years,* he has obviously lost none of his hitmaking touch.

Still, *One-Trick Pony,* the movie, is a chancy proposition. It is a rock-oriented film in a season when such projects are generally on the wane. More important, the story of a one-hit journeyman rocker named Jonah Levin, his broken marriage and traveling band (Stuff—Richard Tee, Eric Gale, Tony Levin and Steve Gadd) is a low-key and dispassionate look at the least glamorous aspects of rock: the seamy center of a career when it's been a long time since your last hit and the trends have started to pass you by.

In this way, the immediate success of "Late in the Evening" is ironic. Jonah Levin never had it so good (which is one thing that's presented a problem for many who've seen the picture). But Simon wanted Jonah Levin to be typical in a way that his creator never was.

"Not since I was a kid have I played in a band," he says a few days later, over coffee in Rockefeller Center. "It's odd to have been in rock & roll all this time and never really been part of a band. I was part of a *duo*—a *vocal* duo—and I played with studio musicians. So I was never part of that life in that way, and that is an essential part of rock & roll. I only know it by being with people who are in it. But I never lived it."

But *One-Trick Pony* doesn't really try to capture Levin's life on the road, even though the sequences with the band (onstage and off) are among the movie's best. What it's really about is what Paul Simon's life (or the life of someone like him) might have been like had "The Sound of Silence" been a one-shot hit, rather than the beginning of a successful career. Because Levin's personality is so closely patterned after Simon's, it's tempting to think that *One-Trick Pony* is autobiography. It isn't, but it is revealing of its creator's personality.

That night in the mixing room, Phil Ramone was working on the film's original ending, which differed drastically from what Simon wound up with. In that first version, Levin apparently reconciles with his wife. Quoting some memorably corny lines from the monologue in "Are You Lonesome Tonight?," the old Presley hit, he tells her that the band has broken up. But that scene immediately jumps to Jonah and the band onstage, playing "Ace in the Hole." Sneak-preview audiences in Denver and New Haven apparently found this ambiguity thoroughly confusing, but a little reflection spells out the message easily enough: Jonah Levin will never quit. What happens in the release print is more certain—and less satisfying.

That desire to have it both ways ties into something Simon said to Ramone that night during a discussion of Billy Joel's *Glass Houses*. "Well," Paul said in that dry, deadpan tone, "I've *tried* to scream. But, you know . . . it's just not in my body to do it."

Back at Rockefeller Center, Simon amplifies this. He has been speaking of his musical roots, and why he approaches his music so eclectically, when out of the blue he flashes back to the very beginning. "One of the earliest thoughts I had concerning music—I was about fourteen, and I *loved* Elvis Presley. And I said to myself, 'I can never, *never* be Elvis Presley. I'll never be as good as Elvis Presley. So I'm never gonna do what Elvis Presley does. I'm gonna go and find somethin' else to do.' And always, what I've worked with is trying to step back and look at the limitations of . . . my brain, my voice, my size, my guitar playing. And given those limitations—which I can try and push, but given what they are—I try to express myself."

It's hard not to be stunned by this. Is Paul Simon the only person who learned from Elvis Presley the opposite of the common lesson: that life was about extravagance, that there *were* no limitations? And yet, the odd shape of Simon's version of Every Rocker's Elvis Obsession seems to be the key to *One-Trick Pony*. Certainly, it explains the character of Jonah Levin better than anything in the film.

The film makes three references to Elvis. Once, Marion (Blair Brown), Jonah's soon-to-be ex-wife, reminds him in the course of an argument that though he's wanted to be Elvis Presley since he was fourteen, it's time to grow up. Later, while the band is traveling in their van, they play a game called Rock & Roll Deaths, the object of which is to name as many dead rock stars as possible. The game ends when Jonah names Elvis, then adds wistfully, "Yup. He's dead all right." And finally, there is that anomalous final scene in which a tearful Jonah recites to Marion what were surely the most hokey lines of Presley's memorably maudlin career: "Honey, you lied when you said you loved me. But I'd rather go on hearing your lies than to go on living without you." Those scenes are clearly meant to suggest Jonah Levin as some sort of Elvis analogue—but one buried under so many levels of qualification and restraint (he's East Coast, Jewish and intellectual) that the source is no longer discernible.

To say that *One-Trick Pony* is a movie without much emotional heat is to speak in the idiom of the film itself: understatement. Sparks fly from time to time, but the characters are too damn polite to ignite them. So, the conflicts that surface—between Jonah's rock & roll dream and his wife's insistence that he give up or grow up; between Levin as a working musician and having to deal with his band as an employer; between Jonah as someone driven to make music and the kind of people who market that music; between the concept of artistry and the concept of work in general—are continually kept in check. They are vital questions, but they aren't treated that way.

This makes *One-Trick Pony* an interesting rock movie, since it is the only one (give or take Godard's *One Plus One*) that eschews flamboyance altogether. And it's nothing if not revealing of Paul Simon's personality. Remember the night he was guest host on *Saturday Night Live,* and he came out for the opening bit wearing a turkey suit? The joke was that though Simon might make any number of rational arguments about why a turkey costume was inappropriate, he would not simply rip it off and stomp away. *One-Trick Pony* is a movie filled with people who would rather wear the turkey suit than make *too much fuss.* The picture has some very humorous and moving scenes—the live footage of "Ace in the Hole": the flashbacks of "Late in the Evening" (which escapes embarrassment due to the sassy Latin brass, which knocks nostalgia into a cocked hat); the ludicrous scenes of Lou Reed, as a hack record producer, screwing up Jonah's music with wrongheaded overdubs; and of industry hotshots trying to explain the intangibles that make hits. Throughout, it's as though a radio is playing songs in Jonah's head, music that he can't play or maybe just doesn't want to, because it's too private or doesn't fit with the joints he's stuck in. Partly, this explains the muted, languid music that makes up the bulk of *One-Trick Pony*'s score, which is divided between songs Levin performs ("One-Trick Pony," "Ace in the Hole") and those that describe his thoughts and feelings ("Late in the Evening," "That's Why God Made the Movies"). The twain don't meet.

Several critics, however, have suggested another reason why so much of Simon's music is this way: his real masters are not rock & roll and rhythm & blues greats but the Tin Pan Alley songwriters. Simon strenuously disagrees. "Pre-rock & roll pop music is the element that has had the least effect on me. There's none of the Tin Pan Alley people that I emulate. My music is recording-studio music.

"What I feel is, you take basic rock & roll as your primary vocabulary," he says. "Now, when I say basic rock & roll, I don't mean heavy metal, I mean the Fifties—doo-wop, Presley, Chuck Berry, Buddy Holly, the Drifters—that kind of urban R&B and rockabilly.

"Now, from there I expand to other textures and rhythms. I expand the harmonic concept, and in that sense I'm influenced a lot by the Brazilians. Jobim is a big influence on me. Also, Fifties West Coast–jazz guys like [Paul] Desmond, Miles Davis, [Dave] Brubeck—that harmonic way of approaching things, and also the use of different time signatures.

"So, I'll take the basic rock things and expand it into different areas musically, and then I'll contract it back to the rock thing. Always coming back to the basics—to either gospel or rock—but goin' away so it doesn't sound like everything. It puts that earlier vocabulary in a different musical perspective.

"Lyrically, what I do is in a sense parallel to the music. I try to combine ordinary speech patterns—a vernacular way of speaking, slang, clichés—with poetic imagery. Lines that you wouldn't say in ordinary speech: 'Boy's got a heart, but it beats on his opposite side.' 'The stars were white as bones.' I try to balance that between striking visual images and ordinary speech. And ordinary speech can be used with the extended harmonic thing to create a sense of irony or contrast, while I can use a strong visual or poetic image with a basic rock & roll thing to undercut. Or I can go the other way: simple speech patterns and simple musical things. I mean, I have all those elements to play with, to see just what I want to create. If I want to say two things at once, I'll go against styles, I'll make 'em rub. I'll put background voices that sound like Jack Scott or the Crickets, and I'll use a line that doesn't sound like them."

It's unlikely that there's another songwriter of the post-Presley generation who could, or would, articulate so completely his working methodology. To some, this may smack of calculation, but it's really just a product of Simon's analytical bent. He is, after all, a man who went back to study music theory after he'd already become an established success. "I had to do that to get out of writing three- and four-chord music. I really feel that one of the most important elements of popular music is melody, and it's very hard to write melodies if you have to stay within the blues changes. Even 'Late in the Evening,' which is written on blues changes, is really not a melodic song, it's a rhythmic song."

Melody has not exactly gone out of vogue since *Still Crazy after All These Years*—there are Billy Joel and Michael McDonald and a new generation of black vocal groups to make sure of that—but all of the important trends (funk, disco, punk and New Wave avant-gardism) place the emphasis elsewhere. Most of this music rejects complexity in favor of a simplicity that can strike the uninitiated or unconverted as simply crude. More than most pop musicians, Simon is insulated from trends (the only time he was really trendy was in the early days of folk-rock). Nonetheless, much of his reaction to the critical response to his new album reflects an awareness of trends.

"It seems like there's great resentment whenever you try to take something simple and make it complex," he says. "It's almost as if this vision of *simple* is that it's naive, innocent. You know, the noble savage. And that's what they admire in rock & roll. But as an artist matures, you can't be an innocent anymore. *You can't be.* You would be like Peter Sellers in *Being There.* You must learn something, and you must try to incorporate that into the world. So, naturally, the way you see things becomes more complex. And in order to express something that's more complex, you need more tools to express it. So what's this insistence on 'It's not good old rock & roll,' as if because it's not good old rock & roll, it can't be good? It's strange, isn't it?"

What Simon is saying may apply equally to Jonah's predicament in *One-Trick Pony*. "Jonah Levin doesn't have the luxury that I have of sitting back and thinking about strengths and weaknesses," Simon admits. "He's out there hustling a buck. And I'm not."

Indeed, that's another factor that drastically distances Simon from the character he's created. Jonah Levin is caught up in rock & roll as a job, in a situation where it's an effort to find paying work and an agony to deal with callous record companies and a producer working to subvert him. For Jonah, just making a friend is a luxury.

That's not Paul Simon's problem. "I wanted to do something other than just record an album. I felt my choices were either to write a Broadway show or a movie. I chose the movie because I thought it would be closer to the process of recording. You get a take, and that's your take. I don't have to go in every night and see whether the cast is performing. Also, I could still record and use the movie as a score. But if I'd written a show, I couldn't have recorded my own stuff—other people would have had to sing it."

Obviously, he doesn't need the money. Simon has had a consistent string of artistic and commercial successes since "The Sound of Silence" in 1965; composing "Bridge over Troubled Waters" alone earned enough to make him financially comfortable. Then there's the new record contract he signed in early 1978 with Warner Bros. That deal meant leaving CBS, where he'd been for fifteen years, and it started a major music-industry feud (some traces of which turn up in Rip Torn's characterization of *One-Trick Pony*'s record-company president, Walter Fox, who's treated as a pondering schlemiel). But the Warners contract also guarantees Simon substantial wealth: for his next three albums, he will reportedly make somewhere between $10 million and $15 million, with complete artistic freedom.

So unlike most rockers gone to the movies (Peter Frampton or Meat Loaf, for example), Simon isn't looking for a way to extend his career once his moment passes. Rather, he seems to have made *One-Trick Pony* for other reasons: because he genuinely felt the need to expand his artistic horizons, and because in the circles in which he now travels (going out with actresses like Shelley Duvall and Carrie Fisher), film is a much more acceptable medium. Even if you're not a one-hit wonder, to the showbiz elite, as long as you're primarily a recording artists, you might as well be— you haven't really made it until you've accomplished something in Hollywood.

But the virtue of *One-Trick Pony* is that it's so completely unlike Hollywood glamour. Like Simon's best music, it's a work in miniature, constantly withdrawing into itself, commenting obliquely, without much sense of grand gesture. In either medium, such a guarded approach can seem smug, or even arrogant (who is this upstart to make a film that takes its audience's interest so much for granted?). And there's no denying that Simon strikes a lot of acquaintances this way.

Yet, like the screams that aren't in him, reaching out for attention more boldly—behaving more obviously—is just not part of Paul Simon's character. Maybe one reason *One-Trick Pony* is about a loser (an anomaly since its creator and his music are both such obvious winners) is that losers aren't obligated to be brash.

The amount of control Simon was able to exert over *One-Trick Pony* is extraordinary. Usually, those powers are reserved only for the biggest stars (i.e., Warren Beatty and Barbra Streisand). Simon may be a big deal on the record charts, but his previous movie experience was confined to contributing songs to *The Graduate* and *Shampoo,* and a role in *Annie Hall.* But the production of *One-Trick Pony* revolved around Simon, as screenwriter and author of the score, because his business manager, Michael Tannen, served as executive producer and because Warner Brothers' movie division financed the film only because of Simon's involvement.

This presented a problem for most of the directors Simon approached—and he approached many before hitting on Robert M. Young. "They all wondered whether there was gonna be enough room for them to direct. I remember having a conversation with Alan Parker [*Midnight Express, Fame*]. He said, 'What would I do here? You wrote it, you're starring in it, and you wrote the music. I don't want to be a yes man. What would my role be?' A lot of people, I think, had that feeling. That wasn't Young's feeling, though. His ego didn't get in the way. He saw room for him to function as a director and be of help to the movie and still feel that he was, you know, in charge."

The biggest surprise, though, was Simon's decision to star. Aside from *Annie Hall,* a 1978 TV special and some work on *Saturday Night Live,* he's done no acting. Yet, Simon says, "I was the only one who had any doubts about whether I wanted to act. Warners really wasn't that interested in the project unless I acted. But I didn't know if I wanted to be so far out there, to be so vulnerable to criticism on a personal level. And I thought, well, if I write it and I write the music, that's plenty. But if I go and star in it. . . ."

The final decision was a product of the mechanics that make casting any rock picture difficult: Jonah Levin isn't a stage singer, he's a rock singer, and with the exception of Gary Busey, there are few, if any, actors who can also sing rock. "At one point, Richard Dreyfuss and I talked about it," Simon recalls. "It couldn't be done. It would have been insurmountable, because I had to give the soundtrack to Warner Bros., and there was no way I could have Richard Dreyfuss singing on it. There was no way Dreyfuss could be in the movie and open his mouth and have *my* voice come out. It would be funny." In the end, Paul says, he felt he did a good job as an actor and even enjoyed it.

So, it's disconcerting to hear Simon's response when it is suggested that *One-Trick Pony* should at least provide a firm foundation for his future movies. "That's true, I guess. But I'm not all that sure I wanna do another movie."

It's hard to say whether that statement is more perverse or ironic. Maybe it's neither; maybe *One-Trick Pony* was just a project, almost an experiment. For one thing, Paul Simon still regards himself primarily as a musician and songwriter; he resents accusations that his involvement in other aspects of the movie caused him to skimp on the score and the album. "I *know* how hard I worked on the music," he tells me. "And I know what's there in terms of melodies and rhythms and time changes."

But there's more to it than that. As it is for Jonah Levin, touring is a bugaboo for any performing musician approaching middle age. It's all well enough to talk about the romance of the road, but there are those souls who'd also like to participate in their children's growing up. If *One-Trick Pony* is a partial excuse—or explanation—for Simon's absence from the concert stage in recent years, then the concept of creating musical projects that work on the screen has a built-in attraction. Theoretically, such work might replace touring. In practice, it doesn't work out that way. Simon says he regrets how little time he's been able to spend, since shooting began, with his son, Harper, who turned eight in early September. Harper, of course, lives with Simon's ex-wife (just as Jonah Levin's son, Matty, lives with his mother), which makes matters even more difficult.

As it happens, Simon is doing a concert tour anyway, to promote the film. It's brief, just a six-week swing around the States. But because Paul is working with a thirteen-piece band and enough electronic tonnage to restage D-day, it involves a couple weeks of pretour rehearsals.

Simon describes the tour as "virtually sold out and way in the red. There's no way I can even come close to breaking even." Others estimate he might lose as much as $300,000 on the tour—only about one-tenth of his record advance, but still not exactly economic good sense.

So what's the point? "Well, the point is . . . I haven't been out there in a while. I haven't made money on a tour in ten years, not since Simon and Garfunkel. I should go out there. I'd *like* to go out there, I'd like to take this band and have a record of it—you know, these guys, at this particular moment, 'cause I don't know if we'll all be together again. It's the movie; it's the album; it's everything."

Mostly, though, it's the movie. *One-Trick Pony* isn't a sure shot at the box office by any means. Warners was slow to schedule its opening, which is never a good sign. But it's a film that deserves to be seen, and as the central creative figure, it's up to Paul Simon to enhance every possibility. Thus, a tour and the film's new, compromised ending.

Yet, one also knows that Simon wants to play again—maybe even that he needs to. A few days before we spoke at Rockefeller Center, Simon was running the band through the new set in a huge soundstage on Fifty-second Street. The scene was streamlined chaos, packing cases towering to the vast ceiling, Phil Ramone's kids toying with Richard Tee's keyboards between songs, secretaries keeping the phones lit up, various crew members testing out equipment.

In the midst of this madness, Simon was working on a medley of "Kodachrome" with a modified reggae accent, and Chuck Berry's "Maybelline," swinging and (of course) understated. Simon was toying with the words of the original greatest hit, sliding off the lines where Berry had punched them home, tinkering with the rhythms, loosening the song up, letting out some slack. Sprung on you like that, flowing so easily out of the nice bright colors of his own song, it was the best kind of surprise. Not necessarily good old rock & roll, you know, but good and rocking. Just your ordinary rhythm & blues, your basic rock & roll. And Paul Simon was up there with an easy grin on his face. As if to say he'll never quit.

TONY SCHWARTZ

IT'S "SIMON AND GARFUNKEL" AGAIN (1982)

"For a long time, I almost needed Paul to be elsewhere," says Art Garfunkel. "He affected me too much, at a time when I really needed to find my own identity. The wish to work together again evolved organically. It was the absence of stuff in the way—your ego, the need for space. I suppose we'd grown up. Paul said, 'Let's sing' and I said, 'It's a deal.'"

"During the 1970s," says Paul Simon, "we were not only competing against the memory of Simon and Garfunkel, but against each other. It was tense. We've always been very competitive, and we obviously have very different musical tastes. But it's mellowed in the past few years, and I saw the Central Park concert as a chance to be positive toward each other, to be good guys, and if we were lucky, to be a popular success."

The story of Mr. Simon and Mr. Garfunkel is a tale about a close, competitive friendship, and how it has influenced the music they've produced, separately and together. It's about how two partners in a relationship that dates back to childhood chose to split up at the height of their success, spent the next 11 years pursuing their own musical interests at a wary distance, and found themselves unexpectedly drawn back together last September.

It was then that Mr. Simon asked Mr. Garfunkel to join him for a free concert in Central Park. A half million people showed up, and the experience proved so satisfying for them that it set the stage for further collaboration. A 90-minute cable television special based on the concert began playing on Home Box Office last week. A record album of the event is due for release this month. Mr. Simon and Mr. Garfunkel have set plans for a half-dozen concert dates together this spring in Europe and Japan. And if all goes well there, they'll return to do a concert tour of the United States, and then record a new album of original material.

When Mr. Simon and Mr. Garfunkel stopped singing together in 1970, they were at the height of their popularity. "Bridge Over Troubled Water," their sixth album of songs written by Mr. Simon, had just been released and was on its way to becoming one of the biggest selling records in pop-music history.

But even then, their interests were diverging. The differences were never articulated, and they never split formally, but "Bridge Over Troubled Water" proved to be their last joint album. Mr. Simon, always the more experimental of the two, wanted to move beyond the confines of two voices and an acoustic guitar to explore other kinds of music. Mr. Garfunkel, who had begun an acting career in Mike Nichols's "Catch-22" during the recording of "Bridge," was also interested in expanding his vocal range. In tandem with Mr. Simon, he had been mostly limited to singing harmony, and he was eager to try recording his own versions of tunes by other songwriters.

Part of the subsequent tension in the relationship stemmed from Mr. Simon's belief that Mr. Garfunkel played it too safe musically—something Mr. Simon views less harshly today than he once did. "Obviously we have a different concept of what an album should be," Mr. Simon says. "Artie works in a narrow range that he does extraordinarily well. He's more of a romantic than me. He likes ballads, as of course we know, tunes that are sweeter and more orchestrated. Sometimes you don't recognize the differences between his songs because he doesn't set them up. It's ballad, ballad, ballad."

Mr. Garfunkel has never offered apologies for his more limited interests, and his preference for lavishly romantic tunes from a small group of songwriters including Jimmy Webb and Stephen Bishop. "I've never felt comfortable doing uptempo songs," he explains. "People say 'Look at how many ballads he does.' Well, ballads are my forte. It's the first tie theory. If you have two ties, and one's your favorite, why go out for a major occasion wearing your second favorite? The artist Kenneth Noland painted stripes, in shades from deep purple to salmon. I'm the same way musically. Others choose to work from a larger palette. My ear just doesn't enjoy the mix of delicate and bombastic.

Mr. Simon apparently does. "Generally I like things rockier than Artie—not heavy metal, or new wave or no wave, but rhythm tunes. Actually I've experimented with a lot of sounds: Latin, gospel, reggae. I even had a Brazilian period." Indeed, Mr. Simon has played with musicians including Urubamba, a South American band; the Dixie Hummingbirds, a group of black women gospel singers; and the famed session musicians from Muscle Shoals, Alabama, who play something Mr. Simon characterizes as white rhythm and blues.

These contrasting musical preferences are also mirrored in their personal styles. Mr. Garfunkel's is more contained and linear, befitting someone who was trained in math and architecture; Mr. Simon's is more eclectic and unpredictable. "Paul typically says something like 'I think it's time to change my friendships' and then does," says Mr. Garfunkel. "I find that interesting. Or he'll decide every five years or so that his apartment needs a whole different look and change it. It's a sense of new era for new era's sake."

But even as Mr. Garfunkel and Mr. Simon traveled on different musical paths through the 1970's, both managed to sharpen their craft and achieve new kinds of recognition. Mr. Garfunkel, long regarded by critics as the less creative of the two, emerged as an original, interpretive singer. "Mr. Garfunkel has become a compelling song stylist and an understated but remarkably musical vocal technician," Robert Palmer wrote in The Times after Mr. Garfunkel's last concert at Carnegie Hall. "He has the rare ability to put a song over with a maximum of feeling, a minimum of fuss and an admirable control of pitch, timbre and phrasing."

Mr. Simon evolved not only into a more sophisticated and resourceful songwriter with compositions such as "Late in the Evening," "Kodachrome" and "My Little Town," but also as a solo performer who could bring considerable energy and feeling to his best songs. Following his release of the album "Still Crazy After All These Years" in 1975, Mr. Simon was awarded a Grammy as the year's best male vocalist.

But if Simon and Garfunkel were each able to build substantial followings in the 1970's, neither one was ever as successful as the two had been together—a fact neither of them were above joking about. When Mr. Simon asked Mr. Garfunkel to join him on a television special in 1977, the comedy show was built around just that theme. In one sketch, co-written by Mr. Simon, Charles Grodin, playing the role of director, calls the two partners over following a rendition of "Old Friends." "The sound of you and Artie singing together is so much better than the sound of either one of you singing alone," Mr. Grodin tells them, blithely oblivious to the hurt he might be inflicting, "that whatever petty differences you might have had in the past, I strongly urge you to take a long hard look at them."

In fact, the two performers continued intermittently to sing together during the 1970's, although never in a full-scale concert. In 1972, they performed briefly during a fundraiser for Sen. George McGovern. Several times in the mid-70's, Mr. Garfunkel showed up on stage at the end of Mr. Simon's concerts, to sing a few songs with him. Twice they even recorded songs together—"My Little Town," Mr. Simon's tune about their childhood in Forest Hills and a new version of the 1959 hit "What a Wonderful World," which they sang with James Taylor.

Several factors prompted the Central Park concert together last fall. On the one hand, the competitive tensions that permeated the Simon and Garfunkel relationship through the 1970's began to dissipate as their individual musical identities grew stronger. Perhaps too, they were more open to a collaboration because each one had suffered a recent and unaccustomed professional disappointment: Mr. Simon over the negative critical and commercial reaction to "One Trick Pony," the film he had spent more than three years writing, scoring and starring in; Mr. Garfunkel by virtue of the tepid sales of his most recent album, "Scissors Cut," and the absence of offers for acting jobs following his role in Nicholas Roeg's 1980 film, "Bad Timing—A Sensual Obsession."

Mr. Garfunkel's receptivity to a reunion was also influenced by a personal tragedy. In 1979, Laurie Bird, the actress with whom he had been living for several years, committed suicide. "I lost the center of my life when I lost Laurie," he says. "After that I was a bachelor again, and that made me more predisposed toward old friends, and one in particular." Finally, there was the simple fact that both Mr. Simon and Mr. Garfunkel were between projects when the Central Park concert offer arose.

Originally, Mr. Simon was asked by promoter Ron Delsener to do the concert alone, and when Mr. Simon first called Mr. Garfunkel, it was to ask whether he might want to join him for a few songs at the end of the concert. "Then I thought," said Mr. Simon, 'Oh boy, I'm going to be the opening act for Simon and Garfunkel and I don't want to do that.'" Instead, they agreed to do the whole concert together, but almost immediately a familiar tension set in. Mr. Simon wanted to use a backup band. Mr. Garfunkel did not.

"It was going to be a very big outdoor show, and I couldn't imagine one guitar putting out enough for 200,000 or 300,000 people," Mr. Simon explained. "Besides, I love working with a band. I love it when it starts rocking."

Mr. Garfunkel, characteristically, was more conservative. "I just felt that the more variables you control in an open air show, the better. I thought we'd be safer if we put all our eggs in three baskets—my voice, Paul's voice and Paul's guitar."

Rehearsals were tense—in part because Mr. Garfunkel had never before tried harmonizing on some of the uptempo tunes from Mr. Simon's solo period, or singing in front of an unfamiliar band. "I kept saying to him, 'Artie, the band will jell, and when it does, you'll want to sing. You'll like it.'" Indeed, Mr. Garfunkel found that in concert, despite a feeling of tentativeness, he was comfortable singing even Mr. Simon's rockier tunes.

Coincidentally, both Mr. Simon and Mr. Garfunkel also turned 40 last fall. If that seems like an advanced age to be performing pop music for an audience largely composed of teen-agers, each of them seemed to have come to terms with the dilemma.

"People ask, 'Can you do this forever?'" says Mr. Garfunkel, "and I say that depends on what 'this' means. Once 'this' was candy-coated, danceable and sexy. Now I'm interested in working in an idiom that's a little more complex, but not so complex that you don't reach people."

Mr. Simon finds himself, at 40, in an unusually positive frame of mind. "I've changed my mind about staying in this field," he says. "You produce good work and it has an impact. You may sell less records as you get older, but so what? Frank Sinatra doesn't often sell a lot of records, but he's a very significant force among a certain group of people. He's not Metternich, but people listen. I've thought about this since John Lennon died. It's funny, because I'm not one who thought he was doing great work, but I was surprised at how moved everyone was by his death, including me. For me it was because he was still going out and trying things, and it's tough to make music for 20 years."

Neither Mr. Simon nor Mr. Garfunkel listens to much current pop music, however. Mr. Garfunkel leans more to Bach, and to favorite 1960's performers such as Joni Mitchell, the Beatles, the Beach Boys and James Taylor. Mr. Simon listens to a smattering of current performers, such as David Byrne of Talking Heads and Philip Glass, but he, too, has a preference for the pop music of the 1960's.

And now Simon and Garfunkel, one of that decade's most popular groups are going to try making music together again. Mr. Simon is interested in writing the sort of ballads he avoided for so long as a solo performer. Mr. Garfunkel is more receptive to singing Mr. Simon's uptempo tunes, and playing in front of a band. Both of them would like to recapture the best feelings of the past, but neither one is willing to settle for that. "There's a Ricky Nelson tune that expresses it best for me," says Mr. Garfunkel. "It's got a line that goes, 'If memories is all I played, I'd rather drive a truck.'"

TONY SCHWARTZ
PLAYBOY INTERVIEW: PAUL SIMON (1984)

Playboy: To your fans, it seemed recently that Simon and Garfunkel had achieved something extraordinary: You reunited after an 11-year split and became a success all over again. The climax was to be a new album together. That didn't happen. Why?

Simon: This is going to feel like that Harold Pinter play *Betrayal,* because to start, we are going to have to unreel backward to late 1980. That was when I finished *One-Trick Pony.* The movie came out to mixed reviews—and the soundtrack album didn't do nearly as well as I'd hoped. It was a period of great depression for me. I was immobilized. And it was about that time that I came under the influence of a man named Rod Gorney who's a teacher and a psychiatrist in Los Angeles. I heard about him from a friend and called him from New York.

Playboy: Was your rapport instant?

Simon: Well, I flew right out to California to see him and went directly to his house from the airport. We sat down and he said, "Why have you come?" I said, "I'm here because, given all the facts of my life, given the fact that I'm young and I'm in good health and I'm famous—that I have talent, I have money—given all these facts, I want to know why I'm so unhappy. That's why I'm here."

We began to talk, and among the things I said was "I can't write anymore. I have a serious writer's block, and this is the first time I can't overcome it. I've always written slowly, but I never really had a block." I was *really* depressed.

Playboy: What made you feel so bad?

Simon: It was many things, but essentially, it was my work and my relationship with Carrie. She and I were breaking up, which we were always doing. Faced with a problem that made us uncomfortable, we were inclined to say, "Hey, I don't need this." We were spoiled, because we were both used to being the center of attention.

Playboy: And you felt you particularly needed attention at that point?

Simon: Definitely. I had a severe loss of faith over the response to *One-Trick Pony*. Also, I had switched labels, from Columbia to Warner Bros., with great trauma. When I left CBS, it became company policy there to make life as difficult as possible for me. And that began a terrible personal battle between me and Walter Yetnikoff, the president of the company. It ended only when I threatened to subpoena people to testify that he had told them he was going to ruin my career.

Playboy: Did you tell all that to your psychiatrist? What did he say?

Simon: When I finished, he said, "I find what you say very interesting and I'd like you to come back and talk some more." Then he asked if I'd noticed the guitar in the corner of his living room. I said I had, and he said, "Would you like to borrow it and take it with you to your hotel?" So I said, "Yes, sure." And he said, "Maybe you'd like to write about what you've said today." I thought, That's an interesting ploy psychologically; so I said, "All right."

Playboy: And that did it for you?

Simon: No, the first night, I never even opened the guitar case. The next day, he asked what had happened, and I said, "You don't understand. It takes me months to write songs." He said, "I only expected you to begin to write a song." I went back to the hotel and I wrote on a piece of paper [the first four lines of "Allergies"]. Just that, with a melody. Went back the next day really excited about it.

But that didn't make me feel the problem was solved. So we just kept talking about writing. And I said, "My problem is that I really don't see what difference it makes if I write or don't write." He said, "Do you want to make a difference?" And I said I did. He asked if I thought *Uncle Tom's Cabin* made a difference to people. I said yes, and he agreed. Then he said, "I think *Bridge Over Troubled Water* made a difference to people. I'm interested in working with you, because I think that you can write things that people feel make a difference. That's the reason I want you writing again."

Playboy: Practical fellow. But what he said doesn't seem particularly profound.

Simon: He was able to penetrate someone whose defenses were seemingly impenetrable. He was able to make me feel that I wasn't there to work just for the satisfaction of having a hit but that there was a contribution to be made. Of course, the reason I'd been blocked was that I felt what I did was of absolutely no importance. He was able to say, "I'm telling you that the way to contribute is through your songs. And it's not for you to judge their merits, it's for you to write the songs." For me, that was brilliant—and liberating.

Playboy: What happened?

Simon: Three or four days later, I went home. And I began writing. Somewhere in the middle of that summer, I got a call from Ron Delsener, the main concert promoter in New York City. He said that the parks commissioner of New York wanted me to do a free concert in Central Park, and asked if I'd be interested. I said yes, but then I began to think it wouldn't work. I was still feeling a little shaky about *One-Trick Pony*. Then I thought, Why don't I ask Artie to join me? Not the usual thing where I sing and he comes out at the end and sings three songs with me. Maybe we'll do 20 minutes, half an hour, a full set. I called up Artie and he was in Switzerland. He travels all the time, loves to walk places. I asked if he wanted to do this concert and he said yeah. Then I realized that if we did half the show as Simon and Garfunkel and I did the second half alone, it just wouldn't work in show-business terms. Which meant *I* would have to open the show. Then I said, "I don't want to be an opening act for Simon and Garfunkel!" So I figured, Well, let's try to do a *whole* Simon and Garfunkel show.

Playboy: What were you working on?

Simon: I was on a real roll with my writing by then, but I stopped to go into rehearsal for the concert. And at the time, we were all in very good spirits. Well, the rehearsals were just miserable. Artie and I fought *all* the time. He didn't want to do the show with my band; he just wanted me on acoustic guitar. I said, "I can't do that anymore. I can't just play the guitar for two hours." First, my hand had never fully recovered from when it was injured a few years ago, when I had calcium deposits. And second, a lot of the songs I've written in recent years weren't made to be played by one guitar. *Still Crazy After All These Years*, for example, is an electric-piano song. And *Late in the Evening* has to have horns. So we got a band.

Playboy: Once you got onstage in Central Park, in front of 500,000 people, did your differences fade away?

Simon: Yeah. We just did what we'd done when we were an act in the Sixties. We tried to blend our voices. I attempted to make the tempo work. I talked a little bit, too, but I found it impossible to hold a dialog with 500,000 people.

Playboy: How did playing for a crowd that size feel?

Simon: In a certain sense, it was numbing. It was so big, and it was happening only once. I didn't have much time for an overview while I was performing.

Playboy: And afterward?

Simon: Afterward, our first reaction was, I think, one of disappointment. Arthur's more than mine. He thought he didn't sing well. I didn't get what happened—how big it was—until I went home, turned on the television and saw it on all the news, the people being interviewed, and later that night on the front pages of all the newspapers. Then I got it.

Playboy: What made you decide to follow the concert with a tour together? To what extent was it just a way to make some easy bucks repackaging old material?

Simon: Well, hey, it *was* old material. But it wasn't cynically done. It wasn't hype. It was done because there was an overwhelming demand. The thing that struck me was that people seemed to like those songs, which I found to be really surprising, because I felt they were dated.

Playboy: How do you feel about the record produced from the concert?

Simon: I don't particularly like it. I don't think that Simon and Garfunkel as a live act compares to Simon and Garfunkel as a studio act.

Playboy: Why not?

Simon: In terms of performing, I've never really been comfortable being a professional entertainer. For me, it's a secondary form of creativity. I'm not a creative performer. I'm a reproducer onstage of what I've already created. I guess everyone who goes on the stage is exhibitionistic, but there are limits to what I'll do to make a crowd respond.

Playboy: What did you expect creatively from a Simon and Garfunkel tour?

Simon: Nothing. I thought I was going to get an emotional experience from it. I felt I wasn't really present for Simon and Garfunkel the first time around.

Playboy: Where were you?

Simon: I wasn't home, the same way that I wasn't present for the concert in the park when it was happening. I mean, a phenomenon occurs and it's recognized as a phenomenon. But because you're in the middle of it, you just think that it's your life—until it's over. And then you look back and say, "What an *unusual* thing happened to me in the Sixties."

So there it was. A chance to go and re-experience, to a certain degree, what I hadn't really experienced the first time. Some of those hits from the Sixties I just had no interest in anymore, musically. But I had an interest in experiencing what it was like being the person who wrote and sang those songs.

Playboy: How was the experience?

Simon: I liked it. And I began to think about the songs. I remember playing a concert somewhere in the middle of Germany. It's strange enough to be in Germany, and when I finished playing, I was thinking, I hate *Homeward Bound*. And then I thought, Why do I hate it? I said, "Oh, I hate the words." So I went over them. And then I remembered *where* I wrote it. I was in Liverpool, actually in a railway station. I'd just played a little folk job. The job of a folk singer in those days was to be Bob Dylan. You had to be poet. That's what they wanted. And I thought that was a drag. And I wanted to get home to my girlfriend, Kathy, in London. I was 22. And then I thought, Well, that's not a bad song at all for a 22-year-old kid. It's actually quite touching now that I see it. So I wonder what's so embarrassing to me about it. Then I said, "I know! It's that I don't want to be singing that song as Simon and Garfunkel!"

Playboy: Why not?

Simon: Because Simon and Garfunkel, as Artie said to me just recently, was the songs of Paul Simon, which people liked, and the voices of Paul Simon and Arthur Garfunkel, which combined to make a sound that people *really* liked. And no question, without Arthur's voice, I never would have enjoyed that success. And so the whole world was big Simon and Garfunkel fans. But I wasn't.

Actually, I'm a rock-'n'-roll kid. I grew up with rock 'n' roll. My main influences in early music were Fifties R&B, Fifties doo-wop groups, Elvis Presley and the Everly Brothers. But Simon and Garfunkel was a folkie act. I liked the blend of our voices, but a significant part of me just wasn't a folkie. What we were doing was too sweet. It was too serious.

When I began making my own albums, the songs became funkier. They were more about the streets.

PART THREE

Graceland

The story of Simon's romance with *umbaqanga* began when somebody sent him an otherwise unidentified tape called Gumboots a couple of years ago. As Simon played it in his car he became entranced, improvising tunes over the simple major-chord changes until he decided he had to work with these guys. Only then did he investigate and find out where the music was from. Simon was a little dismayed: "I first thought, 'Too bad it's not from Zimbabwe, Zaire, or Nigeria.' Life would have been more simple."

FROM ROBERT CHRISTGAU'S "SOUTH AFRICAN ROMANCE," *VILLAGE VOICE*, SEPTEMBER 23, 1986

Despite Simon's ambivalence, he went on to produce an album that won the 1986 Grammy for album of the year, the 1987 Grammy for best single of the year, was listed among *Billboard*'s Top 40 albums for 52 weeks, and sold more than five million copies.

With the release of *Graceland,* recorded partially in South Africa, Simon brought the rhythms of *umbaqanga* to a mass audience worldwide. In doing so, he eased his depression and boosted his career, which was flagging after the mixed reception of *One-Trick Pony* in 1980 and the 1981 album *Hearts and Bones.* He also caused an international controversy. The nature of that controversy and the album itself are the focus of Part Three.

There were two main issues to the controversy. One was whether Simon, by working with black South African musicians, was actually exploiting them; a subject explored here by David Fricke in "Paul Simon's Amazing Graceland Tour." The other was whether he was violating a 1980 United Nations cultural boycott against performing in South Africa by traveling there to record. The UN initially felt that Simon was indeed in violation of its boycott; they placed his name on a boycott list. They removed his name three weeks later, however, after Simon sent a letter to the UN declaring that although he had recorded in South Africa, he had not performed there, nor did he have any intention of doing so.

Elaborating on these events, *Africa Report*'s Michael Maren describes the "sins of Paul Simon," while Ray Phiri and Hugh Masekela are passionate in their defense of Simon and his right to create what he wants, regardless of the opinions of others. Masekela says:

> When God made the world, he just made people and they got into the things they got into without Him. He didn't say, "I'm going to make the world and I'm going to make sure that niggers have a rough time." He just made the world, and Paul just made an album!

Simon, though not inclined to compare the creation of *Graceland* to the creation of the world, seems to agree with Masekela's view. According to David Fricke:

> The very suggestion that his songwriting is politically incorrect makes Simon's blood boil. "Just a minute, man! Nobody can define this. . . . I'm still living in a free society, and you guys," he says, referring to his [South African] critics, "want to tell [me] what I should write politically. Well, what are you going to tell your own songwriters when you get into power? Are you gonna tell them what to write?"

This reaction is in response to criticisms leveled against Simon about, in Fricke's words, Simon's "position on South African government's racist policies, the lack of overtly political songwriting on Graceland and . . . 'the exploitation of the talents of African musicians for the furtherance of Simon's own aims.'"

Among Simon's critics have been students at Howard University. In January 1987 several students accused Simon of among other things "stealing" African music and trying to "culturally diffuse it." In an excerpt from her excellent article, "The Apostle of Angst," Jennifer Allen takes us along to Howard on that cold winter's day.

And lest we forget the album itself, the last piece in Part Three is a review by Robert Christgau. Christgau, too, explores the politics behind the music. But he does so to give a context to music he clearly admires. For Christgau, there is something vital behind and beyond all the talking and thinking that is generated by this particular album. "*Graceland*," he says, "is where Simon rediscovers the rock and roll secret, where he throws down his irony and dances."

DAVID FRICKE
PAUL SIMON'S AMAZING GRACELAND TOUR (1987)

The world is suddenly dancing to a South African beat, much to the dismay of some antiapartheid activists.—D. F.

Paul Simon was sweating bullets. Woefully underrehearsed, playing together onstage for the very first time, he and his twenty-four-member *Graceland* ensemble of black South African singers and musicians were about to make their concert debut, not under a sparkling, starlit African sky but amid the dreary concrete and steel of the Ahoy sports arena in Rotterdam, the Netherlands. Outside, the furor over Simon's controversial journey to South Africa—a trip many antiapartheid activists claim was in violation of the United Nations cultural boycott against that country— continued to accelerate. Inside, disaster, it seemed, was just a drumbeat away, with an evening of strange African bop about to be performed in a dismal setting for a sold-out house of white Dutchmen, some of whom surely hoped to hear at least a few of Simon's old folk-pop hits.

Simon, in the end, did a lot of worrying for nothing. That night, the magic kicked in, and the audience with it. The first heartbeat thump and tingly guitar twang of the party-invitation instrumental. "Township Jive" immediately reaffirmed Simon's faith in the power of *umbaqanga*—the swinging Soweto sound that first lured him to South Africa two years ago—to bring whites and blacks together in a celebration of racial unity and dancing madness. The crack rhythm section, led by guitarist Ray Phiri, put real spring into Simon's rhymin' as the forty-four-year-old singer-songwriter ran through such *Graceland* numbers as "I Know What I Know" and "You Can Call Me Al" with pride and relish, making only minimal concessions to his past ("The Boxer," a high-stepping "Mother and Child Reunion," a zesty reading of an old doo-wop favorite, the Del-Vikings' 1957 hit "Whispering Bells," grafted onto the tail end of "Gumboots").

Special guest star Hugh Masekela, the exiled South African trumpeter, called for the release of imprisoned African National Congress leader Nelson Mandela in his jazz-funk anthem "Bring Him Back Home," while singer Miriam Makeba, a fellow exile, lamented the suffering and repression in her homeland with a soulful torching of Masekela's "Soweto Blues." And the extraordinary ten-man a cappella choir Ladysmith Black Mambazo awed the crowd with its sonorous bass harmonies and lively Afro-Temptations hoofing. Simon and his troupe, in fact, were fueled with so much opening-night nervous energy that they ripped through the Rotterdam show, originally timed to run two and a half hours, in only two hours and five minutes.

"People went wild, just wild," says Simon, still raving about the February 1st blastoff of the *Graceland* tour. "We didn't know what was going to happen. But people went crazy, and we were playing so loud and fast. It was like a dance event, a big rock concert. People fainted, and they got lifted over everyone's heads."

"The people would not let us leave the stage," says Masekela. On the second night in Rotterdam, he says, the audience gave the musicians a standing ovation after their stirring performance of the unofficial African national anthem, "N'Kosi Sikeleli" ("God Bless Africa"). "Then they started singing back to us: 'oh-ney, oh-ney'—like a football chant. We didn't know what it meant, but it lasted about ten minutes. We were in shock. It was amazing."

Indeed, the past few months have been, as Simon sings on *Graceland*, "days of miracle and wonder" for him and his South African collaborators. *Graceland*, the unlikely product of Simon's encounter with a mysterious cassette of South African *umbaqanga* during the summer of '84, is in 6 million homes around the world. (In South Africa, the album has been Number One for nine weeks and has sold 110,000 copies, making it the biggest-selling international release there since Michael Jackson's *Thriller*.) The robust bounce and soulful melodicism of township jive, which gave Simon's brainy lyricism a rhythmic kick lacking in his recent work, has become a daily soundtrack in urban yuppie condos and suburban living rooms and on radio airwaves from Australia to Zimbabwe. *Graceland*'s success has also spawned sister releases on Warner Bros. by Hugh Masekela (*Tomorrow*) and Ladysmith Black Mambazo (*Shaka Zulu*, produced by Simon). The entire world, it seems, is suddenly moving to a South African beat.

However, these have also been days of hurt and anger for Simon. As a result of his musical field trip to Johannesburg in February 1985, during which he recorded much of *Graceland* with the cream of South Africa's black singers and players, he has been publicly censured by the African National Congress and other antiapartheid organizations in the United States and Europe for violating the United Nations cultural boycott of

South Africa. Simon's *Graceland* shows in England this spring were picketed by antiapartheid protesters, and several prominent English musicians, including Paul Weller of the Style Council, General Public's Dave Wakeling, protest bard Billy Bragg and Jerry Dammers of the Specials (who co-wrote the U.K. hit "Free Nelson Mandela") signed a letter to Simon calling for a "complete and heartfelt public apology" for breaching the UN boycott.

Simon, who twice turned down million-dollar offers to play Sun City—the South African entertainment complex located in the black "homeland" of Bophuthatswana—in the past, has never appeared on the UN's published register of performers who have violated the cultural boycott; earlier this year, he wrote a carefully worded letter to the UN Special Committee Against Apartheid, which monitors the boycott, reiterating his status as "an artist who has refused to perform in South Africa" and pledging "to maintain this position in the context of the UN cultural boycott." Nevertheless, Simon has been challenged by civic leaders, interviewers and fellow musicians throughout the *Graceland* tour about his position on the South African government's racist policies, the lack of overtly political songwriting on *Graceland* and—in the words of a spokesperson for the South African antiapartheid group the United Democratic Front—"the exploitation of the talents of the African musicians for the furtherance of Simon's own aims."

"To go over and play Sun city would be like going over to do a concert in Nazi Germany at the height of the Holocaust," Simon snaps angrily, obviously weary of the topic. "But what I did was to go over essentially and play to the Jews. That distinction was never made." The charge of exploiting the South African musicians especially irritates Simon. Not only did he pay the South African musicians on *Graceland* the equivalent of the triple union scale commanded by New York studio vets, but he is not accepting any payment for his *Graceland* concert performances to ensure that the two dozen members of his road band get maximum paychecks.

"The show breaks even as long as I don't get paid," he explains. "Everybody gets paid and makes his or her money. I'm working essentially for free."

But for Simon and the South African musicians at his side, the hardest part of withstanding the slings and arrows of antiapartheid outrage is reconciling the volatile criticism that has dogged every step of the tour with the rapturous audience reception that greets the troupe—not just Simon but Masekela, Makeba and especially Ladysmith Black Mambazo—every night. During the two all-too-brief weeks of rehearsal, says Masekela, "we hoped it would be as good onstage as much as we enjoyed playing it. But the first audience was a sea of smiling faces, giving us ovations and encores. It was very uplifting. And it was great to see South Africa's music get to so many people that would never otherwise have listened to it. A lot of people obviously came just to see Paul Simon. But that he was able to bring so many people to hear my country's music was wonderful."

Nowhere was the dance-floor enchantment and implicit spiritual harmony in township jive à la Simon more evident than in the February 14th and 15th *Graceland* performances in the capital city of Harare, Zimbabwe, nearly a day's drive from South Africa's northernmost border. To be sure, Pretoria cast a long shadow of fear over Rufaro Stadium that weekend. "Miriam said, 'I hope you're going to check the speakers for bombs,'" Simon says soberly. "When one of your main participants asks if you're going to check for bombs, you check for bombs." Security for the shows was provided by the Zimbabwe army.

Yet under a broiling midday sun, with the ninety-plus-degree heat intensified by the hot white television lights (the Zimbabwe shows were videotaped for a Showtime cable special), Simon and company sparked two racially mixed crowds of 20,000 each into joyous fits of shout 'n' shimmy. Whites and blacks alike, many of whom journeyed up from South Africa to see the show, bounced in time to the infectious beat of "You Can Call Me Al," cheered Baghiti Khumalo's spine-tingling zoom-bass runs in "The Boy in the Bubble" and devoutly sang "N'Kosi Sikeleli" with the *Graceland* company.

"The sun was extremely radiant," Simon says with a smile. "On the second day, the sun was so bright that on camera everybody bleached out. There is usually a heavy rain in the middle of each day. But it didn't rain on either day. And the audiences were very festive. Everyone was in a real good mood.

"It was exciting. That's why we went to Africa. Because we thought it would be special. Can you imagine what it would be like if we were able to play in South Africa?"

But *Graceland* guitarist Ray Phiri, the leader of the top Soweto band Stimela, believes that the Zimbabwe shows were a minor victory in a greater battle. "It was the biggest high of my life," he says. "But I knew my people would love it. It's more important to me what people outside southern Africa will think, how they will react and what it will mean to them.

"And when I close my eyes and hear them clap for Ladysmith Black Mambazo, it makes me feel very proud of being part of that. It was this

Jewish man from New York who made it happen for us. Now the world knows about South African music. People out there who feel the emotion in our music know that we are going through trying times. Our music gives the people hope. It keeps them going on hoping that things will be okay."

Things, of course, are not okay in South Africa. Even as young pop fans and old Simon and Garfunkel acolytes spin their copies of *Graceland* at home and Miriam Makeba sings "Soweto Blues" onstage, guns are being fired, blood is being shed, and black men, women and children of all ages are being arrested and detained, often without charge. Internationally, rage is rising over the oppressive measures instituted by the country's white-minority rulers in the face of increasingly violent black-majority resistance. The solution is clear: South Africa's apartheid system of government must be abolished. The method, it seems, is not. "As Miriam says, you have to fight the battle all different ways," says Simon. "Some people have to hit you over the head. Some have to come out and sing beautiful songs. It all contributes to the same thing."

The African National Congress, which has been especially critical of Simon's *Graceland* project, does not agree. "One of the things you should realize is that in South Africa, you cannot in any way separate culture from politics, from economics," says Jeanette Mothobi, a member of the ANC mission to the United Nations, in New York. "All these things, in the context of the South African situation, are closely intertwined.

"It is claimed by some people that this is an artistic endeavor," she says, referring to the *Graceland* record and tour. "But we maintain that at the present moment in South Africa you cannot talk about artistic endeavors when people are dying."

James Victor Gbeho, the Ghanaian ambassador to the United Nations and the chairperson of the Subcommittee on the Implementation of the UN Resolutions and Collaboration with South Africa, believes Simon's "beautiful songs" argument is hopelessly naive. "Hugh Masekela and Miriam Makeba have been singing these songs from South African culture for the past twenty-five years," he says. "How has that changed South Africa? I seriously doubt if it has made any difference."

Both Gbeho and Mothobi are ardent supporters of the UN cultural boycott of South Africa. In 1962, the UN General Assembly initiated a trade boycott against South Africa. That was supplemented in 1980 by a call for member nations to sever all ties with Pretoria—including diplomatic, cultural, military, nuclear, academic and athletic relations—in an attempt to persuade the government to dismantle apartheid.

"We can put pressure on South Africa by cutting cultural relations," says Gbeho, who feels Simon's visit to Johannesburg seriously undermined the UN boycott, no matter how much *Graceland* has done for the spread of black South African music. "When he goes to South Africa, Paul Simon bows to apartheid. He lives in designated hotels for whites. He spends money the way whites have made it possible to spend money there. The money he spends goes to look after white society, not to the townships. This is one reason why we do not want people to go there."

Gbeho says there is no official UN position on black South Africans performing outside the country, as Ray Phiri and Ladysmith Black Mambazo are doing on the *Graceland* tour. But, he continues, "the whole idea of South Africans coming here to sing and therefore change the situation is one we do not think will solve the problem. If you look at the position taken in the recent whites-only election and the subsequent actions of the government there, it does not seem that singing out here makes any difference."

But Hugh Masekela thinks otherwise. The forty-eight-year-old trumpeter, who left South Africa twenty-seven years ago to accept a scholarship at the Manhattan School of Music, in New York, has been active in both the African and Afro-American musical communities and believes music *can* make a difference. "One of the things that made the world realize what was happening to African Americans in the U.S. was music," says Masekela. "At the time, they were being lynched, long before civil rights. Yet Duke Ellington, Count Basie and Miles Davis could make this incredible music in spite of all that. It was through them that you knew about the plight of the people. Even if they didn't say it, it made you wonder, 'How can these people play so great and be treated like that?' There is something to be said for that."

A staunch defender of Simon's links with black South African musicians, Masekela believes that Simon is being unfairly compared to other musicians who have gone to South Africa, like Elton John, Chicago and Rod Stewart. Those artists, says Masekela, "were not moved by the music there. But Paul was moved, and he did something about it." Masekela also feels the public awareness of South African music in the wake of Simon's *Graceland* album and tour is a form of liberation in itself. "In doing this, he was addressing the aspiration of the musicians there," he says. "The part I find hard to understand about this is why these musicians should be deprived of opportunity, the chance of development. Stopping them is a terrible thing to do."

"A lot of our people who have been in exile for quite a long time have become so outdated that they don't know what to do, what we want," says guitarist Ray Phiri. "They are not giving the people of South Africa a chance to tell their story the way it should be told. If they are saying they are helping South African musicians by keeping them away from the world, how is that help?"

Phiri, who has been an active and successful bandleader, producer and sessionman in South Africa's black music community for many years, adds that his participation on *Graceland* has "opened up some gates for me that were not opened before with the white side of South Africa." That is no small accomplishment in a country where black musicians have been victimized for years by the principally white-run record industry through poor management, inadequate legal advice and exploitative royalty deals. "But in the last two years, I have been exposed more than any other black South African musician, because of Paul Simon."

The irony of Simon's predicament is that both Ambassador Gbeho and the ANC's Mothobi concede that if Simon had recorded the exact same record with the exact same musicians outside of South Africa, *Graceland* would not be a political issue now. Mothobi adds that Simon's recording sessions in Johannesburg could have been overlooked if he had written at least one song for the album that directly addressed the issue of apartheid. She cites the example of Little Steven Van Zandt, who wrote "Sun City" as a result of his own musical fact-finding trip to South Africa.

"I would laugh at anybody who says the album has nothing to do with the struggle," counters Phiri, 40, whose given African name, Chikapa, means "wise protector." "That is very stupid and naive. When we talk about a song like 'Homeless,' it is talking about our very present situation, about our situation as exiles 'out there,' homeless. 'Under African Skies' is talking about 'take this child . . . give her the wings to fly though harmony.' You don't get up and say things are bad without giving a solution. I respect people who come up with solutions, not people who come up with big wind that means nothing."

The very suggestion that his songwriting is politically incorrect makes Simon's blood boil. "Just a minute, man! Nobody can define this. That's not the way it is in a free world. I'm still living in a free society, and you guys," he says, referring to his critics, "want to tell [me] what I should write politically. Well, what are you going to tell your own songwriters when you get into power? Are you gonna tell them what to write?

"The whole thing about whether lyrics are political, whether the songs are political," he says with a sigh, "it's almost as if you can't make a significant contribution unless you make things political. But I think we've made more of a contribution than anybody so far, and we didn't do it that way. We did it another way."

When Paul Simon first discussed taking *Graceland* on the road with Hugh Masekela last fall, he was certain of one thing: this would be no ordinary greatest-hits get-down. But outside of that, he had a totally blank slate; he had to figure out how to develop one album's worth of songs into a full two-and-a-half-hour production that would showcase the sounds on *Graceland* while also paying tribute to the musicians who inspired it and the suffering people whose spirit permeates the music.

Inspired by the big-band shows of West African bandleaders like Nigeria's King Sunny Ade and Fela Aniku-lapo Kuti, he decided to form a large group that would include brass, percussion and a full complement of male and female voices, anchored by the *Graceland* rhythm section of Ray Phiri, Stimela drummer Isaac Mtshali and Baghiti Khumalo, who plays fretless bass with the South African group Thotha. Hugh Masekela, best known in this country for his late-Sixties instrumental hit "Grazing in the Grass" (based on a Zambian instrumental), and Miriam Makeba, who enjoyed worldwide success in 1967 with "Pata Pata," were highly appropriate guest stars—prominent South African entertainers living in exile, performing Afro-rooted jazz and blues with a strong political undercurrent. The result was a kind of variety show, not unlike the township jazz revues with which Masekela and Makeba first toured South Africa in the Fifties.

Simon is performing all but two of the songs from *Graceland* on this tour ("That Was Your Mother" was recorded with the Louisiana zydeco band Good Rockin' Dopsie and the Twisters, "All Around the World or the Myth of Fingerprints" with the Los Angeles rock band Los Lobos). But of the roughly two dozen songs in the show, only half are Simon's, and he is only onstage for two or three songs at a time. When he says at the beginning of each concert that "this evening is composed of music from South Africa," he means it.

"I consider myself to be the producer of the show," he says. "One of my main contributions is that I conceived the show. In terms of my stage appearance, I'm not the star."

In fact, no one in the *Graceland* troupe would deny that the real stars of the show are the nine sweet-singing, smooth-dancing members of

Ladysmith Black Mambazo and the group's founder and choirmaster, forty-six-year-old Joseph Shabalala. Hugh Masekela says that on opening night in Rotterdam, the Mambazos, who perform without musical accompaniment and sing primarily in Zulu, had no idea how they would be received. "But they practically ran away with the show," he says. Simon calls Shabalala, the group's songwriter and lead singer, "an enormous cultural treasure, a cultural gold mine." Shabalala says, in halting English, "When we start to sing, the people enjoy. They love our music. It soothes them."

Assuaging pain is an important part of the Zulu choral tradition that gave birth to Ladysmith Black Mambazo. For years, black migrant workers employed in South Africa's cities and in the country's gold and diamond mines have gathered in workers' hostels to sing in amateur competitions called *ingoma ebusuku* ("night music"). They usually sing for prizes—a blanket, a goat, cash—and the material can range from spirituals to contemporary pop songs. But at the root of the vocalists' low, melancholy harmonies, soaring falsettos and vigorous vibratos is a poignant sadness, a yearning for the homelands, families and friends they left behind.

Joseph Shabalala knows that feeling very well. As a teenager, he migrated from his home in the township of Ladysmith to the coastal city of Durban, where he sang with a local group called the Highlanders while working in a factory weaving cotton. In the mid-Sixties, after returning to Ladysmith, he formed Ladysmith Black Mambazo with several relatives and members of other families in the township.

"This is a gift from God," he says during a brief layover on the *Graceland* tour. "The way we arrange compositions, it all came from God. Because among us, nobody goes to school and learns music. It just came itself, like this. Then I assemble the group, ask them to sing and then teach what I feel."

What he feels has struck a resonant chord within both black and white South Africans since the release, in 1971, of the group's debut single, "Unomathemba" (a re-recorded version appears on *Shaka Zulu*). Every one of the Mambazos' twenty-four South African albums has gone gold there (25,000 sales), with some of them going double gold (50,000) and platinum (75,000). The Mambazos are reluctant stars, though. Many of the group members do not have phones; recently, when Shabalala had to get the group together for a last-minute appearance on Dutch television, he put out a "calling all Mambazos" notice on local radio. And Shabalala, who lives quietly in the black township of Claremont, outside Durban, with his wife, Nellie, and eight of their nine children, professes little interest in the worldly rewards of pop success.

"I am not in a hurry to go outside and sing for somebody," he says. "There is something in me, in my veins, that needs music. That's all. To me, it is good to sit down and sing."

The Mambazos' precision vocals—showcased beautifully on two *Graceland* cuts, the a cappella "Homeless" and "Diamonds on the Soles of Her Shoes," the group's first recording with a backing band—are certainly enough to take your breath away. Seven basses form an earthy harmonic foundation, reminiscent of American gospel choirs, topped off with one alto and one tenor, and Shabalala leads the group with vibrant melodic strength, often shifting from a calm, almost whispery lullaby to dramatically sustained bleating on a moment's notice. It is no wonder that the Mambazos' singing style is called *isicatamiya* in Zulu, meaning "stalking approach" or "surprise attack."

Onstage, the Mambazos augment their vocal razzle with physical dazzle—hand and body movements that combine the leaping energy of tribal dancing with fancy Motown-style footwork, all precisely synchronized with the song's story line. "If you do not understand the song," Shabalala says, "we can make the song talk with out hands. You can see how it goes by watching us. If I sing, 'Come back, Nomathemba,' I do this"—he gestures as if pulling something toward him. "If I say, 'Nomathemba is far from me,' I just point. We follow the song with our action."

But the miracle of Mambazo music is that it possesses an emotional resonance that transcends mere technique and choreography, not to mention language. (Paul Simon was first captivated by Ladysmith Black Mambazo when he saw them on a British television special, *Rhythm of Resistance,* singing a song in German.) Shabalala, an ordained minister with the pentecostal Church of God of Prophecy, insists he knows nothing of politics, politicians or cultural boycotts. "We sing for everybody," he says. "Like when you preach, you must preach for everybody. So we just sing, all over. Nobody tells us, 'You must be on this side.'" Still, in his singing and songwriting, he captures with natural choral majesty not only the anguish of his countrymen but their bravery in the face of horrific repression and their capacity for exhilarating joy.

For example, he says that his lyrics for "Homeless," which he co-wrote with Simon, are actually based on a kind of Zulu mating ritual. "If you are a young man and you want to marry, you say, 'I have no house, I have no home, I sleep in the cliff.' When the people heard this song from my home," he says, "they love this song very much. Because it is a song of love." Shabalala admits, though, that lines like "Strong wind destroy our home/Many dead, tonight it could be you" can be applied to the strong wind of apartheid blowing through South Africa.

"Right, the wind destroyed our home. Yes, the wind do that. Many other things like the wind," he says thoughtfully. "That's why I say, you can use the song anyway you like it."

"Joseph is a minister and does tend to see the world in these metaphysical ways," says Simon. But, he adds, "he's not as apolitical as he says."

Indeed, Shabalala tells a revealing story about an encounter he and the other Mambazos once had with the police in Johannesburg. "I remember there was a riot there," he says. "People were fighting, the kids were fighting. But not Black Mambazo. The policeman ask us, 'Where do you come from?' I said we come from singing. They said, 'You are singing while the people are fighting?' I say, 'Yes. They are doing their job. I am doing my job.'"

When the final U.S. leg of the *Graceland* tour ends July 2nd at New York's Madison Square Garden, it will mark the end of a significant chapter in Paul Simon's career. But in spite of everything *Graceland* hath wrought musically, emotionally and politically, pro and con, it leaves plenty of unfinished business in its wake. Just as no one expects Pretoria to dismantle its apartheid system tomorrow, it will be some time before the true extent of *Graceland*'s effect on international awareness of the South African situation and the black music community there can be measured.

The last round of dates, taking in arenas in major cities like Detroit, Philadelphia and Atlanta, was scheduled to address at least two outstanding problems. One was the almost complete lack of black attendance at any of the earlier U.S. *Graceland* shows in Chicago, St. Louis, Los Angeles, San Francisco and New York. "There were so few shows, really, and they sold out so quickly," Simon says. "These final concerts came about really because Hugh, Ray Phiri and Miriam said it was a pity that the black community hasn't gotten to see the show, because they would really get off on seeing it"—although he admits that major obstacle is the fact that in sales *Graceland* was, in his words, "a white record."

Another issue is the South African government's policy of arresting and detaining black children. One-third of the proceeds from the concluding leg of the *Graceland* tour will go to Children of Apartheid, a fund set up by the Reverend Allan Boesak, a South African minister, for child detainees. (The rest of the proceeds will be divided between the United Negro College Fund and municipal charities in each city on the itinerary.) "I feel like nobody could be possibly anything but moved by the thought of children in jail," Simon says, "that everybody could relate to that."

Simon expects to raise $1.5 million from the eight charity shows. He also hopes the benefit gigs will spark similar projects. "Let the ANC put together a tour," he says. "It would be great. Let the musicians who play the songs they approve of get out there. I think that's fantastic."

Also, he believes *Graceland* should not be the last word in the dissemination of black South African music. "It will be the end of this chapter with me," he says of the tour, "but these other bands, like Black Mambazo, will continue to tour." In fact, Ladysmith Black Mambazo has made a video with Michael Jackson and, in addition to *Shaka Zulu*, has three albums available in the U.S. on the Shanachie label. Miriam Makeba will cut a new album of African traditional songs with Russ Titelman, who produced Steve Winwood's *Back in the High Life*. And Simon has been producing an album by Ray Phiri and Stimela for American release.

"Then," Simon adds, "there are all the other groups in South Africa. There's enough now going that they have to come out and keep playing. Other people have to take up the challenge and do this."

Of course, while the music plays on, apartheid continues. But in listening to the ebullient performances of the South African musicians on *Graceland* and their remarkable performances on tour, it is hard to believe that the international exposure these players have received, along with the proud spirit inherent in their music, is not a political action in itself.

"I never said there were not strong political implications to what I did," Simon says. "I just said the music was not overtly political. But the implications of the music certainly are. And I still think it's the most powerful form of politics, more powerful than saying it right on the money, in which case you're usually preaching to the converted. People get attracted to the music, and once they hear what's going on within it, they say, 'What? They're doing *that* to these people?'

"Besides that, a strong artistic community within South Africa is important to ensure freedom of expression. If there is a change in the government or the form of government, there still has to be freedom of expression. The strongest way of ensuring that is to have a thriving community of really powerful, internationally known artists."

And then there is the effect the *Graceland* tour has had on a South

African like Hugh Masekela, who has not been home in nearly three decades. You'd think listening to and playing with young South African musicians and singers like Ray Phiri and Joseph Shabalala would make him terribly homesick. Quite the contrary.

"I close my eyes," he says contentedly, "hearing music in that state, and it makes me feel like I'm back home."

MICHAEL MAREN
THE SINS OF PAUL SIMON (1987)

Did Paul Simon violate the cultural boycott by recording an album in South Africa and touring with black South African artists? While the UN Centre Against Apartheid has not blacklisted Simon for the "Graceland" effort, neither has it embraced the record and tour, putting itself in conflict with the musicians who have gained international notoriety from their association with the American pop star.—M. M.

The next time the United Nations Centre Against Apartheid issues its register of performers to be boycotted because of their support for the government of South Africa, the name of Paul Simon could well be on it. According to the UN, Simon has violated the cultural boycott and much more seriously as far as the UN is concerned, he has refused to apologize for doing so.

To most observers of the South African situation, the inclusion of Paul Simon on such a list would appear absurd. Since the "Graceland" album and tour, Simon's name has come to be associated with black South African music and with the movement to abolish apartheid. Any suggestion that he is supporting apartheid or the South African government is without foundation, and not even his sharpest critics will directly accuse him of that.

Instead, he has been labeled as either naive ("Simple Simon," the hostile British press has come to call him)—the unwitting dupe of the South African government—or exploiting the situation in South Africa in order to further his own career. But the main thrust of the argument against him is that he violated one of the cardinal rules of the anti-apartheid movement by going to South Africa to record the "Graceland" album in 1985.

The fuss stems from a 1980 UN resolution that "requests all states to take steps to prevent all cultural, academic, sporting, and other exchanges with South Africa." And it "appeals to writers, artists, musicians, and other personalities to boycott South Africa . . ."

This has usually been interpreted as not playing or performing in South Africa or the homelands, most notably the infamous Sun City in Bophuthatswana, as these performances by international celebrities are used by the white government in South Africa to imply that their homelands policy has international support and to give the impression that it is business as usual in the country.

Since 1983, the names of artists who have worked in South Africa have been listed in the Centre Against Apartheid's "Register of Entertainers, Actors and Others who have Performed in Apartheid South Africa," the aim of which is to blacklist those who have profited by performing in South Africa. As the introduction to the most recent register states, "Artists have become increasingly unwilling to suffer the adverse publicity of appearing in the Register."

Simon has twice refused lucrative offers to play Sun City—proof enough for most that he opposes apartheid and supports the aims of the boycott. He was also anything but naive in his consideration of the "Graceland" project. He was clearly aware of the political sensitivity of recording in South Africa, and for that reason spoke with black American leaders and entertainers, like Quincy Jones and Harry Belafonte, as well as with South African exiles and musicians before going to South Africa to record the album.

All of these people encouraged him to go ahead with the project, and South Africa's most prominent artists-in-exile, Hugh Masekela and Miriam Makeba, have joined the "Graceland" tour in celebration of South African music.

From the UN's perspective, however, Simon has committed several sins. First, he clearly violated the letter, though not necessarily the spirit, of the boycott by recording in South Africa. And second, he entered into a gray area by touring with a group of South African musicians. Here the wording of the UN boycott lacks watertight specificity and according to Amer Araim, senior political affairs officer at the UN Centre Against Apartheid, the Special Committee Against Apartheid is taking steps to clarify the situation so that there will be no confusion about what is and is not permissible under UN guidelines.

But in the debate over whether or not rules were broken, the UN and those who support the UN's position have clearly lost sight of the original intention of the cultural boycott. Instead, they are considering a violation of the cultural boycott a crime in and of itself, paying little attention to the reality of the situation in South Africa or the contributions that Simon and the "Graceland" tour have made to the anti-apartheid movement.

For now, Simon rates only this footnote in the register: "The Special Committee considered the case of the well-known American singer and composer Paul Simon who was involved in recording an album in South Africa. It decided not to place his name on the register on receiving his pledge that he does not intend to perform in South Africa while apartheid prevails and will maintain this position in the context of the United Nations cultural boycott."

Simon's pledge, as interpreted by the United Nations, came in what one UN spokesman called a "cleverly worded" letter dated January 29 and addressed to Ambassador Joseph Garba of Nigeria, chairman of the Special Committee.

"I write to you as an artist completely opposed to the apartheid system in South Africa. Like millions of people of conscience in that country and around the world who have contributed to the struggle to end the system, I am working in my field toward achieving this goal. As an artist who has refused to perform in South Africa, I reiterate and intend to maintain this position in the context of the UN cultural boycott."

That was enough to keep Simon's name out of the register proper, but the exonerating footnote is a clear statement that in the Committee's view he violated the boycott. The UN interpreted Simon's letter as an apology, and therefore an admission that a violation had occurred. Simon evidently had other ideas.

"What happened after that?" Araim said. "After that, he went to London and started making funny statements, saying 'I did not apologize to anybody'—all of this nonsense."

Simon's lack of remorse was apparently his biggest mistake. The Committee regularly removes the names of entertainers from the register after they have sent a letter of apology. Simon felt that he had nothing to apologize for and that an apology would lump him with the entertainers who had performed in Sun City, banked their money, and then received full pardons.

According to Araim, Simon's refusal to apologize "caused the Committee to doubt his real intentions." "So the chairman of the Special Committee sent a letter to him saying what we mean by the cultural boycott and we were expecting him to acknowledge and support that. He didn't. Until he does that . . ." Araim didn't finish the sentence.

The controversy might have fizzled out had the UN not been drawn into the fray once more in April. Miriam Makeba and some of the

"Graceland" promoters suggested that the tour kick off its charity leg with a concert at the UN itself. The charity leg is an eight-stop U.S. tour that will divide its proceeds evenly among the United Negro College Fund, a local charity in each of the tour's cities, and Children of Apartheid, a fund created by the Rev. Allan Boesak to aid apartheid's youngest victims.

The tour's promoters sought the assistance of several groups including the United Nations African Mothers, an organization composed of the wives of African ambassadors at the UN. After initially responding favorably to the idea, the women's group backed off. "We had nothing to do with that concert," said Evelyn Garba, head of the African Mothers and wife of Ambassador Garba, who chairs the anti-apartheid committee. "We were invited to take part at the last minute and we found out that they were not cleared by the Committee, and we just told them that we wanted nothing to do with it."

The proposal forced the Committee to reaffirm its stand against Simon and the "Graceland" tour, but at a time when the tour had the backing of Boesak, a founder of the United Democratic Front and one of South Africa's most visible anti-apartheid leaders. Boesak stopped in New York when returning to South Africa from a trip to Japan specifically to lend his support to the "Graceland" effort. There he recorded a video tape that was later played at a May 4 press conference announcing the tour.

In the recorded message, he says: "These are among the most troubling and difficult times we have faced in South Africa. Archbishop Desmond Tutu and myself welcome and support the efforts of Paul Simon, Miriam Makeba, Hugh Masekela, and the 'Graceland' tour in raising world consciousness of the effects of apartheid and the plight of the detained children."

"We don't know about the position of Rev. Boesak," Amer Araim said. "But Simon should reply to the letter of the chairman of the Special Committee. If he would do that, we have no problem with his tour or any of his activities."

Boesak's support of "Graceland" could potentially cause problems between him and the African National Congress (ANC), whose position has been to support the rulings of the Committee, but thus far there have been no open conflicts.

London's *New Musical Express* quotes a telex that allegedly came from ANC headquarters in Lusaka: "The ANC fully supports a boycott action against Paul Simon's European and American tours . . . he has singularly done more harm in flouting the cultural boycott against the racist regime."

But what harm had he done? The ANC didn't really have an answer. And ANC representatives in New York declined to talk about it. "I'm not competent to speak on that issue," said Neo Mnumzana, head of the ANC delegation to the UN. "I think the best thing to do is to consult the Special Committee . . . our position is the position of the Special Committee."

"The argument that Simon has helped the anti-apartheid cause is rejected," said Amer Araim. "However, the government exploits these visits to show the people of South Africa that everything is normal. The pro-government *Citizen* newspaper welcomed back Ladysmith Black Mambazo [one of the South African groups that recorded and performed with Simon] as 'South Africa's musical ambassadors.'"

In reality, the only "harm" that has come from the Paul Simon affair has been to the Committee itself and that has resulted from their insistence on trying to apply their authority in a situation where it clearly didn't belong.

The Centre Against Apartheid is supposed to provide guidance for the larger anti-apartheid movement, but as a part of that movement it is also affected by influences within it. According to one UN official who requested anonymity, the Special Committee was "under a lot of pressure from NGOs and London-based anti-apartheid groups, especially Artists Against Apartheid, to issue a condemnation of the Simon tour."

Indeed, the most persistent and vocal critic of Simon has been Dali Tambo, son of ANC head Oliver Tambo and founder of Artists Against Apartheid. Though he does not speak for the ANC, the weight of his father's position sometimes gives his pronouncements an added air of authority.

In an interview with *New Musical Express,* Tambo expressed what is at the root of the backlash against Simon: "What troubles me about Paul Simon—who did he consult with when he went there? He didn't consult with us.

"If you're going into the country, then you must consult with the ANC," Tambo continued. "Because we're saying that we presume that whatever cultural field you're involved in, you don't want it to be used to further the aims of apartheid and the racist regime. Therefore, you consult with us so that we can put you wise about whether or not we think you will be used by apartheid and about the effect of your cultural activities. If Paul Simon had come to us first and discussed this, none of this would have happened."

That is undoubtedly true. Simon's mistake was the diplomatic oversight of not bringing the right people on board as partners in his venture—of not submitting his plans to the politicians for their stamp of approval.

What is frustrating about these charges is how little they relate to the real issue at hand—the abolition of apartheid. Very little of this criticism against Simon has much to do with the stated goal of the boycott—to isolate the regime in Pretoria. And certainly, the net effect of "Graceland" has in no way compromised that goal.

If anything, the scene of a huge mixed race audience north of the border in Harare, dancing to the songs of South Africa, must not have been a comfort to Botha. Simon's exposure of some of South Africa's musical talent has already opened the floodgates for other South African music to reach the West, carrying with it news and information about South Africa.

Simon has been criticized for not explicitly condemning apartheid in his lyrics—but that has never been his style. Even without the overtly political songs of Miriam Makeba and Hugh Masekela and closing the show with "Nkosi Sikeleli Afrika," the "African National Anthem," the "Graceland" concerts are clearly making a strong political statement. "No one can walk out of the 'Graceland' concert and not feel a personal connection to South Africa the next time they see an article about it in the newspaper," said one observer of a "Graceland" show.

The controversy has brought as much criticism to the Committee as it has to Simon. It has been revealed that the Committee did not consult with any South African artists before drafting its guidelines. Certainly, Hugh Masekela and Miriam Makeba, the two most prominent exiled South African artists, were not consulted and both have been vocally critical of the Committee in this affair.

In many ways, this application of the cultural boycott does the work of the South African government. Like the government's heavy-handed control of the foreign press, the UN's measures are an attempt to control the flow of voices and information from South Africa.

The battle over the definition of the cultural boycott is destined to be fought in the trenches of the anti-apartheid movement. Oliver Tambo and the leaders of the ANC or UDF are unlikely to clash over an issue that should be considered trivial. Whether or not Paul Simon is included on the next UN register will probably not affect the public's perception of his politics nor will it have much of an effect on the ultimate solutions in South Africa.

By using its boycott weapon against Simon and by extension, against Masekela and Makeba, the UN has only blunted its own sword.

A CONVERSATION WITH RAY PHIRI (1987)

Ray Phiri, the gifted South African guitarist whose band, Stimela, tops the charts at home, provided musical direction and lively guitar solos to "Graceland."—M.M.

On Paul Simon and South African music:

Paul Simon needed a tap that he could open and out pours water. I wasn't in his plans when he went down to South Africa. It was by pure chance that he went to Soweto to one of the *shebeens* and heard one of my records being played there and everybody was dancing to the tune. He wanted to know who the band was and they told him, Stimela. Somebody from London had sent him a pirated copy of South African music, the Gumboots Jive and Rhythm of Resistance albums. That's what got him involved with Ladysmith Black Mambazo. For two years, he was listening to this music and trying to find out where it comes from, then Warner Brothers got in touch with the company which recorded Gumboots Jive. Then he went down to South Africa and started working with them. After a week, things weren't working really fine because there was a musical communications breakdown between the guys he was working with. He was looking for a tap, not just musicians, but people who would give him ideas.

People who say he has stolen our music, that's nonsense. They should have accused me of that because I arranged it all. I think "Graceland" is the best thing that ever happened to South African music, moreover to the black community. Right now we are heroes back home. We have had people who have been out of the country for more than 20 years and they have done nothing for our musicians, they have done nothing to bring our music out, so this guy went down at the right time and started working with the right people. This is the best thing that ever happened because Paul Simon worked with people who believe in their music and who needed to let the world know that we also have something to say in our special way through music, South African music.

Today each and every South African should be very proud because now the world has realized that it is not only Miriam Makeba and Hugh Masekela that gave us a name. I've got so much respect for Hugh and those guys, but they have done nothing to help the musicians at home. But I can forgive them because they have never been given a chance. They never had a chance like Paul. Paul had the money, had the ways of doing it. They have been exiled, they would have been arrested for going back to South Africa.

South Africans know that every headline says Paul Simon and his South African musicians. That says something! He is the only small white boy in a cast of 25. It is more like our show than his show. And he is proud to be part and parcel of this, that's why he always takes the third seat and gives us all the glory. It is up to us to take it any further. There will be quite a lot of South African musicians who will benefit from this collaboration, so they must stop saying that he stole South African music. Paul had to tell them that all the musicians are getting royalties, which means that we've got to flaunt our checks to them and say this is how much we got, and then they'll turn back and say we sold out for money! I've earned this, I've worked hard for it, so nobody has the right to tell me anything.

On the opposition to the Graceland tour by some antiapartheid activists:

It's a case of the left not knowing what the right is doing. My record is clean. I have never collaborated with the system and I would never do that. I wouldn't have had my records banned in South Africa if I was a collaborator with the system. I have always been outspoken. That's why today in South Africa people say my band, Stimela, is the people's band. I don't write political songs because to me that is outdated. I will never make use of the name of Nelson Mandela to further my aims and fatten my bank balance. I respect that man too much to use his name to further my own aims. He has given up his freedom for one thing—to unite us all, including those so-called leaders who are outside the country who are making a lot of noise and who don't want to see any young guys coming from South Africa with a positive way of doing things. They feel threatened by that power. It makes me really sick sometimes. . . .

MARGARET A. NOVICKI AND AMEEN AKHALWAYA
AN INTERVIEW WITH HUGH MASEKELA (1987)

One of South Africa's best-known musicians in exile, trumpet player Hugh Masekela was among the artists who toured with Paul Simon's

"Graceland" concert. In an interview with *Africa Report,* Masekela expresses strong views about the criticisms of the Simon effort by the overseas anti-apartheid movement, which, he maintains, has made decisions affecting the lives of South African musicians without their consultation.—M. A. N., A. A.

* * *

Africa Report: How did you get involved in the Paul Simon tour, because there's a lot of confusion about who stands where?

Masekela: Who stands where is not important to me because at this point I am so pissed off that I don't care about what people think. I am saying to them, "What have you done for South Africa lately? If the Graceland tour hadn't come up, what would we have heard from you about South Africa?" It's almost like the Graceland tour is the scapegoat for everybody taking a political stand about South Africa!

Paul Simon is an old friend of mine and we have followed each other's works for a long time. We were produced by the same producer in 1966. So when Paul was promoting this album when it was first released in London, he said, "I want you to hear what I did." First he played me the album. I've always loved Ladysmith Black Mambazo and that old style of South African music that it captured. I told him that he had really captured the mood and translated it very well into American and it mixes great. So he asked me, "What do you think the next step should be if this record makes it?" He said, "Do you think they will boycott us?" I said I didn't think it matters. "You didn't take money from South Africa, you took money there, you paid royalties, you are sharing writers' credits with everybody, you put us in the forefront and you put the music into the ears of people who would otherwise never even bother about Africa." So based on that, it is a very positive step.

For us, coming from the townships, only a collaborator is a sell-out as far as I am concerned. In South Africa, when you are born black, you make the statement when you are born that you are oppressed and don't like it. If you become a collaborator or a policeman, then it's another situation. But if you don't willingly go out to collaborate . . . A lot of people in South Africa are just ekeing out a living.

I met this South African lady in England. She's in exile, she comes from a very rich family in Cape Town, their money was made off our backs. I don't care if a person is in the ANC, when they were at home, they lived at home as Europeans and didn't suffer what we suffered. In the anti-apartheid movement, there's a lot of people like that, and to a certain extent, I resent their morality because they don't know the townships and they don't consult us. So this woman said, "There goes the cultural boycott." I said, "What do you mean?" I said we want to work with people from home. And I don't take orders from anybody. I'm in touch, I'm beamed into Soweto, Guguletu, Crossroads. I know all those people and they say, "Go ahead, we like it." I take my orders from home.

So to this woman, I said, "I'm tired of people like you coming out and telling us what to do, because when you lived in South Africa, although you helped us, you made your money through our oppression. I appreciate that you came overseas and you are now in the anti-apartheid movement, but it would be nice to consult with us." So she said, "We send forms to all the musicians in the townships to sign to say they denounce apartheid." And I said, "Who the hell do you think you are to send a form? You are here in Hampstead in your duplex apartment and you are going to send the form to somebody in Soweto?"

That is the basic stance—that you *must* make a statement against apartheid. When I was born, that was my statement! From there on, every day of my life, if I am living in those hovels, that is my statement. The day I go and sell out, then I should be accused. But no one should expect somebody who lives in the townships to denounce anything, because they have families. People tell me, "Hugh, I'm political, but I'm looking after my mother. If something happens to me, my mother won't eat." I can't say to him, "I won't talk to you, you are a traitor." I have to understand his position.

The feelings of the people were exemplified when those people did that "Let's work together" video in South Africa. They burned their houses and they took them out of town. If the people were not proud of those who worked with Graceland, they would have done the same. These guys have been working with Paul for three years, and every time they go home, there are super welcomes. The street people are on their side, are buying the record, like what they've done, they are proud of them. That's more important.

But the movement outside—I'm not going to accuse the ANC—but allies of the ANC who say they work on their behalf have given these people a hard time. I admire the fact that some of them have been on Robben Island, but it doesn't mean if you suffer, you should come and take out your wrath on people who didn't go to jail because everybody suffers in one way or another. The Mandelas and Sisulus who are in jail don't have that kind of spirit. They have a spirit of reconciliation. The stand of the people who are nitpicking on Graceland is so inflexible that it has caused the biggest division ever among South Africans that I have ever seen.

Africa Report: What has been the ANC's reaction to your involvement in "Graceland"?

Masekela: I told the representative I spoke to the other day exactly what I'm saying to you. And he said, "Hugh, our problem is that there are a lot of people overseas who are lobbying for certain things. And when you are lobbying, you are extreme. Anything that makes waves in your lobby takes away your credibility." So there are the extreme supporters of the boycott in the movement and there are the other extremists who like it. I said to the ANC guy, "I don't know where you are coming from because you should decide whether you are against Paul or against certain members in the group. Tomorrow you're going to be after me and you will say, 'Don't go to Hugh Masekela's concert because he played in Graceland.'" But when people like something, they will go and see it. And this concert is a very powerful one. In our second tour in June and July, we are raising money for children in prison in South Africa and we are going to come up with a very substantial sum of money. We wanted to inaugurate that program at the UN, but the UN committee turned us down.

Africa Report: Despite the fact that Paul Simon is not on the UN blacklist?

Masekela: He was never blacklisted. They haven't decided whether he should be blacklisted or not. That's why he hasn't apologized. There was never a clause which said you can't record there.

Africa Report: In the U.S., is the criticism coming mainly from under the UN aegis?

Masekela: We don't know where it is coming from because nobody is showing his face. It is just coming out in the press that so and so said this. There are some guys at the UN who have been here for more than

20 years and who have never been in a township. I don't think they know who Mahlathini is or who the Dark City Sisters are. At one time, Miriam Makeba went to the UN with Elizabeth Sibeko to look at the statutes and to try and meet these people. They made her wait for hours. And later they said in the papers that she never came, she is lying. It comes back to one thing: Representation without consultation, especially in our case, is like dictatorship in exile, and we do not want to be dictated to from that platform by anybody! Nobody mentions the Pan Africanist Congress, the United Democratic Front, black conscious-ness or any of the other movements who have supported the show.

Africa Report: In South Africa, the pro-apartheid media tried to use "Graceland" to say that the cultural boycott has failed, that the thou-sands of South Africans who went to Harare for the concert don't sup-port the cultural boycott.

Masekela: We don't regard ourselves as part of the cultural boycott. We don't regard ourselves as being wrong. We think that the people who want us boycotted are well-intentioned and we stand on common ground, but if anything we are more in touch with the townships than they are because we are working with people who live there, we are in touch with people at home, and we ask them about this.

Second, there is a certain naivete here because the South African government will use anything, any time there is divisiveness, to come and put in the wedge. I am sure they have infiltrated and I think a lot of the press is coming from those elements. They have a very sophisticated international network of public relations and they have played havoc with the press because most of the people in the press who knock us don't know what they are talking about.

They have described me as being very vitriolic because I give them hell in press conferences. I say, "Next week when Graceland is not there, I wonder if you will still be worried about South Africa. I know you'll be talking about something else." I know that the South African press is taking advantage of this. There are people in the show like Ladysmith Black Mambazo, who come from the core of Inkatha terri-tory and everybody knows the violence that happens there. Anybody who expects them to martyr themselves right now is kidding himself because these guys want to sing, they want to be in show business, and they are getting attention. Inkatha doesn't need the necklace, they go further than that, and if they want you on their side, you can't be anywhere else. These people are *the* Zulu group, so I'm sure that they are intimidated as far as wanting to say whatever. They are not famous for making great political statements.

But people who don't make political statements are not necessarily apolitical. Ray Phiri is a member of the UDF and he has had a lot of problems with the police, so it is very funny when he is accused of playing for the SADF in Namibia. Miriam Makeba and myself have been living with a cultural boycott before it happened. At the risk of our careers, we have knocked the government for 27 years while overseas. In those days, we were considered "communists" and it put our careers back so far that I have always said that my musical career will not start until we are free. Now, I'm just of the people through the people. I don't see any way that I can inspire anything because *I* am inspired by the struggle of the people. If the people get any inspiration from me, it is a blessing that I am not looking for. I wouldn't have a song, I wouldn't have a name, a language or a tongue, without them.

I think that the people who are on the cultural boycott scene can't tell their Paul Simons from their Harry Oppenheimers. Harry Oppenheimer can go to Lusaka, but they won't talk to Paul Simon! Paul Simon gives, Harry Oppenheimer takes away. And what Harry Oppenheimer takes is BIG, but who knows Harry Oppenheimer in the press today? Paul Simon is the arch-devil when it comes to South Africa. He looks even worse than Botha!

Africa Report: Did the decision to do another tour to raise funds for detained children come about as a result of the controversy or was it planned before?

Masekela: No, we went into this tour with the controversy already there. And we don't recognize the controversy, so we're not doing anything to placate anybody. We think that we have a right to represent South Africa. If Joe Garba can be a spokesman for South Africa, then I can also talk for South Africa and I think I have better claim to it. What happened was this: We were in Los Angeles, and myself and Ray Phiri were dissatisfied about the fact that when we looked in the audience, we saw people mostly of European origin. I said to Ray that I felt that we should take the show to the inner cities. If we still don't get African-Americans, then at lest we will have tried.

But not only should we extend the tour, but we should give something to the South African cause because our good luck and good fortune from this show has come from South African art. We should show that we are grateful for whatever little we have gotten out of it. We should find a cause. At that time, we didn't know what it going to be. So myself and Ray went to talk to Paul and said we should take the tour to the inner cities—to Washington, to Detroit, Chicago, and New York. We then chose the charity.

Africa Report: One of the criticisms was that Paul Simon should have used his music to make some political statements.

Masekela: That is as ridiculous as saying that God should be castigated and all churches in Africa should be closed down because He gave Africa a bad deal and after all, He did create the world, didn't He? It is no different. Just say, "To hell with God, why was I born in South Africa? If God is God, if there is a creator in this world, God should be put down for making us Africans!" But when God made the world, he just made people and they got into the things they got into without Him. He didn't say, "I'm going to make the world and I'm going to make sure that niggers have a rough time." He just made the world, and Paul just made an album! He didn't know it was going to be a hit and if it hadn't been a hit, we wouldn't have heard from anybody. I am positive about that. I don't know of any artist who has ever made an album and called to ask permission and ask what kind of lyrics he should write! The guy says he was moved by the music. To me, that is a statement on its own, because Paul knew what South Africa is about. He is a masters graduate of Queens College, he is an art collector, he is a very well-read person and he is very articulate. He has written brilliant songs in the past.

One of the things that people miss culturally about us is that they want to typify us. I think it is a mistake that Castro made. Today, Cuba is looked at like a clenched fist, bearded, cigar-chomping, fatigue-wearing country, but it's not really that. But they want us to have that same kind of Savimbi look. They want us to all sound like the group Amandla. But South Africa is not about that. We have a wide spectrum of music, and even though we are in a war, we have to show our music as it is, and if there is one song that says it to me, it is "Homeless."

The fact is that Paul Simon was moved by the music and dealt the fairest of any musician that ever went to South Africa. He stuck with it for three years, despite all the castigation. He had a clear mind and he has made great friends with these guys. Paul is not going to abandon these guys. He says to me, "Hugh, Joseph Shabalala and Black Mambazo and Ray Phiri are my friends. I've been to their homes, I've lived with them for three years. They've helped me and I've helped them and we are going to be life-time friends. These people are saying I shouldn't play with them because they are from South Africa. What do they want from me? I refused to go to Sun City and do a tour of South Africa. I love these people's music!"

If that is not a statement, then what is? Did Ray Charles do it, did George Benson do it, did Tina Turner and Millie Jackson do it? Millie Jackson told them to go to hell. She went to South Africa twice and the same people who are castigating us forgave her. In other words, you can go to South Africa and take $3 million, but if you come back and say I'm sorry, Mr. Garba, Mr. ANC, then that's OK. That's nonsense!

JENNIFER ALLEN

THE APOSTLE OF ANGST (1987)

"Happy?" says Paul Simon. "That's a dumb question."—J. A.

It is a cloudless, bright January day, the kind of morning in Manhattan when the buildings look as if someone had scrubbed them and polished their windows during the night. Paul Simon steps into the padded quiet of the limousine outside his Central Park West apartment. He wears a chesterfield coat, khakis, and a wide, soft scarf swaddled around his neck. He has a cold, and he dreads that it will linger until next week, when he has to begin rehearsals in London for his eighteen-city concert tour.

Today he will talk with a group of students at predominantly black Howard University in Washington, D.C., about *Graceland,* his first million-selling album in nearly a decade. He likes speaking to students; he has done it recently at UCLA and at NYU, and he is looking forward, he says, to getting the "black reaction." *Graceland* is a collaborative effort; most of its songs were recorded with black South African musicians, and that country's voices, its rhythms, are blended with Simon's dense and quirky lyrics. His use of South African musicians has generated considerable controversy since the release of the album in August—questions have been raised in the press about his possible violation of the cultural boycott against performing in South Africa. But he has answered his critics with confidence, explaining that he did not perform there, has turned down offers to play in Sun City, supports the boycott. He seems unworried about what may transpire today.

Graceland has been near the top of the charts for months, and has received widespread critical blessing. Simon is irked that radio stations have not been playing it, but he is almost certain that it will get a Grammy nomination today for Album of the Year (as it does, along with three other nominations). Ebullience, however, is not his style. When he talks about *Graceland,* it is to say that he is getting bored with performing its songs, as if to deny that after all these years it is sweet to have a hit.

And now, gliding through the city, he talks about the charity work that has kept him busy of late—planning benefit concerts for the homeless and raising money for a medical van to minister to poor mothers and children—and he says, "The world is pretty hopeless. I'm coming to that conclusion."

At the Pan Am shuttle terminal, he meets Charlayne Hunter-Gault, of *The MacNeil/Lehrer NewsHour,* who is working on a profile of him and plans to film today's events. He grabs a free *Wall Street Journal* and, smiling, reads aloud a headline: "TALK SHOW CRISIS: TOO MANY HOSTS, TOO FEW GUESTS. Yeah, I *told* you there weren't going to be enough guests! You said we'll have enough guests and I said no, no, there won't be enough guests!"

Most of forty or so students are dressed conservatively and look slack, sullen, as if they are sitting through a required orientation lecture.

Simon gives his speech without notes, telling about how the album was made, how he paid the musicians triple-scale American, how he agreed to share royalties whenever they collaborated on the writing of a song, how he learned after his arrival that the black musicians union had held a meeting and decided they wanted him to come. He talks about his visit to Soweto. He talks about the cultural boycott, about the "guilt" he felt while he was in the country. He shows them the video of "Homeless," a song from the album that he sings with the ten-member a cappella group Ladysmith Black Mambazo. He finishes his talk and pleasantly invites their questions.

A boy in an orange sweat shirt is first to stand. *"How can you justify going there and taking all their music?* For too long, artists have gone and stolen black music—you're taking it and bringing it back here and throwing it in my *face!"* The boy is yelling, jabbing the air with his finger, his face filled with rage. "You're telling me the Gershwin story of South Africa! It's nothing but stealing! You have not been to South Africa yet! If you did you would not be *alive!*"

"Could I respond?" says Simon. "Have you ever been to South Africa?"

"I know what it's all about, though! I live there!"

"You live there?"

"I live there, I live in Bed-Stuy!"

"Okay, so, metaphorically speaking. First of all, I was invited there by black musicians."

"They wanted money!"

"You think it's easy to make a hit? 'Oh, I know a great way to steal some money. I'll go to South Africa?' You don't think it's possible to collaborate?"

"Between you and them, no. You don't understand the music at all!"

"You can't say no to me, I know these guys."

"You bought these guys!"

The student moderator interrupts to nervously ask for the next question. Another boy stands and takes objection to the video that Simon has shown. "This is going to be used to make people forget the violence," the boy says.

"I don't see that," says Simon.

"You don't see that because you're part of the plan, my brother."

A South African student demands to know "what made you somersault" after turning down Sun City. And another, the chairperson of the South African student union, takes offense at Simon's mention of wealthy blacks in Soweto. ("But they *existed,*" Simon will say later.) Another South African parodies the Zulu dancing on the video with a bump-and-grind.

One student seems more tempered. "I'm not going to crucify you," he says. "Thank you," says Simon, smiling.

"But even Jerry Falwell was invited to South Africa by liberal blacks, so it doesn't mean that much."

Cole Porter's name comes up, and so does Sting's, neither of them flatteringly, and phrases like "art for activism's sake." Five television cameras record all of it, reporters scribble. Bathed in the hot lights, Simon sits on a stool, taking occasional sips of water and telling them, over and over, that this album is a beginning, an attempt. "This is a motion toward helping. It exposes a culture, a people. . . . I'm trying to be in the dialogue. . . . It's an experience to sit here and have people come to you and attack you. It's hard to know if you're being attacked as an artist or as a person. . . ."

After an hour, the moderator calls not so much an end to the meeting as a truce. "Well," says Simon, "it's been, it's been an education." The moderator then presents him, on behalf of the students of Howard University, with a Howard backpack and T-shirt, a moment so awkward that Paul Simon actually blushes.

Charlayne Hunter-Gault chews a piece of gum and shakes her head. "It's the poor liberals," she says, "who take all the shit."

ROBERT CHRISTGAU
SOUTH AFRICAN ROMANCE (1986)

A rock-and-roll equivalent of unimaginable vitality (and industry) and complexity is somehow thriving in apartheid's face.—R. C.

Though it's giving in to the album's most suspect tendencies to begin this way, I'm here to tell you that Paul Simon's *Graceland* is a tremendously engaging and inspired piece of work. If you like him thorny it's his best record since *Paul Simon* in 1972, if you like him smooth you can go back to *There Goes Rhymin' Simon* in 1973, and either way you may end up preferring the new one. Simon-haters won't be won over—his singing has lost none of its studied wimpiness, and he still writes like an English major. But at least *Graceland* gets you past these usages, because it boasts (Artie will never believe this) a bottom. For Simon, this is unprecedented. *Graceland* is the first album he's ever recorded rhythm tracks first, and it gives up a groove so buoyant it could float a loan to Zimbabwe.

Well, not exactly. Only in metaphor, you could say, and a metaphor of suspect tendency at that, because it implies that music transcends politics. Which, as it happens, puts it near the epicenter of what *Graceland* has to be about even though there are only two or three vaguely political moments on the entire record—the protesty title "Homeless," a terrorist bomb metaphoring by, like that. Simon recognizes his dilemma. As he has already amply publicized, *Graceland*'s groove doesn't come from nowhere—it's indigenous to black South Africa, in support of which the aforementioned Zimbabwe recently lost its U.S. aid. Now, despite what Simon-haters may expect or even claim, the artist's relationship to the Soweto-centered "township jive" known generically as *umbaqanga* is deep and committed. I'm not just talking about the way he treated his musicians, paying them triple-scale American in Johannesburg and handing out composer's credits and bringing the Zulu ingom'ebusuku chorus Ladysmith Black Mambazo to New York for a *Saturday Night Live* spot and a lovely gig at S.O.B.'s. I'm talking about the music itself. This isn't the mere exoticism that flavored past Simon hits with reggae and gospel and Andean pipes. It's a full immersion. And still there's reason to wonder whether it's enough.

At first I didn't think so. I was annoyed by the radical incongruity of the thing, the way chatty lines like "Aren't you the woman/who was recently given a Fulbright" or a modernist trope like "staccato signals of constant information" bounced over a beat specifically intended to help half-slaves forget their loneliness. But for several years I've been listening greedily to what little *umbaqanga* I could get my ears on, and pretty soon I was won over. On its own idiosyncratic terms, this is a real *umbaqanga* album: the rhythms and licks and colors that define the style can't go unchanged in this alien context, but I swear they remain undiluted. Yet at the same time it's a real Paul Simon album: the guy is too bright, and too fond of himself, to try and go native on us. Nor would I call it a fusion, because somehow each element retains its integrity. To use the term favored by David B. Coplan's study of "South Africa's black city music and theatre," *In Township Tonight!*, *Graceland* is genuinely syncretic: it reconciles different or opposing principles, at least for the duration of a long-playing record.

Of course, I'm judging as an aspiring aficionado of the township groove. Other listeners may hear *Graceland* as either utterly normal (song-poetry-with-a-good-beat) or unutterably beyond the pale (revolutionary savagery), but to me that groove sounds fresh and inevitable, with as much affinity for r&b as for the West African polyrhythms beloved by the tiny claque of U.S. juju and soukous and Afro-pop fans. That claque still includes me, but my allegiances have shifted. *Graceland* crystallizes a suspicion that had its inception this spring, when musicologist Charles Hamm offered me a hurried phonographic introduction to the tart, rich harmonies and far-reaching clarity of singers who had previously been names in obscure books and articles, most memorably the Soul Brothers and Steve Kekana. The three *umbaqanga* anthologies assembled by Earthworks in England and released Stateside by Carthage and Shanachie—including *The Indestructible Beat of Soweto,* my favorite LP of 1986 so far—emphasize energy and drive, but the axiom that the music of southern Africa is voice-based rather than drum-based was what jumped out at me in Hamm's living room. Over that ebulliently indigenous groove, the voices reached for and attained some sort of international identification, and suddenly I realized that a rock and roll equivalent (and industry) of unimaginable vitality, complexity, and high spirits was somehow thriving in apartheid's face.

The story of Simon's romance with *umbaqanga* began when somebody sent him an otherwise unidentified tape called *Gumboots* a couple of years ago. As Simon played it in his car he became entranced, improvising tunes over the simple major-chord changes until he decided he had to work with these guys. Only then did he investigate and find out where the music was from. Simon was a little dismayed: "I first thought, 'Too bad it's not from Zimbabwe, Zaire, or Nigeria.' Life would have been more simple." But Juluka producer Hilton Rosenthal sent him more tapes from Johannesburg and he was hooked. After consultation with the likes of Quincy Jones assured Simon that as long as he respected the music and the musicians he'd be all right, he immersed, booking several weeks of studio time in South Africa, where he cut five tracks with musicians from varying tribal traditions and put together a trio to come to the States for more recording. Eventually there were guest appearances from exiled pennywhistler Morris Goldberg, Sunny Ade steel player Demola Adepoju, Senegalese star Youssou N'Dour, the Everly Brothers, Ralph McDonald, Linda Ronstadt. Although the accordion Simon loved on *Gumboots* doesn't play a large part on *Graceland,* two American bands that feature accordion, Los Lobos and a zydeco outfit from Louisiana, back up the two final selections, which Simon hopes hit home with compatriots who find all this a touch strange.

The two American cuts are plenty lively, and would have done wonders for Simon's 1983 *Hearts and Bones,* but on *Graceland* they fall a little flat, partly because they're not lively enough and partly because they're not strange enough. Why liveliness should be an issue is obvious. *Hearts and Bones* was a finely wrought dead end, caught up in introspection, whimsy, and the kind of formal experimentation only obsessive pop sophisticates even notice—the rest of us just wondered why the damn thing never left the ground, and in the end so did Simon, leaving him vulnerable to *umbaqanga*'s three happy chords. But the strange part requires more explanation. In remembrance of Rene and Georgette Magritte dancing to doowop's "deep forbidden music" on *Hearts and Bones,* Simon could have made like Billy Joel, who produced a vaguely "'50s" album after the heavy concepts of *The Nylon Curtain* failed to go triple platinum. but if Joel is rock's (would-be) Irving Berlin, Simon is some postfolkie cross between Cole Porter and Lorenz Hart, constitutionally incapable of doing things the easy way. By the late '70s he'd already applied 12-tone theory to pop composition, so in 1985 he found himself trying to fit first melodies and then lyrics to apparently elementary structures that kept tripping him up as he went along. At some semiconscious level he understood quite well that exoticism on this level was a hell of a roundabout way to return to the simple things, and in the end that's one of *Graceland*'s subjects. It's lively, and it's also strange.

Musically, the strangeness inheres mostly in the continuing integrity of the African and American elements, which makes for that radical incongruity. The beat is still African yet a shade less driven, more buoyant if you approve and lighter if you don't, intricate like pop funk more than juju. Longer melody lines, less chantlike and circular verse-chorus structures, subtler arrangements, Roy Halee's 48-track mix, guest accents, the way Ladysmith's curlicues stand in for straight response singing on some cuts—all contribute to the effect. Since African beats are rarely heavy, this may well make *Graceland* less European/urban rather than less African, but it's sure to palliate Simon's fans and probably Simon, so it bothered me at first. Soon, though, the buoyancy carried me away. Simon and Halee have found new resources in these musicians, and with the basic trio—guitarist Ray Phiri, bassist Baghiti Kumalo, and drummer Isaac Mtshali, all players of conspicuous responsiveness and imagination—the discovery was clearly collaborative. The record's virtuosic syncretism—juxtaposing Sotho and Shanga and Zulu, *umbaqanga* and ingom'ebusuku, and then moving north and west, with the African Beats' steel guitar no less striking than Talking Heads' synth guitar—is unusual, too, though it's seamless enough that sometimes you have to stay alert to be sure it's there. But Simon's effortlessly conversational singing on top, so free of rough spots that you know it's a careful fabrication, is truly disquieting; annoyance evolves into uneasy acceptance of this abrupt musical and cultural disparity. And of course, the voice comes bearing words.

Simon may write like an English major, but he's long since stopped writing like he's still in school. His ironies can be arid and too often his ideas aren't as big as he thinks they are, but this doesn't make him any worse than the average *New Yorker* poet, and he's got the music to bail him out—to transmute cliché into reality just as it does for countless more hackneyed lyricists. What the music does for him here, however, goes well beyond the salutary effect of decent melody and rhythm and vocalization on most verse. *Graceland* is where Simon rediscovers the rock and roll secret, where he throws down his irony and dances. There are many ways to describe this secret—sex or youth or the primitive, spontaneity or simplicity or directness. With Simon, the terms I'd choose are faith and connection, themes that keep popping up on *Graceland*. Though the title song describes a journey "through the cradle of the Civil War" to Elvis's mecca, which is never attained, it also hints (as Simon agreed when I asked) that somehow the world's foremost slave state is a haven of grace. In "You Know [*sic*] Me Al," an American beer-belly ends up saying amen and hallelujah in an African marketplace. In "Under African skies" there's the blessed assurance that "the roots of rhythm remain."

And by leading with "The Boy in the Bubble," his most acute and visionary song in many years, Simon sets up every resonance. Here, the African images—lasers in the jungle, a deathly desert wind, a baby with a baboon heart—are no way merely South African, because this is a song about "the way we look to us all." Here the terrorist hides his bomb in a baby carriage and wires it to a radio in a world run by "a loose affiliation of millionaires/And billionaires"; here a boy wants to live so much he seals himself off from that world in a plastic bubble. You can hardly tell the horrors from the miracles, they're everywhere, and for a climax we have the rhetorical "and I believe" that precedes Simon's final repetition of the long refrain. Borne on yet another pulse of Forere Motloheloa's tireless accordion, it sounds like real faith to me, and it cements our connection to all this ironic joy-amid-pain. Simon has done the near impossible—brought off a song about the human condition. Looking for "a shot of redemption," he escapes his alienation without denying its continuing truth, and it's really like the Warners press release says: *Graceland* "is *human* music. It celebrates the family of man." I perceive only one problem—Simon found his redemption not in all humanity but in black South Africans. The problem isn't ruinous—as I've been saying, the man is fascinated by the subtleties of his debt and out front about its extent, and he's done plenty to pay it back. But it does deserve detailed attention.

Umbaqanga is an awesome cultural achievement. Even to call it the reggae of the '80s, as Simon has for explanation's sake, is to diminish it slightly. Those who know that in South Africa (even more than on the rest of the continent) reggae is the pradigmatic political pop, while state radio promotes a vigorously self-censored *umbaqanga* to divert listeners from messages of freedom beamed across the border, may consider this a perverse judgment. But *umbaqanga* was and is created under far more duress, and anyway, Simon is talking musical influence, not politics, and in that respect reggae has its shortcomings: maybe just because its drug of choice is cannabis rather than alcohol, it's less active and less up. As Simon evidently believes, *umbaqanga* is the most joyful and redeeming rock and roll equivalent in memory. The way this music contravenes apartheid's determination to deny blacks not just a reasonable living but a meaningful identity seems almost incredible. But that doesn't make it some strange accident.

Compared to most black South African pop, which emulates American pop, soul, funk, and jazz (though by now South Africa has a jazz heritage of its own), *umbaqanga* honors traditional forms, which fits apartheid's fantasy of the harmless native just fine. But it's by no means tribal or rural—just like Chicago blues and rockabilly and early soul, it's a conscious urbanization. Its capacity for affirmation in the face of horror is an old story in black music (see Albert Murray's *Stomping the Blues*), and while it doubtless serves some as an escape, it just as doubtless serves others (or the same ones at different times) as a respite, a transfusion, a promise. Pretoria may think it's harmless, and Pretoria may be wrong—so accustomed are the overseers to disdaining bush rhythms that I doubt whether they can discern just how potent this groove is. As Neo Mnumzana of the African National Congress told me: "We have to grant the validity and legitimacy of genuine forms of expression. The regime may not see them as dangerous, but they are strengthening the people in their resistance."

Southern Africans are more interested in voices than drums, but that doesn't mean they don't regard rhythm as one of life's primaries, and *umbaqanga* is about the beat. By rock standards that beat is pretty elaborate, staggering ostinatos over a jumpy 8/8; the bass is usually high in the mix, leading the groove rather than stirring it up reggae-style, and as Simon discovered when he tried to write metrically identical verses, the songs' rhythmic shapes often evolve incrementally. But by juju standards, say, it's kind of square, which is just why it might appeal to Americans, with our crude tastes in propulsion. And though the beat is southern African first, it's also specifically South African. It must have been bent some by Afro-American models—almost all the music in Soweto is—but there's also the likelihood of direct European influence back in its prehistory: because South Africa has been industrialized for so long, it's always attracted large concentrations of fortune-seekers from England, Ireland, Germany, Holland, Portugal. *Umbaqanga* reflects the way South Africa has mixed African tribes; it reflects the forced flow of South African life from phony homeland to official slum; it reflects South Africa's industrialization, and its cruel prosperity too. It testifies to the resilience of apartheid's victims, but like everything else in South Africa it also grows out of apartheid. It could no more come from Nigeria, Zaire, or even Zimbabwe than Elvis could come from Johannesburg. And neither could *Graceland*.

"I'm no good at writing politics," Simon told me. "I'm a relationship writer, relationships and introspection." And of course this is true, yet the romantic isolation he transcends on many of *Graceland*'s songs is also social isolation, and he's pleased enough to acknowledge that South African subtext informing many lyrics as well as the album's gestalt. So why exactly Simon has steered away from politics proper on the album and in interviews is a question that troubles anti-apartheid activists. I spoke to about a dozen all told—black and white, South African and American—and not one was inclined to be judgmental. Merely by recording in Johannesburg Simon violated the letter of the U.N. cultural boycott (not deliberately, he claims). Yet except for exiled pianist Abdullah Ibrahim, who was clearly displeased but declined to comment on Simon's "personal decision," the only one who came close to insisting that Simon was flat-out wrong was Amer Araim, a non-South African "international civil servant" at the U.N. Committee Against Apartheid. Elombe Brath, who's been on the picket line ever since Pretoria's *Ipi Tombe* scam a decade ago, admitted "mixed emotion" because it seemed Simon's "intent was honorable"; Jennifer Davis, a 20-year exile active with the American Committee on Africa, kept using the term "gray area" and pointed out that "you can't have nice neat official statements in a situation of tremendous flux"; the ANC's Neo Mnumzana went so far as to suggest that "it's quite possible he might be doing a service to South African culture." Clearly, no one wanted to see black musicians (and black South African culture) denied a chance at exposure, a chance that strictly speaking is forbidden any cultural product of a corporation cooperating with the regime (the cuts on *The Indestructible Beat of Soweto,* for example). But all were dismayed that Simon remained no good at writing politics under these circumstances. In many ways the most striking testimony came from Charles Hamm, a grandfatherly political moderate who like Simon was in South Africa at the time of the second Sharpeville massacre, which set off the current state of emergency. The experience radicalized him, and he can't quite comprehend how Simon remained insulated. "I have trouble accepting all these lyrics about Paul Simon. It's not so much what he says as what he doesn't say."

Simon doesn't claim to be apolitical as a person—only as an artist. He has his views on South Africa, and he intends to keep them to himself. The reason, he says, is to protect the friends he's made there, especially the black friends: "I'm not gonna open my mouth. I open my mouth and they get a firebomb in their house. These people are living there. They don't like their life—but it's a life." And while several people who don't live there tell me the regime rarely gets that blatant with nonmilitant blacks who are known outside, it seems understandable that Simon and his friends aren't so sure. Still, I'd be curious to know just what Simon's views are, because I detect in him an ideology of anti-ideology that I simply don't trust.

This is a man who supports Amnesty International and twice turned down dates in Sun City; it's also a man who's done fund-raisers for Ed Koch and refused to sing on "Sun City" because the demo he was sent named artists who'd played Pretoria's showplace of bogus integration, including his friend Linda Ronstadt (the names were eventually dropped when other artists insisted, but Simon was so offended he didn't even try). This is a man who says he "would never knowingly break the cultural boycott"; it's also a man who calls reluctance of the world music biz to handle South African artists and product "double apartheid," which even if you find the letter of the U.N. boycott misguided is very loose language. Like almost everybody who thinks about South Africa he dreads the bloodbath: "Let's keep pushing to avoid the battle. Millions of blacks could get killed." But his sharpest political statement was on a subject closer to home: "Authoritarian governments on the right, revolutionary governments on the left—they all fuck the artist. What gives them the right to wear the cloak of morality? Their morality comes out of the barrel of a gun. Try and say bullshit on their government, write a poem or a book that's critical of them, and they come down on you. They make up the morality, they make up the rules."

No matter how true you think this is, it's truer than you want it to be for sure. How important it is, however, is another question—very important if you're an American accustomed to going off at the mouth like me or Simon, less so if you wake up every morning with nothing in your belly and a boot in your face. Which makes it an idea that isn't quite as big as Simon thinks it is, an idea typical of all those headstrong individualists whose considered distrust of politics turns them into centrist liberals by default. The depressing saga of Linda Ronstadt in Sun City exemplifies this mentality: I have no doubt that Ronstadt sincerely opposes apartheid, but there comes a time when sincerity is meaningless, when it's reasonable to demand humility if not solidarity or tactical smarts. So it has to be significant that Ronstadt gets a personally designed cameo on *Graceland,* dueting with Simon on the verses of "Under African Skies," one of which evokes the youth of Ladysmith's Joseph Shabalala in general terms, the other of which evokes Ronstadt's girlhood with marked specificity. The song is attractively straightforward, dealing directly with the religious theme that's alluded to elsewhere, but even if I admired Ronstadt's crystal harmonies as much as Simon, I'd object to the evasive family-of-man-ism implied by the parallel verses. The offense is compounded, of course, by who Shabalala's sister-in-song happens to be: a prominent violator of the Sun City boycott. Even if her lyric called for total U.S. divestiture, Ronstadt's presence on *Graceland* would be a slap in the face to the world anti-apartheid movement—a deliberate, considered, headstrong slap in the face.

Sincere opponents of apartheid may feel I'm making too much of this, so let me add that it doesn't ruin the album or even the song for me, at least not yet. The music is that good, the salvation through musical synthesis that original. But *Graceland* does nevertheless circle around an evasive ideology, the universalist humanism that is the secret intellectual vice of centrist liberals out of their depth. It's not so much what Simon says as what he doesn't say. Apartheid's propensity to distort everything it touches comes damn close to doing this album in right now, and in a decade, when the consequences of Simon's tactic are history, it could make the beautiful music of Simon and his black friends unlistenable.

Simon wants the music to speak for itself, but the most eloquent music can only say so much; he wants to "try and bridge cultures," but he can't determine who controls the bridge once it's built. Pretoria broadcasts this music on state radio—"Homeless" and "Under African Skies," not "The Boy in the Bubble"—because Pretoria thinks it's harmless at worst and a vinyl Sun City at best, a demonstration that their hideous system doesn't preclude meaningful racial cooperation. And who knows, this time Pretoria may be right. I don't believe politics transcends music, but I don't believe music transcends politics either. They're separate realms that impinge on each other, and in times of crisis they impinge more and more inescapably. I hope Simon has succeeded in reconciling opposing principles for more than the duration of a long-playing record, because I want to be received in Graceland myself. But there's reason to wonder whether he's done enough.

PART FOUR

Brazil,
Broadway,
and Beyond

How does a musician evolve in his fourth decade of composing and performing? For Simon, the more he follows his muse, the further he goes back to his roots.

It's safe to say Simon would agree. "I don't know that I've had a really new idea since the '60s," he says, in a 1987 rock documentary for the BBC. "What's new is a deeper understanding of the idea, and a greater sense of control." In a 1993 interview with Tony Scherman, he elaborates. " 'Cecelia' had the same idea as *Rhythm of the Saints*: no melodic instruments, no bass, no drums, just percussion. I remember having the thought... 'who cares if it comes from South America? Who cares where it comes from? If it sounds good, it's a song!' "

Part Four: Brazil, Broadway, and Beyond attempts to give a context to Paul Simon's most recent projects: *The Rhythm of the Saints* and the Broadway-bound musical *The Capeman*. Several articles explore the process behind the creation of *The Rhythm of the Saints*. In a piece from *Newsday*, Wayne Robins calls the album "a continuation of Simon's infatuation with exotic musical cultures, steeped in the moody, spiritual percussion of Brazil and West Africa." In "Songs of a Thinking Man," Jay Cocks looks at Simon's "penchant for self-reflection—self-immersion sometimes" and the way in which he chooses to "undercut and play against it." And engineer Roy Halee, having worked on nearly every album of Simon's, gives his perspective on *The Rhythm of the Saints* in a rare interview he granted to Paul Zollo.

In another Paul Zollo interview, a highlight of Part Four, Simon describes the evolution of *Saints*. When asked how he decided to combine African and Brazilian music, Simon says, "They are actually connected. The Brazilian drumming is from West Africa, so I'm just going backwards, really." He also describes his process for writing the songs: how he makes a musical track first and then writes the songs to the finished tracks; the same process he used in creating *Graceland*.

This method of songwriting, however, goes back much further than 1985. In an article for the *New York Times* in 1972, Simon says:

> "Peace Like A River" was written off a loop track—a conga loop. I was working with some Puerto Rican musicians here—they were playing stuff called *plenas*, Puerto Rican folk music—and I brought them into the studio to do "Me and Julio." It did not work, so I said, "You play what you want to play and I'll see what I can come up with." They played great stuff but I couldn't come up with anything. Then I noticed that the conga player, Victor Montanez, was playing this thing—dunk dunka, dokka dunk; dunk dunka, dokka, dunk. So I picked that out, made a tape loop out of it, let the loop play for three minutes and a half and wrote the song to it.

Simon also has roots—or at least, long-dormant seeds—in musical theater, the genre he's exploring right now. As early as 1968, a *New York Times* article noted that Simon was slated to write songs for a Murray Schisgal play called *Jimmy Shine*, starring Dustin Hoffman. (John Sebastion eventually wrote the music.) In that same year, Ralph Gleason declared in *Jazz & Pop* magazine: "If any of the new generation of songwriters is going to write a musical, Paul Simon is the most likely." In a 1972 *New Yorker* article Simon is quoted as saying, "Eventually, I'd like to write for the stage." And in a 1975 *Newsweek*, Simon laments:

> The staple of American popular music is all three- or four-chord, country- or rock-oriented now. There's nothing that goes back to the richest, most original form of American popular music—Broadway and Tin Pan Alley—in which sophisticated lyrics are matched by sophisticated melodies. . . . It's no fluke that me, Berlin, Gershwin and Kern are all Jewish guys from New York who look alike.

At the time of this writing, very little has been published about *The Capeman*. Included here is the charming "Doo-wop Tells a Story of the '50s," which describes the process of auditioning for *The Capeman*. Simon's collaborator on the musical is Nobel prize–winning poet Derek Walcott. The show is based on a true story, the murder of two teen-age boys in New York City. "It's a Puerto-Rican story and I'm working with a lot of Latin musicians and composing kind of in the way I do now," says

Simon. He also includes doo-wop numbers, as once again Simon looks to music he has long loved as he continues to experiment with technique, form, and spirit.

PAUL ZOLLO, FROM <u>SONGTALK</u>,
THE JOURNAL OF THE NATIONAL ACADEMY OF SONGWRITERS
RECORDING WITH ROY HALEE (1990)

"Roy Halee is a genius," said both Paul Simon and Art Garfunkel about the man behind the board for all of their albums. He engineered every album by Simon and Garfunkel as a team and also most of their solo albums. He also co-produced all of their albums beginning with *Bookends.* The distinction between engineer and producer is not an easy one to make, and whether he is listed as engineer only or engineer and producer, Roy Halee's contribution to the work of Simon and Garfunkel is immense.

He's the guy who captured Simon and Garfunkel's amazing vocal blend on tape, a process that he explains was only possible when both men sang at once. He also worked with both Simon and Garfunkel on their solo albums, no easy feat after the breakup of one of the world's biggest and most beloved bands. And he traveled around the world with Simon to record the tracks for *Graceland* and now for Simon's new album, *The Rhythm of the Saints,* which Simon says is Roy's "crowning achievement."

Roy Halee began his career as a musician; he studied classical trumpet and wanted to take his place in a symphony orchestra but didn't feel he was good enough. "So I gave it up and got into sound and audio work," he said. He worked for many years in the New York audio department of CBS TV before their move to Hollywood, at which time he got a job as a staff engineer at Columbia Records in New York.

At Columbia, even before hooking up with Simon and Garfunkel, Halee worked with the just-signed Bob Dylan, recording "Like a Rolling Stone" among other Dylan songs, an experience Halee didn't find entirely enjoyable, especially as opposed to the studio perfectionism that was his inclination and which he was able to attain with Simon & Garfunkel. "Dylan was not easy to work with in the studio," Roy recalls. "He liked to do things very quick and very disorganized. He'd say, 'I want to do a vocal over here by the drums' and stand next to the drummer. And you'd say, 'Hey, look, it's kind of hard to isolate you by the drums when you're standing right next to him and he's beating his brains out,' but he didn't care."

Simon and Garfunkel *did* care about every facet of the recording process, and their collaboration with Halee was a three-way partnership that has resulted in some of the most wonderful music the world has known. We first met up with him in New York, where he was busy recording Simon's newest album, and spoke a few weeks later, over the phone, from his Connecticut home.

Paul Zollo: Do you remember hearing Simon and Garfunkel for the first time?

Roy Halee: Yes. And I was floored. I thought that the sound of the voices was very, very interesting and unique. I loved the blend of the two voices. And, of course the writing, that goes without saying. I thought it was very, very different and it appealed a lot to me.

In the sense that I was classically trained and here were two guys who really sang and their harmonies were beautiful, it was in tune, it had a rock beat, it had everything that I loved. Plus the two individuals were a joy to be with.

PZ: Was it a challenge to record that particular blend of their voices?

RH: No. It was never a challenge to get that blend as long as they were singing on one microphone. There was a time that we ran into when Artie wanted to do his vocal separately or Paul might want to do something separate and I always had to fight for the right for them to sing together, because no matter how well it was recorded, there always was that seam in the middle when they did it separately. Something happened to the sound that just wasn't right, it wasn't as good as when they did it live.

The blend of their sound hitting that microphone was very unique. It changed it and it sounded separated when they didn't do it together. It was never quite the same. So I had to battle a little bit for that right. But I won, most of the time. [*Laughs*]

Which means they both had to perform at the same time and no one could do their part over; if one guy made a mistake, they both had to do it over. So, Artie in particular, would like to take his time and take a little more time and do it separately. But he gave in. Because I proved it to him that the sound just wasn't the same.

It's like if you put ten microphones on an orchestra or one microphone, one microphone will always sound better. It's a fact. And they're finding that out with digital recording of orchestras and they're going back to less microphones.

PZ: You've both engineered and produced their albums—

RH: Production is a vague word, what a producer is, what his role is. It really encompasses a lot: getting the best out of the artist, organizing the recording, organizing the music; he's in charge of the control room to a large extent. It's very tricky.

And it's always harder to produce and engineer at the same time.

PZ: You went from engineering and producing their most successful album, Bridge Over Troubled Water to working with Simon on his first solo album. What was that like?

RH: It was tough for a number of reasons. Here's a guy who's going out on his own and emotionally it was hard. But I've always had faith in Paul, in Paul Simon. Of course. Because he's a great writer and a great musician. I guess I was a little worried. Sure, like everybody, I was a little concerned, because Simon and Garfunkel was so successful at that time. But then I swallowed it. They both are very talented guys and I knew they could do well by themselves.

PZ: Was it your intention to make his first solo outing a more simple production than the hugeness of Bridge?

RH: Yes. His solo album was much simpler than a Simon & Garfunkel album. Paul purposely wanted to go a very simple route; get the lyrics out there and let's not hide anything; let's not hide me, let's not hide anything with production, let's keep it simple. Which was a very *bold, brave* move on his part, I thought.

I remember distinctly thinking, "Jesus, this guy's got a lot of balls. It's great. Let's do it." Less, sometimes, is best. You talk about production: less is best sometimes. It's fuller, you get the most out of the instruments. It's tough to mix a *lot* of stuff in pop records so that you *hear* everything distinctly.

PZ: Paul's present process is to create songs by recording the track first. Does that make your job hard?

RH: It is difficult to record a track first before a song is written. The first time we did that was with "Mother and Child Reunion" which we recorded in Jamaica. It's more difficult for Paul than for me. I can be helpful in putting the track together; editing the track, making sure everything is recorded properly and is in tune. But he has to write the song. It's a process that's tough; it's very hard on him.

PZ: Simon explained to us that one of the reasons he came up with this new approach is that he was disappointed with Hearts and Bones, which you worked on, both in terms of its production and how well it sold. Do you share that feeling?

RH: I do agree with Paul that some of the songs on *Hearts and Bones* could have been better. Like that song "Cars are Cars." I think that's an embarrassment, that song. It's not a good song. It's not well recorded. And then you have a song like "Magritte" on there which is fabulous, and I think that probably could have been recorded better, too.

That was a rather hurried and rushed project because Paul was involved with the [*Simon & Garfunkel*] tour at the time, and then Artie was going to be involved in the record, and then he wasn't involved in the record. So it was kind of hectic and scattered, which comes across on the record. That it's not really in the pocket, it's not really organized.

"Hearts and Bones" is a killer. I love it. But if we were doing that record now, we wouldn't have put "Cars are Cars" on the record.

When I think of that record, I think of the songs "Magritte," "Hearts and Bones," "Train in the Distance." "The Late Great Johnny Ace." I thought "Allergies" didn't really comes across; it was too pop, it didn't have that raw edge that I like. There are things that are a little too slick. When you hear the new record, you'll hear what I mean. It's more earthy and it's got a better feel to it.

Since we record track first now, it's been a long time since I've had the luxury of having him come in and say, "I've got a song. What do you think?" I remember when he came in with "Bridge Over Troubled Water" and played it for me on guitar and said, "What do you think?" I thought it was a killer. I still have the demo of that around here. My reaction immediately to "Bridge" was to record it with a gospel piano. Immediately.

PZ: Did you enjoy recording in South Africa?

RH: It was hard. It's always hard going into strange environments with strange musicians, strange studio, strange equipment. And especially in Africa. [*Laughs*] It's not like you're going to Hollywood to Sunset Sound. It was quite a challenge.

PZ: But did you know that what you were recording was going to turn out so well?

RH: In the very beginning of the *Graceland* project, I loved what we were doing. But I was not convinced that it was going to be great. In the beginning, anyway. I loved the music we were recording. But there were no songs written yet, so it was shaky ground as far as I was concerned. But I loved the feel of that stuff. And then we brought it back and edited the hell out of it. The digital editing worked very well for us in that respect. It makes doing involved editing much easier. On that project, without it, I would have been in serious trouble.

PZ: Do you have a favorite track on Graceland?

RH: For a long time, "Boy in the Bubble" was my favorite track on *Graceland*. It most represented that feel and that record. Then I'd switch over to "Graceland" and keep switching around. But I think "Boy in the Bubble" is probably my favorite on the record because it encompasses the whole magilla to me.

PZ: After recording all those tracks, were you at all surprised by the greatness of the songs that Simon then wrote to them?

RH: I'm never surprised by anything Paul Simon does. I've come almost to expect it.

PZ: How does the new album differ from Graceland?

RH: This new album is different than the *Graceland* project in that the tracks that we cut first are all percussion without any other instruments. We recorded percussion grooves. On top of the percussion grooves, musical grooves are happening. So you have the West African musical groove going against the Brazilian percussion groove. Which makes it *really* different, man, wait until you hear this stuff! Oh, man. Oh, boy.

We just got back from Paris and recorded some tracks there. We recorded one track with two guitars, keyboard, bass and drums. It's a very interesting track, with guys from Cameroon. It's the only one that we didn't do percussion first. The rest is all percussion: all congas; bass drums, batas, Jesus . . . everything imaginable.

PZ: *Do you have a current favorite song on the new album? Simon said that he thought "Cool Cool River" may be one of his best songs ever.*

RH: "Cool Cool River" is great. The track is *amazing.*

Today my favorite song on the new album is a song called "She Moves On." It's a killer. It's all percussion, no trap drums, with Vince playing guitar, and also Ray Phiri, the guitarist from *Graceland,* and it's also got Michael Brecker doing some saxophone work on it. It's a good song. Paul has outdone himself on the lyric.

JAY COCKS
SONGS OF A THINKING MAN (1990)

Paul Simon's musical wanderings have taken him from Africa to Brazil and to the deepest, farthest reaches of himself.—J. C.

It's an old question. It goes back as far as *Bridge Over Troubled Water,* when Paul Simon gathered some unexpected, tropical-inflected rhythms around him and first really found his voice. His lyrical voice, that is: the tart, tempered combination of irony and melancholy that would turn him into one of the best writers of his generation, either in the grooves or on the page.

There have been, intervening, two decades, a couple of marriages, one son, a hurtful professional divorce and a group of exquisite albums. But that *Troubled Water* question, framed as an up-tempo goof but phrased suddenly like a suicide note, still stands. Let's consider it more benignly, as a kind of standing offer: "Why don't you write me/I'm out in the jungle/I'm hungry to hear you." And take him up on it, at last.

"Dear Paul: How you doing? I suppose we can all hear for ourselves. Another wonderful new album, *The Rhythm of the Saints.* A stone beauty.

Another stone beauty. They seem to roll around every few years or so, and since *Graceland* in '86, they seem to come from new territory. Sort of rare and familiar at the same time. Must be you're still in the jungle, if not exactly on safari. Africa for *Graceland,* Brazil now. All those strange, haunting sprung sounds, gliding guitars and drums echoing like distant dreams. Is this the way your dreams sound? Percussive and persistent? The kind that linger into the daylight, aren't they?

"And while we're at it: What did the Mama Pajama see Julio and his friend doing down by the schoolyard? How come we can call you Al? And in this new song *The Obvious Child,* what is the cross doing in the ball-park?

"Yours sincerely . . ."

"It got me thinking when that first popped out," Paul Simon says, sitting in the living room of his Manhattan duplex, watching an early moon come up over Central Park. "'The cross is in the ball park.' The first thing I thought of was Billy Graham, or the Pope, or evangelical gatherings. But I came to feel what that's really about is the cross that we bear. The burdens that we carry are doable, they're in the ball park."

Neat enough, especially for a 49-year-old, 5-ft. 5-in. rock 'n' roller who still plays a court-singeing game of one-on-one and pledges allegiance to the New York Yankees. He is, after all, the man who sang yet another, still more famous question ("Where have you gone, Joe DiMaggio?"). Settling in to watch the Yankees close down a dismaying season a few weeks back, he speculated on the chances for one heavy hitter to grab off a bit of individual glory. "I'm not confident he's going to hit tonight. I saw him last night, and he had that look of defeat in his eyes. I could tell. Popcorn?"

That's a knowing bit of self-mockery you hear in the voice, making room for the accent that would brand him as a sure New York boy even if his music weren't so uptown all on its own. Simon is well aware of his penchant for self-reflection—self-immersion sometimes—and knows how to undercut and play against it, as anyone who's seen him larking around on his producer pal Lorne Michaels' *Saturday Night Live* shows over the years can instantly attest. The man who wrote *Me and Julio Down by the Schoolyard* and *You Can Call Me Al* and *50 Ways to Leave Your Lover* knows how to have a good time with a lyric, but only Paul Simon could write a tune titled *Have a Good Time* that's a deliberately dippy paean to incidental ennui and spiritual indifference.

"*Rhythm of the Saints* doesn't have an overall theme," he suggests. "It jumps around from subject to subject within the songs, slips from verse to verse. There are a lot of personal references: family, friends, some love-affair stuff. I know what all the lines mean in direct relationship to my life."

Lots of others think they know too. It's one thing to work into the new record musically, as Simon's friend Quincy Jones does when he says, "Paul goes straight for the throat. And he's smart enough to understand the African motor, which has driven pop music for so long." But it's another to cast the lyrical runes for references to his personal turmoil, especially when he is hands-down champion of the Confessional Songwriters, Elliptical Division. Perhaps it's just another kind of standing invitation.

Even Simon, who is adamant about protecting his privacy (and thus his best material), has become a little less guarded of late. The release of *Rhythm of the Saints* coincides with a couple of loud flourishes from the career of his second wife, the writer and actress Carrie Fisher, with whom he is not, at the moment, on speaking terms. This doesn't stop either of them from writing about the other, however. There is a Simonized character named Rudy in her current best seller, *Surrender the Pink*. But her ex-husband, who has read the book, acts like a man who was let off easy and maybe got in the last, best licks as well.

"It's not really stuff I talk about casually," Simon says, measuring the words like a jeweler weighing gold. There is a *Saints* love song called *She Moves On,* in which a man falls victim to a woman's witchery and pays the price. But the pain, which undoes him, also releases him: Simon takes the high ground. "That song is close to my heart," he admits. "Too close to the heart. It's about men being afraid of women's anger. It felt pretty real."

Along with all those effulgent rhythms, it's the finesse of the language that lofts songs like this out of the arena of gossip and retribution into something far more formidable. "In its literary context, his writing is very important," says the poet Derek Walcott, to whom Simon dedicates a *Saints* song called *The Coast.* "Most poetry is sedate, quiet, self-concerned. His imagination is much bolder and more refreshing. He reminds me of Hart Crane."

It takes some effort on Simon's part to stay in such heady company. His apartment, elegant and ordered, always has a guitar handy, but there are books of poetry (Wallace Stevens, Philip Larkin) open all around the living room, within easy reach, like so many cerebral snacks. In case this sounds a little rarefied for a rock guy—even a rock guy who sang a few tunes to Derek Walcott's poetry class at Boston University—it should be added that Simon also enjoys listening to music as various as Miles Davis,

Prince and Public Enemy. It's not always the sounds of silence up there on Central Park West.

It was those very sounds, of course, that made stars of Simon and his best friend from Forest Hills, Queens, Art Garfunkel. Under the *"nom de 45"* Tom & Jerry, the boys had a minor hit single in 1957, then followed the folk-music trail into the new decade. Oft-told rock legend #192: how a house producer at Columbia Records without Paul's knowledge added electric guitar, drums and bass to an earnest, intimate, acoustic ballad of Simon's; and how *The Sounds of Silence*, with its new rock underpinnings, became a No. 1 single in 1966. It was a fluke, but Paul and Artie were smart enough, gifted enough and fast enough to build on it and go for a long, sweet ride.

"My best memories go back to the *Parsely, Sage, Rosemary and Thyme* days, when we were beginning to make albums more carefully, that we really liked," Garfunkel says of those post-*Silence* days. "When we sat back and listened to the playback of that record, it was a high point in my career." The highest came in 1970 with the release of *Bridge Over Troubled Water*, which remains in the top 50 best-selling albums, of all time. It was also the last album Simon and Garfunkel would make together.

"We never thought Simon and Garfunkel was going to break up," Garfunkel says. "We just thought we'd take a break from each other." "Going out solo was my decision," Simon says now. "But I was nervous about it." The record company had a case of the corporate faints: Simon was busting up an act whose last record had sold 10 million copies. But the boys were having problems. Garfunkel was getting absorbed in acting, while Paul was taking his first turns down various lightly charted musical byways. "There was stuff I wanted to do anyway that Artie wouldn't have done," says Simon. "He wouldn't have gone to Jamaica to do *Mother and Child Reunion*. I know that he wouldn't have thought it was interesting." On *Bridge*, Simon adds, "maybe we sang four [songs] together. The rest is his solo or my solo. Artie and I were over by January 1970. We were really over before the '70s began."

The sympathetic imagination didn't have to strain to see the break coming. Simon's writing then was a vulnerable, and quite a bit more open, as anything he would do until his travails with Fisher resulted in his terrific (but commercially problematic) 1983 album, *Hearts and Bones*. It was Garfunkel, working down in Mexico on *Catch-22*, about whom Simon seemed to be singing when he asked, "Why don't you write me," just as it was very probably Garfunkel who was being addressed in *The*

Only Living Boy in New York, an intensely wistful ballad about the encroachments of loneliness and the first endings of a vital friendship. "I've never asked him if any of the songs he's written were about me and our split," Garfunkel reflects. "But *So Long, Frank Lloyd Wright* [also on *Bridge*] may be. I was an architecture student. And *Why Don't You Write Me* sounds a lot like, 'Where the hell are you, Artie?'"

There has been a little work together during the years since, including a memorable reunion concert (and resultant high-selling live album) in Central Park in 1981, but altogether, their relationship now follows the course of a Simon song, where endings are lingering but emphatic, and pain, like some rare vintage, grows keener with age. "He does things that I could never understand," says Garfunkel, who lives right across Central Park from his old friend. "He called me up one day and said, 'Artie, I'm dropping your vocals on *Hearts and Bones*. It's not turning into the kind of album I want it to. And by the way, I'm marrying Carrie on Tuesday, and I want you to come.'"

Simon's rejoinders to such talk are kept out of conversation and stashed where they can do the most good: in his songs. Simon does work at it, though, as far from public scrutiny as he can manage. "Paul's been famous since high school," says Lorne Michaels, "so he may have gotten soured on the way his image has been portrayed." The 18-year-old son of his first marriage, Harper, has temporarily left school and spends a good deal of time living with Carrie Fisher in California, where he can be near his girlfriend. When he comes East, his father, an inveterate night owl, rouses himself early to cook breakfast. "There's very little bullshit between them," Michaels observes, and Harper, a Grateful Dead fan, appears to be finding his own way.

But there is a stillness that goes beyond quiet in that apartment overlooking the park. There is a prevailing inwardness, a tone of twilight reflection, that seems to mirror Simon's own tenuous spiritual equipoise. "We see very little of each other now," Art Garfunkel says. "I see him about four times a year. I miss him. We have very complex feelings toward each other. We're not close friends anymore. But we are friends at the bottom of it all. There is a great love for each other that would snap into place on a dime."

Simon, however, is not a man who carries a pocketful of loose change. "*Rhythm* is reflective of what's happened in the four years since *Graceland*," Simon says. "And then there are aspects of my personal life and my family's personal life that are more grave than they were four years ago. And that's in there. It was on my mind, it had to be in there.

There's something about having a very big hit that's happy, like *Graceland*, that makes me think a little bit. I couldn't get more happy. That would really be manic." This is also, mind you, the author of that rueful piece of self-analysis with the memorable chorus, "Maybe I think too much [about thinking too much]." But that's it, after all. The essence of Simon's music, what makes it last and what makes it so directly personal. This is the soul of a thinking man.

WAYNE ROBINS

SIMON SAYS: *THE RHYTHM OF THE SAINTS* STARTED WITH THE SOUND OF BRAZILIAN PERCUSSION. THEN CAME THE MUSIC, AND LAST, THE WORDS (1990)

It was early September, and Paul Simon was beginning to feel that familiar hand-wringing sensation, that nagging uncertainty, those last-minute doubts. His new album, "The Rhythm of the Saints," had been finished for a while. But as Simon pondered the imminent release of the record, he made a decision: Not yet.

It had been well over four years since Simon's last album, "Graceland," brought him back to the eminence he had achieved in the 1960s with Art Garfunkel and in the mid-1970s as a solo artist. But Simon didn't seem worried about matching the success of "Graceland," which won Grammies two years in a row: Album of the Year in 1986, Record of the Year, for the title single, in 1987.

After all, "The Rhythms of the Saints" is a continuation of Simon's infatuation with exotic musical cultures, steeped in the moody, spiritual percussion of Brazil and West Africa. It's the next step in the progression from "Graceland," on which Simon adopted the buoyant beats and heavenly harmonies of South African pop.

It wasn't as if there were a major problem. It's just that Simon thought some of it sounded better on headphones than on speakers. There was something about it that gave him an undefinable uneasiness. He decided to tinker. "I'm pushing it back a few weeks," Simon said, "I think I can fix some of the mixes and make them a little better, and maybe re-sequence [change the order of the songs]. I'm not really sure. I might end up coming right back to where I am now. But if I don't give it a try, I won't really be at peace with myself."

That meticulousness has long characterized Simon as a songwriter, musician, and bandleader. "He's very methodical, takes his time, doesn't rush," says pianist Richard Tee, who performed on a number of Simon albums in the 1970s and will be part of "The Rhythm of the Saints" touring band. "He works at his own pace. If he's not sure, he'll say, 'Let me think about this, and tomorrow I'll let you know.'"

Saxophonist Michael Brecker concurs. "One of his talents is enormous patience," Brecker said of Simon. "He's willing to take the time to solve a problem that maybe can't be solved with a quick fix."

"The Rhythm of the Saints" finally will be released on Tuesday, but Simon questioned the finished product until the very last moment. "I was so careful about putting the record together that the last phase of mixes went a little too fast, because I was trying to make a deadline that I promised the record company," Simon said. "Now I'm not sure I made absolutely correct decisions."

Simon was sitting in his gentleman's clubhouse of a midtown office, walls lined with career curios: a poster advertising a concert by "the Joshua Levin Rand" (the fictional group from his movie "One Trick Pony"), a rare 78-rpm copy of "Hey Schoolgirl," by Tom and Jerry, the pseudonymous 1950s doo-wop duo of Paul Simon and Art Garfunkel.

Simon selects his words as carefully as he chooses the musical mix of his albums. "I don't think of myself as a perfectionist," he says. "But I can understand the case being made that I was. I think: It's either right, or it's not right. If it's right and sloppy, it's still right, as long as something in me says, 'I like that; that's musically satisfying.' Or, something says, 'I don't know why, but I'm not perfectly at ease with this.' When that happens, I don't think it's [seeking] perfection. It's trying to root out some irritation. Something bothers me about it. Sometimes you just have to accept that you made an imperfect piece—it's not possible to make a perfect song. It's just not possible. I've never done it."

Wondering if anyone had ever written a perfect song, Simon recalled an anecdote he'd heard about Irving Berlin. "Well, his famous quote was, 'White Christmas' wasn't just a good song; it was the best song that anybody had ever written.' Maybe he's right: It is a really great song."

On "The Rhythm of the Saints," Simon is hardly dreaming of a "White Christmas." "In the bottles and the bones of the night . . ." he sings in "Can't Run But" on which Simon is backed by the Brazilian group UAKTI. "The composer and leader of that group is an inventor of instruments," Simon said, "so the instruments you hear, a lot of them are his invention."

In other songs, Simon did live recordings of Brazilian percussion groups as the structure for what he'd eventually compose. "I recorded two tracks in Rio of traditional drums, and one track in Salvador, Bahia, with a group called Olodum. That track we recorded in the street, no studio," Simon said. "There were fourteen drums: ten bass drums, four snares."

The rhythms helped dictate what Simon would compose. "Because the drums are tuned, they imply a key," he said. "This album is essentially in the key of B flat. So the track would start with drums, and the drums would imply a key, then we'd go to the guitar, compose a structure, then I would improvise melodies hundreds and hundreds of times until I found a melody I liked. Words would sometimes come with the melody, sometimes they wouldn't come for a long time. I have a book of images and phrases, lines that I keep. If there was a line that fit somewhere musically, I'd connect it up to whatever the story was, or begin the story with that line, almost like a skin graft. And that way, the song forms. It's not preconceived. It's much more me following the trail of the sound on the track and what my subconscious is stimulated to erupt."

Recording an album with such a heavy Brazilian percussion influence was not Simon's initial plan. After "Graceland," Simon set out to do something completely different.

"I was working on a Broadway musical, and I thought I would begin to record this stuff as a break from working on this musical," Simon said. "If I got stuck, or burned out, I'd have another project to go to." Simon spent about a year and a half on the musical, and figures he's about halfway finished. He declined to answer questions about what the musical was about, or who any collaborators might be. "I'd rather not talk about it, because I'll come back to it when I finish the tour," he said.

No matter how exotic or cerebral Simon may have been over the years, he's developed a lighthearted trademark that helps keep his current work grounded: He works with musical cues from the 1950s. Phrases from the Penguins and Little Richard and the melody line from the Del-Vikings' "Whispering Bells" appeared in "Graceland" songs.

The first single from the new album, "Obvious Child," finishes with a falsetto flourish copied from "Desiree" by the Charts; another new song, "The Coast," appropriates a riff from the bass vocal line of Frankie Lymon and the Teenagers' "Why Do Fools Fall in Love"; if you use your imagination, the new, uptempo "Proof" seems to borrow elements of "Unchained Melody" and Ray Barretto's "El Watusi."

Doo-wop provides the backdrop to some of the 48-year-old Simon's fondest memories of growing up in Queens in the 1950s. "I remember when there was no Long Island Expressway," Simon said. "I could look out the window of my house and just look at fields stretching all the way to the World's Fair grounds. I remember playing softball as a kid in the 'under-five-foot' league—you had to be under five feet tall to play. I used to like to go to the playgrounds, I used to hang out there and sing, sing with doo-wop groups. I remember going to an Alan Freed show in Brooklyn; it was a big adventure, taking the train, going all the way to Brooklyn, the Brooklyn Paramount. I saw Bo Diddley, Frankie Lymon, the Cleftones, Big Al Sears on saxophone, Buddy Holly, good show . . . The Cleftones were like local heroes. I went to Forest Hills High; they went to Jamaica High School. But they were like the local group that had a hit, so everybody wanted to be like the Cleftones."

To get away from summer in the city, Simon's parents, Louis and Belle (dad was a professional bassist), took him out to Montauk, where Simon is now an on-and-off year-round resident. (He also has an apartment in Manhattan.)

"You can't find land, more space here," Simon said during a recent walk around the East End horse farm where he was to stage a benefit concert for the nearby Montauk Lighthouse. "I live up on the cliffs. It's the only place on Long Island I know where cliffs occur on the beach. It's not a swimming beach, but it's a nice place to walk. It's nice in winter, very private. I write a lot out here."

At the Montauk concert, held at the end of August, Simon debuted the multi-national, multi-ethnic (Cameroonian, Brazilian, South African, as well as North Americans of every shade) band he'll begin a tour with later this. In addition to songs from "The Rhythms of the Saints" and "Graceland," the band also renovated—with pumping horn lines and polyrhythmic percussion—a number of Simon's earlier hits, such as "Still Crazy After All These Years," "Kodachrome," and "Bridge Over Troubled Water."

"I like the version we did of 'Kodachrome,'" Simon said. "It actually came out of Armand's [Sabal-Lecco's] jamming on the bass, a certain groove that fit 'Kodachrome.' I like singing 'Still Crazy After All These Years.' I haven't done it for a long time. 'Bridge Over Troubled Water' I never sang with Simon and Garfunkel because it was always Artie's solo. So that's sort of fun to sing, reclaiming my most famous song, in a way."

There are other Simon songs he'd just as soon allow to gather dust. "I don't have an easy time singing '50 Ways to Leave Your Lover,'" he said.

"I don't mind the record too much, but I don't seem to be able to sing it live in any way that's satisfying. Of the Simon and Garfunkel songs, I'm not inclined to sing 'Mrs. Robinson.' I think it's dated. On the other hand, I'll bet 'Scarborough Fair' would be nice with all those Brazilian sounds: percussion and bells. I think that would create a good 'Scarborough Fair' atmosphere. That might work."

If Simon sometimes seems obsessed with musical details, there are other situations in which he manages to let himself go—just a little bit.

"In some aspects of my life, I'm real sloppy," he said. "I can't get straight who called when I'm supposed to call back, I write down messages and forget them, I'm absent-minded and I'm not a real neat person in my house."

And yet: "On the other hand, I like it when the lighting is right, and I like a sound system that sounds good. If I'm at somebody's house, I'll tinker with their sound system to make it sound as good as I can make it. So there are things where I absolutely don't see things that irritate other people, like I'm very indifferent to food. But there are other aspects where I say, this should be like this, and this, and this."

Simon believes that if it isn't broken, don't fix it; the problem is deciding whether or not the thing's not broken. "It's not like I say, every instrument has to be perfectly in tune, and every phrase exactly right. It's either musical and alive, in which case it's fine and you leave it alone. Or it's not, and you try to figure out what it is, and bring it back to life."

PAUL ZOLLO, FROM SONGTALK,
THE JOURNAL OF THE NATIONAL ACADEMY OF SONGWRITERS
**PAUL SIMON—THE *SONGTALK* INTERVIEWS,
PARTS ONE AND TWO (1990)**

N. B.: *Paul Zollo's interviews have been edited for this book, and will be reprinted in their entirety in the expanded version of Zollo's* Songwriters on Songwriting, *a collection of interviews with songwriters forthcoming from Da Capo Books—S. L.*

From Part One

This is the first part of our two-part talk, a conversation continued on two coasts, connecting east and west as his music spans the globe. It's an account of explorations both internal and external, and of songs from the sounds of silence to the roots of rhythm. It's about the abstract and the ordinary, the dissatisfaction inherent in any quest for perfection, and the fortune he's found: the discoveries of the heart and of the mind.

Paul Zollo: Does your best work come from active, conscious thinking about what a song should say?

Paul Simon: About what the song should say? No, not any more. Not in my writing in recent years. I don't consciously think about what a song should say. In fact, I consciously try *not* to think about what a song should say.

PZ: Why is that?

PS: Because I'm interested in what . . . I *find*, as opposed to . . . what I'm planting. I like to be the audience, too. I like to discover what it is that's interesting to me. I like to *discover* it rather than plot it out.

So I let the songs go this way and that way and this way and whatever way it is and basically what I do is be the *editor:* "Oh, that's interesting. Never mind *that*, that's not so interesting, that's good, *that's a good line.*

And the *most* that I can do is say, "There's a good line," and the rhyming pattern, I don't know, let me see how I will set up that line. And that's the most I'll do. To construct the first half of a thought that's the set-up to the second-half.

A lot of time the whole thought comes. Not connected to the thought before it in any appreciable way. And then you say, "Well, what *will* this connection be?" And by the time you get your choice of the third thought, you're off in a direction. Because *three consecutive thoughts imply direction.* They don't necessarily imply *meaning.* But they imply direction.

And I think direction is sufficient. When you have a strong sense of direction, then meaning clings to it in some way. People bring meaning to it. Which is more interesting to me than for me to *tell* meaning to somebody. I'd rather offer options to people. Options that have very pleasing sounds.

So the first impression is that the sound of something is nice. You don't have to think about what it means at all. And then when you do think about it on the first level, it could mean a lot of different things.

And that's really the way I write. Where there are a lot of different meanings that are available. And *valid*. I mean, there have been people who have interpreted some of my songs in ways that I hadn't really thought of. But were absolutely valid. All of the evidence was there and it was valid. And it was more interesting, sometimes, than some of the thoughts that I had, which just happened to be from *my life*. They had a more interesting thing happen in *their* life.

PZ: I'm sure you've had the opposite happen, too, in which people come up with perverse ways to read your songs?

PS: Well, yeah, that's true, too. But to *sustain* those interpretations, you'll find that people just have to twist themselves into a pretzel to do it. I mean, there was a whole period of time where "Bridge Over Troubled Water" was supposed to be about heroin.

PZ: Yeah. "Silvergirl" was supposed to be a syringe.

PS: That's a tough one. It's a tough one to *prove* cause, of course, it's absolutely not so, so how are you going to do it?

PZ: It was said that "The Boxer" was written about Dylan. And "lie la lie" had to do with the lie of his name. Did you ever hear that one?

PS: No, I never heard that. [*Laughs.*] But, of course, that's not so, either.

In fact, for me, I thought that "lie la lie" was a failure of song-writing.

PZ: You did?

PS: Yeah. I didn't have any words! Then people said it was "lie" but *I* didn't really mean that. That it was a lie.

But, it's not a failure of songwriting, because people like that and they put enough meaning into it, and the rest of the song has enough power and emotion, I guess, to make it go, so it's all right. But for me, every time I sing that part . . . [*softly*], I'm a little embarrassed.

PZ: *That's hard to believe, since the song is now so much of a classic. Do you remember writing it?*

PS: All I can remember is a time on a plane. I had taken a bible from one of the hotels and I was skimming through the bible and I think I saw the phrase "workman's wages." That's all I remember from that song.

PZ: *You described sitting in a room and tossing a ball against a wall while working on the songs for Graceland. What effect, if any, does that physical activity have on your mental activity?*

PS: I think it's very calming. It's like a Zen exercise, really. It's a very pleasant feeling if you like playing ball. The act of throwing a ball and catching a ball is *so* natural . . . and *calming* that your mind kind of wanders. And that's really what you want to happen. You want your mind to wander, and pick up words and phrases and fool around with it and drop it . . .

As soon as your mind knows that it's on and it's supposed to produce some lines, either it *doesn't,* or it produces things that are very predictable. And that's why I say I'm not interested in writing something that I thought about. I'm interested in *discovering* where my mind wants to go, or what object it wants to pick up.

It *always* picks up on something true. You'll find out much more about what you're thinking that way then you will if you're determined to say something. What you're determined to say is filled with all your rationalizations and your defenses and all of that. *What you want to say to the world* as opposed to what you're thinking. And as a *lyricist,* my job is to find out what is it that I'm thinking. Even if it's something that I don't want to be thinking.

I think when I get blocked, when I have writer's block (though I never think of it as writer's block anymore), what it is, you have something to say but you don't want to say it. So your mind says, "I have nothing to say. I've just nothing more to say. I can't write anything. I have no thoughts." Closer to the truth is that you have a thought that you really would prefer not to have. And you're not going to say that thought.

Your mind is protected. Once you discover what that thought is, if you can find another way of approaching it that isn't negative to you, then you can deal with that subject matter.

PZ: It's funny that you've written two songs called "Think Too Much" (on Hearts and Bones) and yet you are striving not to think too much in your songwriting.

PS: Well, the fact that I had two songs called "Think Too Much" is just a joke. I write one song called "Think Too Much" and I think, "That isn't even the way I should write it. I should write it *this* way." [*Laughs*] It's just another example of never letting it go and thinking too much. That's why I did two songs.

But they are two entirely different songs. One was saying, "I think too much and ha, ha, it's a joke. Look at that. Maybe I think too much." That's the fast song. [*"Think Too Much, A"*]

Then I finish and I say, "Well, maybe it isn't a joke. Maybe the point is that you think too much and you're not in touch with what you feel. And the *proof* of it is that you've written this *joke song* about a very serious subject." So now I wrote a song that is all about feeling on the same subject. So there were two ways of approaching that subject.

PZ: Was the entire Graceland project an attempt to not think too much in your writing and to feel more?

PS: Yes . . . yes. That's so. But at the same time, I was using a different technique in writing, which in a way started with *One Trick Pony* but really you could see clear evidence of it in *Hearts and Bones*.

The language starts to get more interesting in *Hearts and Bones*. The imagery started to get a little interesting. What I was trying to learn to do was to be able to write vernacular speech and then intersperse it with enriched language. And then go back to vernacular. So the thing would go along smoothly and then some image would come out that was interesting and then it would go back to this very smooth, conversational thing. So that was a technique that I was learning.

There was a touch of it in *One Trick Pony*. There's a song called "Oh Marion" where I wrote a line, "The boy has a heart but it beats on his opposite side." That may have been one of the earlier times when some piece of imagery was striking.

It didn't have anything to do with logic or anything. I don't know where it came from. But on *Hearts and Bones* there's more of that: "Magritte" has more of that; "Hearts and Bones" has more of it.

"Train In The Distance" is in itself that kind of speech: "Everybody loves the sound of a train in the distance. . ." That's imagery and that's the title.

By the time I got to *Graceland,* I was trying to let that kind of enriched language flow naturally, so that you wouldn't really notice it as much. I think in *Hearts and Bones* you could feel it, that it was coming. You could sort of see it. Whereas in *Graceland* I tried to do it where you didn't notice it, where you sort of passed the line and then it was over. And let the words tumble this way and that way. And sometimes I'd increase the rhythm of the words so that they would come by you so quickly that all you would get was a *feeling*. And so I started to try and work with moving feelings around with words.

PZ: "You Can Call Me Al" seems like the perfect example of that combination of the colloquial with enriched language. The chorus is conversational, set against enriched lines like "angels in the architecture, spinning in infinity . . ."

PS: Right. The songs starts almost like a joke. Like the structure of a joke cliche: "There's a rabbi, a minister and a priest." "Two Jews walk into a bar. . . .: "A man walks down the street." That's what I was doing there.

Because the beginning of a song is one of the hardest parts about songwriting. The first line of a song is *very* hard. And I always have this image in my mind of a road that goes like this [*motions with hands to signify a road that gets wider as it opens out*] so that the implication is that the directions are pointing *outward*.

It's like a baseball diamond; there's more and more space out here. As opposed to like this. [*Motions an inverted road getting thinner.*] Because if it's like this, at this point in the song, you're out of options.

I want to have a first line that has a *lot* of options. And the other thing that I try to remember, especially if a song is long, *you have plenty of time.* You don't have to kill them, you don't have to grab them by the throat with the first line.

In fact, you have to wait for the audience—they're going to sit down, get settled in their seat . . . their concentration is *not even there.* You have to be a good host to people's attention's span. They're not going to come in there and work real hard right away. Too many things are coming at you: the music is coming, the rhythm is coming, all kinds of information that the brain is sorting out.

Easy words and easy thoughts. Let it move along and let the mind get into the groove of it. Especially if it's a rhythm tune. And at a certain point when the brain is loping along easily, then you come up with a thought or image that's different. Because it's entertaining at that point.

So "You Can Call Me Al," which was an example of that kind of writing, starts off very easily with sort of a joke: "Why am I soft in the middle when the rest of my life is so hard?" Very easy words. Then it has a chorus that you can't understand. What is he talking about, you can call me Betty, and Betty, you can call me Al? You don't know what I'm talking about. But I don't think it's bothersome. You don't know what I'm talking about but neither do *I*. At that point.

The second verse is really a recapitulation: A man walks down the street, he says . . . *another thing.* You know?

And by the time you get to the *third* verse, and people have been into the song long enough, now you can start to throw abstract images. Because there's been a structure, and those abstract images, they will come down and fall into one of the slots that the mind has already made up about the structure of the song.

So now you have this guy who's no longer thinking about the mundane thoughts, about whether he's getting too fat, whether he needs a photo opportunity, or whether he's afraid of the dogs in the moonlight and the graveyard, and he's off in, listen to the sound, look what's going on, there's cattle and . . .

PZ: Scatterlings . . .

PS: Yeah, and these sounds are very fantastic, and look at the buildings, there's angels in the architecture . . . And that's the end of the song. It goes "phooom!" and that's the end.

* * *

PZ: Gerry Goffin told us recently that since his life has become so comfortable, it's not as easy for him to write. He felt he needed some turmoil in his life to stimulate him. Do you find you need turmoil or can you create when things are calm?

PS: Well, that's a very good question, really. It's a very hard question to answer.

I'm not really sure. Turmoil does provoke or illicit emotions more. But I wouldn't purposely put my life into turmoil in order to write. There's plenty of turmoil that you contain with you for years and years and years that you can tap into. And not every song is about turmoil, anyway.

But, yes, that's true that when you have an active emotional life, there's more subject matter. I think that's so.

PZ: Randy Newman said that you are one of the few writers from your generation who has never let the quality of your writing diminish. Do you have any thoughts as to how you are able to do that?

PS: I think that, for me, . . . I'm as interested in the subject of writing and making records as I ever was. From when I started, which was at the age of fifteen, I've been very interested in this. So I'm blessed, really. I'm never bored. I'm always interested in problem solving in this area and I can always seem to go from one problem that I want to solve to another.

I mean, *Graceland* led me to West African drumming and West Africa led me into Brazil and the Caribbean. Because the Southern Africans are reputed to be the great singers of the continent. But the West Africans are the great drummers of the continent. So one piece of information is adjacent to another.

You sort of just follow whatever's interesting to you. And my interest level on writing and making records has never diminished. It's as strong as it ever was. I think that describes what happens with me in my work.

With the other guys, I don't know if they're as interested or not. I don't know. But I know it was very helpful for me to go and play with musicians from other cultures. That was *very* stimulating for me.

If I had to sit and play songs that I wrote on guitar, I don't know if I'd be as interested. I'm stimulated by other musicians. But I've always been interested in music from other places. Since I was a little kid, really. That's just my natural inclination to be that way.

PZ: You, Dylan and the Beatles almost simultaneously brought the song to a new place. What influence, if any, did the Beatles' writing have on your writing?

PS: I didn't think they influenced me a lot. I think it was inevitable; they were so powerful that you couldn't really escape the influence. But I tried as hard as I could not to be influenced by the Beatles or by Bob Dylan. Or the Rolling Stones. Which made it hard to stake out some territory that was your own. Because between them, they [*laughs*] really had covered the map. And I thought that Simon and Garfunkel, we just *barely* got a wedge in there. Which I then tried to expand. But it was just impossible not to be influenced by that.

PZ: Did you ever recognize your influence on them? McCartney said recently that when he first heard "Bridge Over Troubled Water" he attempted to write a song like it. The song he wrote was "Let It Be."

PS: [*Surprised*] McCartney said that? Well . . . I didn't know that.

But, they [*The Beatles*] listened to everything, too. Much more than Bob [*Dylan*] did. So whatever it was that struck them . . . "Bridge Over Troubled Water" is influenced by Gospel writing. So it's not really my influence, it's really Gospel writing. But maybe he heard it from me.

PZ: But you took it and put it in a new form. It sounds different than a Gospel song.

PS: Not very. Not very. I mean, I think the way that Artie sings it is different. But if you listen to Aretha Franklin, who recorded it a year later. She's singing it just the way it would be played.

And as for Bob [*Dylan*], I don't know. He's like the most mysterious of all the people of our generation. He's sort of impenetrable, really.

PZ: I read in a book about you that once you went to his house and looked through his garbage to see "how Dylan did it."

PS: I did? [*Laughs*] I would *never* do that to anyone. *I heard that.* Yeah, I remember that. It's absolutely not so. Absolutely not so. I remember that being said. I don't know why anyone would think that they could find out anything by looking in his *trash*. No, I never did that.

PZ: Earlier you described the way your father showed you chords when you were a kid, and explained the pull of the relative minor, the movement from the I chord to the VI chord. Those are changes you've used in many of your most powerful songs. Any explanation why that is such a powerful pull to our ears?

PS: No, but it seems to be. The same with a IV chord to a I chord is going to do it. Or a I to a IV. If you use it in the right way, it's going to have an emotional kick. If you don't use it in the right way, it's a cliche. But at a certain point, when you want to convey some emotion, those changes, if they come at you like a surprise, they'll do it every time.

I don't know if that's a generational thing or not. But it certainly is for me. As simple as they are, those become a key element in my writing and I always experiment with them. I don't always use it but I always try and see if I can use it.

PZ: *The I-IV or the I-VI?*

PS: Both.

PZ: *In "Slip Slidin' Away" the theme is the inevitable movement towards death, as in "That's Why God Made the Movies." Yet in "Graceland" your attitude seems to have shifted. You say, "We all will be received in Graceland." Has your attitude changed?*

PS: Well, I don't have one attitude. I have many attitudes that incorporate opposites. Now I try to get all the opposites into the same song, if I can. I try to resolve it one way or the other, but opposites—having two very strong feelings about the same subject—we *all* have that.

So that's a good thing to have in a song. Then you don't have to pick. You can just describe how you feel on both sides of the issue.

* * *

PZ: *Do you think that there is any limit to the imagination?*

PS: To one person's imagination?

PZ: *To your imagination, or to a songwriter's imagination.*

PS: Yeah, I do think some people have shallower pools to draw the water from. It's true.

PZ: *Do you ever find that your own pool has gone dry, that there's nothing left there to draw from?*

PS: Yeah, sure, all the time. On every album I say that. And one of these days that's really going to be true. At least that's my fear. But so far, it's been that if you have enough patience, it will come.

PZ: *Patience is the key?*

PS: I think so. Patience, persistence . . . whichever. Sometimes you have to be very *tenacious* and sometimes you have to give yourself a break and not beat yourself up and say, "Where is it? Where is it?" It's not here, you know. It'll be here when it gets here, and that's it. There's nothing more you can do.

Sometimes you say, "Try and work a little harder. Maybe you'll get a little more." And sometimes you will. [*Softly*] Sometimes you won't . . . Those are different strategies you can use to provoke yourself.

PZ: *Randy Newman told us that he has to make himself sit there on a daily basis to get it to keep coming.*

PS: Well, lately I don't do that. I used to do that but for the last few months I've been finding that the work comes at absolutely unexpected times.

I had one period last summer where every day for four days I woke up *exactly* at 5:30 in the morning *with lyrics!* I didn't set an alarm. I woke up at 5:30 every day with some song in my head from this album and lyrics. It was like, "Wow . . . this is great!" Then I began to expect it. I woke up one day at 5:30 and there was nothing. [*Laughs*] That was the end. It didn't happen again.

Then big periods of time would go by when I would get nothing then I'd get a bunch of lines on several different songs for a day to two or maybe three and I'll think, "Okay, here we go," and then it stops. And that's been the pattern now for many months.

PZ: *So you feel now that it's more beneficial not to force yourself?*

PS: I haven't felt that it's done me any more good to do that. But I think this is because I have somehow come to believe that the only lyrics that I'm really interested in are the lyrics that I find, not the lyrics that I invent. If it doesn't come to me in that surprising way, I don't tend to believe it or get excited about it.

But then, I guess I'm really talking about certain types of lines and phrases or images that are really interesting. They're sprinkled through-out the song.

Most of the song is not that. Most of the song is just meat and potatoes. Lines that are either moving the narrative forward or setting up these other lines which are observations. And so I have pages of these lines that aren't in songs, that are just interesting lines or images or combinations of words. I keep playing the songs and looking at the lines to see if they will fit anywhere rhythmically; will they belong?

PZ: So you're actually working on several songs at once?

PS: All of the songs at once.

PZ: All? How many are there?

PS: Ten. I start the album from the beginning and I play it through and I try to work on each song. Because I'm working on the album as a whole as opposed to ten different songs.

PZ: You said that you're more interested with what you find in songs than with what you invent. How do you draw the line between discovery and invention? Don't they overlap?

PS: Yes, they do. [*Pause*] You just have no idea that that's a thought that you had. It surprises you. It can make me laugh or make me emotional. When it happens and I'm the audience and I react, I have faith in that because I'm already reacting. I don't have to question it. I've already been the audience.

But if I make it up, knowing where it's going, it's not as much fun. It *may* be just as good, but it's more *fun* to discover it. So that's what I go for.

I mean, it may be that that's what is slowing me down to such a slow pace, you know, that I keep waiting for this stuff instead of just writing. But just writing what? How do I know what I'm going to write if I don't discover it? If I make up what I'm going to write, all I'm going to write is what I saw on television or what I read in the paper or what I saw . . . it's not going to be from the underground river of your sub-conscious. Because that just comes to the surface occasionally and you have to capture it when it happens.

PZ: Do you ever feel that these thoughts that surprise you come from beyond you?

PS: No. Beyond? No. I don't know what that means.

PZ: Many songwriters, including John Lennon, have expressed that they feel like channels, and that songs come through them from a source that is beyond.

PS: Well, it's coming from their subconscious. Unless you believe that someone is sending you a signal from another planet or another sphere. But maybe that's an explanation for your subconscious. I don't think that way.

PZ: But doesn't it ever seem to you that the process is rather magical?

PS: Yes, and that's why it's more fun to write that way.

PZ: But that magic is something you possess?

PS: You don't really possess it. That's the feeling that it comes through, that you're a transmitter. It comes through you.

PZ: So you do feel that?

PS: Yeah, but you don't possess it. You can't control it or dictate to it. You're just waiting. You're just waiting . . . waiting for the show to begin.

PZ: Have you ever felt, after completing a song, that it doesn't exist in a physical form, that you create something that's not really there?

PS: I never think that. The only thought I ever have about it is: here's a piece of tape that was actually blank at a certain point and now *it's* the same but it's filled up with all these . . . *sounds*. They didn't exist and now they all exist in some digital, magnetic form.

That's it. That's all I think about in terms of . . . No, I do have another thought that's sort of in that area that you're talking about, which is when I finish a song in my head, I'm always afraid that I'm going to get killed . . .

PZ: Before you can record it?

PS: Yeah, that's right. Get hit by a car, or something . . . Before anyone's heard the song. It makes me very nervous.

Although I have now four or five songs for this album and I haven't put them down on tape. People have heard me sing them but they're not on tape.

PZ: Does that worry you?

PS: A little bit.

PZ: Earlier you described discovering a thought and then consciously trying to think of the beginning, or set-up, to that thought. Doing this are you creating an illusion that the song appeared in order when in a sense it was written backwards?

PS: Well, backwards is still an order. That's not out of order. I think a piece surges forward and backward and forward and backward until finally it stops. And sometimes things will have that classic form where they seem to build to a certain peak and then conclude. I think people are very satisfied by hearing that form.

But I think that's just one of the forms and it doesn't necessarily satisfy me.

Sometimes I'd rather hear a shape closer to life. Amorphous is a closer shape to life than symmetry.

PZ: It seems that much of the greatness of songs is that they are perfectly ordered—

PS: When they're right. When they're really right. Then they do something to us. They make us feel really good.

PZ: Your current work is so much more concerned with rhythm than melody. Is it your feeling that melody is no longer important?

PS: We're long out of the age of melody. Long out of there and we probably won't be going back into it.

PZ: You don't think so?

PS: I don't think so. Something literally earth-shattering would have to happen for us to *change direction* away from rhythm. You can't have melody without more interesting changes. It's very heard to have melody over mechanized *drums.*

PZ: Don't you think we'll tire of hearing those rhythms and we'll hunger for melody again?

PS: It's possible. But I don't think so. I'd like that to happen, but I don't think it will.

    I think the opposite will happen. People will forget about melody and they won't hunger for it. They won't know what it is.

PZ: That's a startling thought. It seems to me, though, that the desire to hear melodies is an inherent human need. It's something we can't do without.

PS: Well, you don't see it much reflected in music. What you see reflected in music is *rhythm.*

PZ: But don't you feel that nowadays, with the emphasis on rhythm, people feel especially relieved and nourished when they hear a good melody?

PS: Yeah, I *do.* I think people are nourished and relieved to hear interesting lyrics, too. *Any quality at all* that comes their way is really appreciated given the fact that it's a world where the quality of life is being eroded. The quality of *everything* is being eroded except technology.

    And as the marketplace expands to a world-wide marketplace, it's not like the market is going to have any effect upon the writing. Because the writing can get worse and the sales will go up. So there's no easy way to make a big movement. Certainly the corporations don't care.

    So who will be the melody writer? Where are they going to learn it from?

PZ: Isn't it possible that they might listen to some old records? Or CDs?

PS: Well, that's what would have to happen. But, you know, people don't read history, people don't listen. Some do. *Most don't.*

When we take this generation now and go a generation past this, they won't be listening before that. It took me a long time to listen to music that existed before rock and roll. A long time. And the people who were born years later, even they can't seem to go back beyond the sixties. They don't listen to the fifties rock and roll, which had its own melodies. Fifties music had its own melodies. I really liked that kind of melody.

Early fifties music also had a different kind of melody, more melodic. But then you're closer to the age of melody.

Because the Big Band era and post-war, that was still all about melody.

The days of Irving Berlin and *those* great songwriters was about *melody.* Nobody's come close to writing melodies like *they did.* Nobody . . [*Pause*] Maybe Paul McCartney.

PZ: He's the one you would choose?

PS: I think he was probably the most notable melody writer . . .Stevie Wonder, also, is a notable melody writer. I don't know anybody else that was really—

PZ: Jimmy Webb?

PS: Yeah. Jimmy Webb is a good writer, you're right.

PZ: How about yourself?

PS: Not in the same league with Paul McCartney. But I still have memory of melody, so I mean, I do write melody. But I think he had a really great gift, Paul.

* * *

PZ: Is there one song you would consider to be your best?

PS: [*Pause*] No. I don't know how to answer that.

There's a song on this new album that's one of my best. It's called

"Cool Cool River" or "The Cool, Cool River," I'm not sure which yet. That seems to be a very good one.

PZ: Are you looking forward to the songs to come?
PS: Oh, yeah. If I can get them out. If I can write them it will be better. When they come, they seem to be better.

But anyway, I don't have to think about that. I don't think it's something that I *want* to think about either.

I mean, writing songs is what I do and I enjoy it. I'm grateful that people are . . . *still interested* after all this time. That I can keep doing it. That they will keep letting me make records.

It's great. I've been interested in writing songs and making records since I was thirteen years old. And I'm still absolutely enthralled with it.

From Part Two

* * *

PZ: Why have you chosen The Rhythm of the Saints as the title for your new album?

PS: This album is about drums, about drumming. It's about West African drumming. And the West African religion of the Yuruba people was exported with the African Diaspora into the New World because of slavery. So that culture and those religions, the West African deities, were syncretized with Catholicism so that West African deities would have a corresponding Catholic saint. So that when the slave-master came in and said, "I told you guys not to be playing drums," because the drum was forbidden, especially the holy drum, the bata, they would say, "This is not about Chango, this is about . . . Santa Barbara." So it became an Afro-Catholic religion.

The inspiration for the album comes from the West African drumming as it is expressed through Brazilian psalms. So I called the album The Rhythm of the Saints.

PZ: You've titled this album before finishing all of the songs. Was the title "Graceland" a title you had before writing those songs?

PS: No.

PZ: Do you remember when it occurred to you that using the name "Graceland" would be the key to that album?

PS: Very late. Very late in the thing. After everything was finished, I had no title for the album. In the chorus where it says "Graceland," I fought for a long time to get rid of it. I didn't like it.

PZ: Why?

PS: Because I thought it was distracting. I figured people would think I'm writing about Elvis Presley, and this is a South African record and I'm now writing a song about Mississippi and Graceland . . . I took a long time before it settled and I got comfortable with it and said, "Oh that's fine. You're not writing about Elvis Presley and it doesn't matter if they think you are. Those that get it will know that you're not, and those that don't get it won't care, they'll be just as happy that you're writing about Elvis Presley. It's not going to do any harm and in fact, it's kind of fun in a way." And once I got comfortable with that, then it wasn't that hard to come and say that was what the album really should be about. The album was about that, but it takes a while before everything settles down and you can understand what it is that you've done. On this album, I've had the title "The Rhythm of the Saints" for a long time, though. Graceland didn't have a title very close to the end.

PZ: Have you written lyrics yet to all of the songs for this album?

PS: A few of the songs are more or less finished. More or less. There's about four songs pretty finished. I'm a little closer on a few.

PZ: How did you decide to combine African and Brazilian music?

PS: They are actually connected. The Brazilian drumming is from West Africa, so I'm just going backwards, really. The Brazilians are great drummers. And then [I'm] going backwards and putting the West African over the Brazilian rhythm, as opposed to having the West African drummers. Because the West African drummers usually have less in the ensemble. Brazilians will go anywhere from six to eleven drummers.

PZ: You explained how you are writing all these new songs the way you wrote the songs for Graceland, by making a musical track first and writing the songs to the finished tracks. When you make these tracks, how much guidance do you give the musicians? Do you write out lead sheets?

PS: No. [I] sing it. I sing the guitar parts. I wrote that [shuffle] track; all the staccato stuff. I just rewrote the bridge yesterday. The structure of the song is set. We've spent a couple of days trying different structures but now that's set, so I'll write it to that. This has been the pattern now with the whole album so I'm a little faster now in making these structures. It was harder in the beginning.

PZ: As a songwriter, that seems like an extremely tough challenge to create the song to a finished track. Do you find that?

PS: It is, but I don't think it's any tougher than doing it the other way. Depending upon how high your standard is for what you want to accomplish. The reason I did that was after the *Hearts and Bones* album, I said, "I don't want to be in a situation again where I write a really good song and don't make a really good record of it." So from now on (and of course I'm going to say "from now on," "it doesn't mean anything. [Laughs] It just doesn't mean anything. It means the next thing that I do), I'll make a good record first. And if the song comes out good, then everything is fine. But if the song isn't good, then I'll probably throw if away and write another song. But that record is still going to be good. The track is going to be good.

PZ: You're saying that there are songs on Hearts and Bones *that you don't think you recorded well?*

PS: Right, the whole album. [Softly] The whole album.

PZ: Does that feeling come from the fact that it didn't sell as well as your other albums, or did you feel that at the time?

PS: No, it wasn't my feeling at the time. But at the time, it's very hard to have a perspective because you're working on something for so long. You become so invested in it that you just can't come up with a negative opinion about it or you couldn't go forward. Of course, at a time I had a lot of confusion in my life, so I also wasn't paying a lot of attention. I probably paid less attention to that record than probably any record I've ever made.

PZ: That's surprising to hear that album has such a strong thematic unity, the idea of thinking too much, and the dichotomy between the heart and the brain.

PS: Yes, that's true. But in terms of making the record, I let things go on that record that really if I was paying attention I shouldn't have let go.

PZ: Anything particular?

PS: Just the way I made the tracks. They weren't really good rhythm tracks. But I didn't have a good band. I didn't have a band. My best records have always been when I worked with a really good rhythm section.

PZ: Do you spend any time at all writing songs by yourself on guitar?

PS: No.

PZ: Why?

PS: A couple of reasons. Number one, my guitar skills have deteriorated considerably. From lack of playing. Which I suppose I could get back from practicing, which I always mean to do but I don't. I mean, I'm on this record, I play on about four or five tracks but that's it, really. And I work with guitarists who are brilliant, so there's no reason for me to be brilliant at it. I make up the stuff in the studio now, over the course of days or week, or sometimes more. Which is the same process as making up songs with a guitar, and making up whatever, chord structure . . . It's the same thing, really. You're improvising against your hands with a guitar. So here I'm improvising against, you know, somebody's else's hands.

* * *

PZ: Scott Eyerly, in his ShopTalk column a few issues back, clocked every song on Graceland on a metronome to show the huge variety of tempos that you used to break up the album. Is that an important concern?

PS: Yeah. Not only that, but key is one of the most important factors, even more than tempo. Key relationships, the similarity of tempos won't bother you as much. That's one thing to keep in mind.

Another thing to keep in mind is the length of a song. If every song is four minutes and 45 seconds, you're going to feel it in some way. Maybe not in the first four or five songs, but you're going to feel it.

I think you ought to vary all of that. For what I'm doing, you want to vary it. Because I want people to pay attention and be comfortable. I don't want them not to pay attention.

PZ: You sometimes will rise in keys from one song to the next, moving up a whole-step.

PS: Or a half-step. Half-step, whole-step, it depends. This album, *The Rhythm of the Saints*, goes B-flat, B minor, F, F# minor, F major, A-flat major, A minor, B-flat, C-sharp minor . . . I think that's it. [Simon later resequenced the songs in the following order of keys: A-flat, A minor, B-flat, G C-sharp minor, B minor, F sharp minor, G, C.]

PZ: Four songs in minor keys?

PS: Yeah.

PZ: Do you have lyrics yet for this track? [While talking, from the control room we could hear Roy Halee working on an edit of a track in process then called "the shuffle tune" and later titled "Thelma." Simon excluded this track from the final album.]

PS: No. Nothing's coming. First I get the melody.

PZ: When you think of a melody, do you try to immediately attach words to it?

PS: Yeah. I try and find words that will fit immediately. I think it would be great if I could do that. [Softly] This song is a little bit too long, because the second song and the fourth song on the album are both long songs and serious songs. So this has got to be light and easy and that's why I cut it that way and in that key and everything.

It had to be in F or C. But it had to be that way anyway, because that's where the drums were. [Simon used tuned bass drums on this track.] So when you get the keys right and get the tempo right and get the length right, all you have to do is write the song. At least when you write the song, all of that stuff is right. As opposed to doing it in the wrong key and now you can't fit it in somewhere.

The space between tracks, that's not an arbitrary thing. They used to always make it three seconds. It's dictated by the song that begins with an upbeat on what is apparently a downbeat.

Sometimes a song will begin on an upbeat, you know. You have to keep that in consideration, too. You don't want to put a song that begins with an upbeat on what is apparently a downbeat.

And there are other subtleties that you can work with. Some songs will sound better if you fade a phrase on the second beat of a bar pass, and you begin the next song on the one beat of the next song. Some songs will be better if you fade on the fourth beat of the bar and then the next song comes right in.

So that little area between tracks is not a no-man's land. It's something you can control and make it work for you. It'll work against you depending on how you're doing it.

PZ: Did you do that on past records?

PS: No, not consciously. But maybe by instinct. But surely there have been mistakes. Every album has had mistakes in that area.

PZ: In 1972 you said that "Bridge Over Troubled Water" was your best melody to date. Do you still feel that?

PS: Well, it's a very . . . very strong melody. It's hard to know now, now that the song has become . . . it's a Gospel standard. Maybe it's a standard in pop records, I don't know, I don't have a perspective on it anymore.

* * *

PZ: *In your songs you've expanded the vocabulary of chord changes used in pop songs. You made a comment in the past that you really aren't interested in two or three chord songs.*

PS: Well, that's probably a comment from a decade or so ago. Graceland is almost all three chord songs. It's just that the chords come in different places. This new album is not quite as three-chordy.

When you're dealing with rhythm, you're more naturally inclined to go to the simple chords because the rhythm . . . dominates. You can do some interesting changes, but it's a lot harder. And what I found with Graceland is that the African way of using three chords was so different that it was fresh.

* *

PZ: *If you met someone who didn't know your work at all, who had never heard even one of your songs, and you wanted to give them an idea of what you do, what song would you play them?*

PS: I would have to see who the person was. That would be my somewhat dormant performing instinct, to try and puzzle out who was the audience and what would please them.

I took a trip on the Amazon about a year ago, and we stopped in this Indian village. It was bigger than just huts; it had houses. It had two streets in it. And we passed a store where two kids were playing the guitar, a boy and a girl. They were maybe late teens or early twenties. And I was with my son. And they sang "The Sound of Silence." In Spanish. And they didn't know who I was. So then we sang "The Sound of Silence." They said, "Oh, you know that, too?" I said, "Yeah, I know that, too." Then I sang "El Condor Pasa." Which they, of course, know the Spanish version of. But again, though, you could guess that audience.

* *

PZ: *You've shown us in your work that there are a myriad of topics people can use in songs; ideas most people would never consider using.*

PS: The subject of popular songs has been the same forever. And if you put it in the right setting, that is the subject matter of popular songs. People need it. They never get tired of hearing . . . songs about love. It's one of the big things that we think about, and this is one of the areas where we can express it.

In today's writing, the songs are really about the rhythm. And the subject matter of songs, with the exception of rap, is usually not important. And nobody seems to object.

I feel like if you can satisfy people's rhythm jones, then why not say something interesting? As long as that doesn't take away from the satisfaction you can get from the rhythm. If it does, then you're defeating the purpose. But if you say something that's interesting or provocative along with rhythm, it's going to be a much better song, obviously.

For the rappers, I mean, when they get onto an interesting subject or interesting set of imagery, that's key because they don't have the element of melody. You've only got words and rhythm. So you've got to make those words say something. But in terms of other popular songs, you've got rhythm, melody and words, and the words are the least important. Unless you can make those words so interesting that people really enjoy it.

PZ: Did you like the song "Biko" by Peter Gabriel?

PS: Yeah, it was a very powerful song.

PZ: He took African music and used it with an African theme, as opposed to what you did by combining it with American concerns.

PS: I don't think that "Biko" had a particularly African feeling. It was an African theme. . . . I don't know if it was powerful to African ears, but it was powerful to our ears. And that's fine. He has a talent for that. But I don't.

PZ: The one song on Graceland that mentions Africa is "Under African Skies." But that is really more about music than Africa, about remembrances of where music comes from.

PS: Yeah, but in "You Can Call Me Al," the guy is in . . . "Maybe it's the third world, maybe it's his first time around . . ." I thought it was interesting to combine what was on my mind with that music. I thought it would be interesting to an African audience, if they could get to the point of hearing it. And they did, once the album became a big hit. It was a huge hit in South Africa. It had all the biggest bands in South Africa on the record.

So here's all these songs with what must be relatively strange subject matter, and I guess on the frivolous subject matter, like "I Know What I Know," maybe it's meaningless. But the "Boy in The Bubble" with that imagery, that must be pretty interesting to somebody that's hearing it there. That's not the way songs are coming at them.

So I thought it was interesting. I always try to be interesting to everybody. I always talked about what I knew and I was trying not to pretend to be an expert about something that I didn't know.

PZ: I loved the way, in "Africa Skies," that you tied together the African verses with Linda Ronstadt's remembrances of discovering music in Tucson, Arizona.

PS: Linda Ronstadt is also very interested in that subject and music of other cultures, and does it very well. She's very seriously involved in it. She researches it, likes to sing it. Yeah, she had a pretty big influence on me, too, Linda Ronstadt. She sort of just left rock and roll and went off and did whatever she was interested in. Which is what I wanted to do, and when I saw that she was doing it, it made me feel better about doing it, too.

PZ: Earlier you said that using truth in a song will give it more resonance, yet the songs in One Trick Pony weren't true to your own life.

PS: Yeah, but it was about people that I knew.

PZ: Was it difficult to write an entire cycle of songs based on someone else's truth?

PS: It was a different problem to solve. It didn't seem any more difficult than the other but I think the question is was it any better. I don't know that it was any better because I wrote on one subject.

Usually when I'm finished, I don't go back. Usually once I'm finished I'm really happy to be finished. I know I felt that way with

Graceland. I was happy to let it go. A little bit emotional and all that after the tour and all . . . but it has to be done. You're with it a long time.

It's enjoyable when you're doing it. I love to work. I really have a good time. Some of it more than the other. Like going to Brazil to record. I mean that's just pure fun. The hard thing is writing the song. But even that has its really good parts because when something comes, you're happy.

I saw Bruce Springsteen last night and he said he was really happy because he wrote a new song and he felt it was really good and he really liked it and felt really happy. So that's great.

PZ: How long does that feeling last for you after you've written a good song?

PS: Well, it can last for years, once it's a fact.

PZ: To get back to One Trick Pony, did you write some of those songs as the character of Jonah Levin?

PS: Yeah, "Soft Parachutes" was. Yeah, I was writing it as like what was in his mind.

PZ: Would "Ace in the Hole" be a Jonah Levin song?

PS: That was like a performance song. It wasn't supposed to be autobiographical as much as it was supposed to be a song in his repertoire.

PZ: It seems that some of the songs on the album are so sophisticated that he wouldn't have written them, or if he could, why would he have only been a one-trick pony? I think of the song "Jonah." Could Jonah have written "Jonah"?

PS: I think that's a valid point. I think that's a weakness in it. Whose voice are we hearing? Who is the narrator of this tale? Although he wasn't supposed to be a character who didn't have talent, he was supposed to be a character who is out of style. So even if he wrote that song "Jonah" I don't think he'd be a hit off of that.

There are songwriters who are very sophisticated songwriters who don't have enormous careers or mass popularity. They're very sophisticated but there's not a big audience for that.

PZ: That seems more common than your career. There are many instances of great, artistic songwriters who have small, cult audiences, but there are few examples of someone writing songs at your level who is able to communicate to the masses. Do you see that at all?

PS: [Pause] Yes and no. Because most of the stuff that were hits were the easier songs. And the more sophisticated stuff wasn't a hit. It really wasn't until Graceland where it was sophisticated and simple at the same time that it starts to spread across boundary lines.

And that—getting things sophisticated and simple at the same time—that's an objective. Try and do that. Try to simplify and simplify without losing what was really interesting.

PZ: When you are in the midst of writing, do you give any thought to who will hear the song, and how it will be received?

PS: I think when people write, they have an imaginary audience in mind. A lot of times you hear a song on a record and you know it's aimed at a certain audience, people communicating with their group. And when I started to combine groups that hadn't been combined before, the songs became richer. They were a little more exciting to a lot of people. And they were more antagonizing to a lot of people, too.

I think that's part of what this discussion is about: cross-cultural musical experiments. When you use elements of one culture to address elements of another culture and vice-versa. I take traditional African rhythms and sounds and address an American audience. I take what works for an American audience and address an African audience and that was upsetting for a lot of people. And stimulating to other people.

But I believe that there's a very basic feeling that music gives to all people and we're all connected on this very basic, emotional level by music, rhythm and harmony. And that many, many people can understand you when you're using that vocabulary. Or maybe they don't understand you but they still listen because the sounds are inviting and they're familiar, they don't threaten. And then whatever it is that you start to say with those sounds, that's where the fur starts to fly.

But how can people begin to communicate if we don't begin to appropriate a wider vocabulary? If you can't speak in someone else's language, how are they going to hear you? So I'm somebody who speaks . . . broken music.

* * *

PZ: *Was there a point in your writing when you consciously made a change from writing what were essentially pop songs, such as "Hey Schoolgirl" to more artistic songs such as "The Sound of Silence"?*

PS: [Long pause] Well . . . I'm trying to find out if there's anyone besides Bob Dylan who could have influenced me. But I really can't imagine . . . that there was. It might not have been Dylan directly but it was the folk scene of Bleecker and Macdougal [streets, in Manhattan's Greenwich Village]. But [Dylan] was so dominant a force in it that in a way you can attribute it to him. Although, I'm sure that he was influenced by the street, too.

Anyway, it was that scene which I was hanging around but not penetrating, coming from the disadvantage of Queens. That scene probably influenced that kind of writing.

And I think as a writer, since my writing was very much connected to record making, that one of the things that's characteristic of my work is that I have a very strong aural recall. I really remember sounds of a lot of things. Much stronger than visual. And so I remember how records went and I can remember obscure records and what part of the record that I liked; did I like the drum sound?

These were thoughts that I had when I was fourteen. And I've kept that and really, I'm always recapitulating those early sounds in records today. All the time. I mean, I doubt that anyone would hear it but me but I know exactly what those sounds are connected to, and they go back to adolescence almost every time.

In terms of really major influences, I don't think there's anything of really major significance past the sixties. With a couple of notable exceptions.

PZ: *Such as?*

PS: Antonio Carlos Jobim. He had a big influence on my thinking.

PZ: Did you study his music?

PS: Yeah, I studied it. Lyrically, I've had a lot of influences since the sixties. Lyrically things are going on all the time but really not in terms of making records and writing music.

Even the African music I heard has something akin to fifties music. The harmonies—they're different, but that's how I first heard it—but when I actually went to get the harmonies, they were a lot more difficult than when I first heard them. They're simple chords but when they came, that was very different. But the notes and the melodies are basically major scales. And major scales are like Christmas carols and Sam Cooke, though he used the sixth a lot, the sixth of the scale.

Gospels quartets . . . that came later, but really Gospel quartets was the completion of my education that Doo-Wop started. Doo-Wop came from Gospel quartets which I didn't know when I was thirteen years old.

PZ: Who influenced you lyrically since the sixties?

PS: Different poets that I read. [Pause] Wallace Stevens. Derek Walcott. I read a lot of his poetry. A poet from St. Lucia. Caribbean influences, a wonderful poet. Seamus Heaney, an Irish poet whose work I like quite a bit.

PZ: One of my favorites.

PS: Yeah? Then you'd like Derek Walcott's work a lot.

PZ: Ted Hughes?

PS: I read some Ted Hughes. Of the English poets, I like Philip Larkin. And various other people. John Ashbery's a good poet whose work I like.

I read quite a lot of poetry. But those people all, in some way, influenced my thinking. Or allowed me to go some place, that really was my instinct to go to anyway. Once I saw that I had a model that I could . . . absorb.

In fact, I just met Derek Walcott which was very . . . very pleasant for me. His work had a lot to do with this album because he writes a lot about that part of the world and the Caribbean. I usually carry his stuff with me. I don't think I brought it this time but I think I brought Seamus Heaney with me . . . and a book on Yeats . . .

PZ: *Have you ever written any poetry?*

PS: A couple times, yeah.

PZ: *Do you think that's an easier thing to do than to take words and music and try to put them together?*

PS: No. I think the only kind of writing that I'm really good at is writing songs. I've never really tried to do other writing, but I did write a screenplay.

PZ: *It was once written that you were working on a novel. True?*

PS: No. No, I don't think I could write a novel.

PZ: *Is it true that you and E.L. Doctorow have been working on a musical together?*

PS: Well . . . no, there isn't any truth to that. But he is a friend of mine and he did give me advice on a musical that I was working on before I put it aside to finish this album. I took advantage of his generosity to ask a lot of questions.

PZ: *Is that a project that you are going to return to?*

PS: Yes, oh, definitely. As soon as I finish the album, go on the road, do a tour, then I'll definitely go back. I'm about a year and a half into it. I'm quite into it.

PZ: *Are you writing the book and the songs?*

PS: No, I'm not going to write the book. It's a story that's true so I'm doing research on the story. I've done a few collaborations with songwriters but I'm not sure yet where I'll end up . . . I don't have to address it until I finish this project. It's sort of on the back-burner now.

PZ: *Would you be in the musical, performing the songs?*

PS: No.

PZ: *Are you conceiving of it in the old-fashioned musical form, with people singing—*

PS: Well, I would hope that it would not be an old-fashioned form but yes, people would be singing. There would be a story and people would be singing and dancing and speaking. And any way that I could tell that story, I would.

PZ: *Are you writing these songs on the guitar?*

PS: No. It's a Puerto-Rican story and I'm working with a lot of Latin musicians and composing kind of in the way I do now.

You know, if I have to solve a problem that I can't do in my head, I will pick up a guitar and play the notes and the chords, if I can't hear it clearly. To give myself other choices of notes, to be able to see it and touch it at the same time instead of just imagining it? But most of the problems I deal with are in my head. I can hear it most of the time.

PZ: *Are you writing these songs differently at all because you don't intend to sing them yourself?*

PS: I'm not writing them differently. But I suspect I'm going to be in trouble because of that. I'm writing songs for women and I'm probably writing them in the wrong key. But I really don't know that yet. I don't know how to write for different voices or for different instruments. I really don't know that.

PZ: *Do you think your writing has been affected by writing for yourself as a singer as opposed to songwriters who write for other singers to perform?*

PS: Not that much. Because I've written a lot of songs that weren't that great for me to sing. Because I felt like writing those songs. The most notable example is "Bridge Over Troubled Water" which I didn't sing. It took me years to sing that song. I heard it but it wasn't something that my voice wanted to do very well.

"Late in the Evening" is not a song that my voice is particularly great on, though that's a nice track.

A song that is very good for my voice is "Diamonds on the Soles of my Shoes." I think it's natural. But there are other songs where it's . . . unfortunate that I'm the person who's going to sing them. As a song-writer, it's too bad that I have to be represented by that guy as a vocal-ist. Because I can hear a lot more.

At this point in time, my voice has been around for so long, that people are familiar with that voice itself. That's probably an advantage. But in terms of interpreting a song, I don't have a lot of range. I do cer-tain things well and that's it. Other things, finding a way around it or an alternative way of singing it, I don't do well.

PZ: That's surprising that you say that, because you seem to have a very large range.

PS: Yeah, I don't have a problem with range in terms of octaves, I have a decent range. I tend not to sing anything above an F#, really, but I can get up to an A-flat. An F is really as high as I like to go. And I like to sing a little bit lower now. I don't mind singing in the bass register.

PZ: I love how on "I Know What I Know" you sing way down in your range on the reoccuring line "who am I to blow against the wind?"

PS: Yeah, I'm more comfortable doing that now. Singing a little bit more. I used to feel that you just have to sing the song like . . . Shaker furniture. Just like that. Don't make it more about your voice and your singing. Just service the song. But I feel after being on the road for a long time, I just got more comfortable singing and doing more things with my voice.

* * *

PZ: Do you think a technical knowledge of music theory is important for songwriters?

PS: It can't hurt. It can help. Yeah, there are some problems that you solve by information that a teacher can give you. You'll have a much harder time solving those problems without that information. You might solve them, anyway. But why reinvent the wheel when the information is there?

PZ: Is it possible that the knowledge can get in the way of the spontaneity? I'm conscious when I'm going out of a key, for example, and maybe not as free because of it.

PS: I guess it can go the other way. But certainly in popular music and rock & roll, that's not the problem.

PZ: Many great songwriters, though, never studied music, such as Paul McCartney.

PS: No, he didn't study. But he's very, very musical. He thinks clearly about it. He thinks about the shape of it. Yeah, I heard him describe music in terms where he understood the shape. He plays a few instruments. And his ear is very fine. When I was working on "Graceland," on the tracks, writing the song, I saw Paul. He said, "What are you working on?" And I said, "This stuff." "Can I hear it?" I said, "Yeah, sure, yeah." So we went into my car, and I was just playing him the tracks. And I'd finished quite a few of those songs and I had spent a lot of time writing them, and I played those tracks for him and he began to improvise melody, and many of them were really good. I mean, they weren't as good as the melodies that I had but I had reworked these melodies for a long time. His first impulse was very musical. He got it, sang easily, effortlessly, over the top of it. He's a very musical guy.

* * *

PZ: When Graceland was released to almost unanimous critical acclaim, the press often praised it by pulling down your past work. Did you notice that?

PS: Yeah, there was revisionism and *Graceland* in a way brought it out. But the style of music had changed a lot. And the generation of writers who were writing, they were coming from that same place.

But, like I say, fortunately it's not my job to describe how I am and where I stand. Whether one piece of work is good or not. And I know this: if they tend to dismiss a piece of work, it'll be rediscovered.

PZ: You do feel that?

PS: Yeah. I think *Hearts and Bones* is a great flop. What I learned having had *Hearts and Bones* and *Graceland* come right next to each other, and it was a hard lesson, [softly] it didn't matter that much whether you had a flop and it didn't matter that much whether you had a hit. The only thing that mattered was the power to write the song. And that was after you were playing on your own field, you were making up your own game and your own rules and it was comfortable. It was more responsibility but it was more comfortable.

I'm very critical but at least I can stop short of being brutal. Whereas when it's in other people's hands, if you believe it, it can get brutal. People can be brutal.

I don't think it's very good for a serious songwriter to pay attention to what [critics] say. It's just too hard. And it's not informative. They don't know what they're talking about. And can't know what they're talking about, by definition. Unless you write songs and make records, you just really can't know what it's about.

A critic is not capable of distinguishing between a safe move that is executed and an interesting mistake. An interesting mistake is by far the more valuable.

PZ: Hearts and Bones came out at a time when there wasn't much else going on, and it was a nourishing album for a lot of people.

PS: Yeah, it was obviously a relatively small group of people who felt that way. That was an important thing. A larger group were getting nourishment from another area. I think it's important not to take to heart, that people get nourishment from some other area. Keep going. In fact, it's good if people stop looking at you for a little while.

It was easier to make *Graceland*, by far, than it is to make *The Rhythm of the Saints*. Everybody's looking.

Had *Hearts and Bones* been successful, I don't think I would have made *Graceland*.

If *Hearts and Bones* had been successful, I would have taken that rhythm section and gone and written some more songs. The same way that I wrote songs then.

It was the thought that I spent time making songs and I didn't make a good record of them that set me up for the thoughts about *Graceland*. I don't think I would have gone and done a whole album. I might have done one cut, like I did "Mother and Child Reunion" or "Loves Me Like A Rock." But as the album wasn't a hit, and there was no pressure, no expectations, no . . . interest, I said, "Well, I have nobody to please but myself. So I'm going to do exactly what I find interesting. And I don't have to explain it to anybody because nobody's interested."

PZ: But you don't have any sense that you have a following that is eager to get anything new?

PS: Yeah, I do have that sense. I thought there was an audience that would be about as big [as that] for *Hearts and Bones*.

I mean, there are examples of recording careers that become significantly diminished. People who have enormous success and then it tapers down to . . . nothing. That's how it goes: it's about two million, then 400,000, then 200,000, then 25,000 and then that's who you are.

PZ: That's actually more common than your career, in which you've been able to continue to surpass yourself. Graceland was an entirely new direction in your career, it was hugely successful.

PS: I was totally involved in what I was doing. I never thought this was a come-back. I never thought, how interesting at your age, to get back on top. I don't think age has anything to do with it.

I really don't know. I don't know that there are any hits on this album, because this album is in less of a format than "Graceland" and "Graceland" wasn't in any format.

So we'll see. We'll see if people think these songs are as good. I think they are. I think they are.

I've given myself a deadline to finish it, though I've never made a deadline. I'd like to finish it in June and have it out by August. [The album was both completed and released in October 1990.]

I wonder if there's a player here. I'll play you a cut.

DOO-WOP TELLS A STORY OF THE '50s (1995)

"Tell you the truth, I don't know who Paul Simon is," says Benji Rosario, age 16. Wants to be a big musician, Benji Rosario. At first glance, wrong as usual, he appears to be just one more kid who drags phonograph needles across vinyl records to make the skin-crawling backbeat for rap songs.

This morning, he and his group, Lost Boyz, will audition for Simon's new Broadway musical, "The Capeman."

No surprise that Simon is writing music that will sound like, well, music. But stand by: Teenage singers are trying to outdo each other with sweet harmonies. Not only are the Lost Boyz auditioning, but so are 250 other groups, all of them ages 14 to 20.

What numbers are the Lost Boyz rehearsing for the audition?

"We're doing, 'Earth Angel,' and 'In the Still of the Night,'" says Rosario.

He and the other Boyz let fly: "In the still of the night/I held you, held you tight."

As they harmonize in a teacher's office, the four a capella voices of Lost Boyz rise into one song that rolls into the hallway and bounces off the tile walls, smoothly as a cue ball against the felt walls of a pool table.

Other kids crank around to follow the sound back to its sources. Harmony lives.

Simon is handing out $10,000 in prizes to the top singers who show up at the Nederlander Theater. His motive is pure: he wants to flush out the best a capella singers in the city to perform in his musical.

"There's a big resurgence of the streetcorner form—Boyz II Men helped," says Vicki Sanacore, drama teacher at Hostos-Lincoln Academy, an alternative high school in the South Bronx. "That, plus a lot of the kids have a very romanticized view of the '50s."

On the radio, KISS-FM has turned into an outlet for smooth soul and R & B—a fine tonic for the baby boomers who dropped out of popular music when it turned into one jarring screech about rape, murder and alienation. The Internet, whatever that is, is jammed with news about doo-wop singers. Now it looks like the stampede to harmony and melody is being joined by teens, the people who are perpetually in charge of pop music.

"Everyone around here, they love to hear the doo-wop," says Isaac

Cruz, a senior at Hostos-Lincoln, and the bass voice in Lost Boyz. "If we're in the office singing 'Still of the Night' or a Boyz II Men song, they'll walk in and say, 'Who's that?'"

If they make it into the musical—a long shot, like most things in the performing arts—the Lost Boyz will find themselves in the middle of a murder story that once shook New York.

"One instant, in 1988, it came to me to do a musical about the Capeman," said Simon. "It was an idea that wasn't there one instant, and was there the next."

The Capeman was Salvatore Agron—at 16, the youngest person ever sent to Death Row in New York. On an August night in 1959, Agron and a buddy knifed two other kids in a Hells Kitchen playground. He used a silver dagger and wore a red-lined black cape. The 1950s may not have been so innocent as people remember them today. But two murders by teenagers in a night—probably shrugged off in a few paragraphs today—devoured the seven New York City newspapers for weeks in 1959. Commissions were formed. Prominent people issued pronouncements about juvenile delinquency. That Agron was Puerto Rican, perhaps a member of a Puerto Rican gang called the Vampires, drove the pitch even higher.

Agron's death sentence was commuted by Nelson Rockefeller. He became a prison poet. He was paroled in 1979, and died from a chronic illness in 1986, at the age of 42.

"All I remembered was that the Capeman murder had happened," said Simon, then a 17-year-old at Forest Hills High School who was harmonizing with his buddy, Art Garfunkel.

Simon tore into the Capeman story. He interviewed Agron's family and friends, tracing them back to Puerto Rico, where Agron's father had been a Pentecostal minister. He is collaborating on the story with Derek Walcott, the Nobel Prize–winning poet.

"Once I was able to piece together his story, the music became more apparent," said Simon. "There will be doo-wop music, and plenas and bombas from Puerto Rico. The story for the show is finished, but the music isn't."

"I know the show is about Capeman, a Puerto Rican guy in a Puerto Rican gang," said Isaac Cruz. "We're all Puerto Rican in the Lost Boyz."

The other two members of the group are Enrique Carmona, the alto who founded the group, and Manny Sanchez.

"They not only know the doo-wop, they're also heavily influenced by the salsa sounds," says Vicki Sanacore. "If they don't win, I'll kill them."

"I have heard Paul Simon's 'Graceland' music," says Carmona. "With the African beats. And also the 'Rhythm of the Saints.'"

"Paul Simon—I heard a couple of his songs," said Isaac Cruz. "That one with the video—'If you be my bodyguard, call me Al'—with Chevy Chase in it. That's the one I know. I love Boyz II Men, and the Carpenters."

Simon groaned, slightly. "People's idea of the '50s is 'Happy Days' and 'Grease,'" he said. "They don't know the mystery of what the street produced."

Chronology

1941	Born October 13, 1941, in Newark, NJ. Raised in Queens, NY. Son of Louis (a musician and college professor) and Belle (an elementary schoolteacher). Has one brother, Eddie, four years younger.
1956	Simon and Garfunkel meet at Forest Hills High.
1957	Simon and Garfunkel, as "Tom and Jerry," appear on Dick Clark's "American Bandstand." Their first hit, a pop tune called "Hey, Schoolgirl," stays on <u>Billboard</u>'s Top 100 for nine weeks. The duo records followups through 1959, but they stiff; they separate c. 1960, with Garfunkel eventually working as a carpenter in the Berkeley, CA, area.
1960–62	Simon continues to try to break into the writing and recording fields, working under various pseudonymns, including True Taylor, Jerry Landis, and the mock group, Tico and the Triumphs. Cuts demos with young Carol Klein (aka Carole King). Garfunkel records as Artie Garr.
1963	Simon cuts his first folk protest song, "He Was My Brother," under the pseudonym of "Paul Kane"; Garfunkel returns to New York and reunites with Simon.
1964	Simon and Garfunkel are signed to Columbia; album <u>Wednesday Morning, 3 A.M.</u> is released; fails to sell. Simon goes to England, "where his heart lies." Remains through 1965, recording the solo album, <u>The Paul Simon Songbook.</u>
1965	Columbia issues "The Sounds of Silence" as a single with overdubbed electric guitar, bass, and drums; it shoots to the number-one spot on the <u>Billboard</u> Top 100 chart. Simon returns to the U.S. and reunites with Garfunkel. The duo hurriedly records an album to cash in on their success.

1966	Sounds of Silence released; Parsley, Sage, Rosemary, and Thyme recorded and released; Simon approached by Mike Nichols to score his upcoming film, The Graduate.
1967	Touring. Simon begins composing songs for The Graduate and the duo's next album, Bookends.
1968	Bookends and The Graduate soundtrack released.
1969	Wins Grammy Awards for best album with The Graduate, and best performance by a pop vocal group; Simon marries Peggy Harper. Garfunkel goes to Mexico to appear in Mike Nichols's film, Catch-22; duo works on their next album when possible.
1970	Wins Grammy Awards for best album and best performance by a pop vocal group with Bridge Over Troubled Water, and best single for "Bridge Over Troubled Water." Increased tension, over Garfunkel's acting career and Simon's desire to write music in a different style, leads the duo to break up.
1971	Releases Paul Simon, first U.S. solo album.
1972	Son Harper is born.
1973	Hits with "Kodachrome" and "Loves Me Like a Rock."
1975	Divorces Peggy Harper.
1975	Wins Grammy Award for best album for Still Crazy After All These Years. Hits number 1 on the Billboard charts.
1977	Acts in Woody Allen's Annie Hall, portraying a sleazy recording artist.
1979	Leaves Columbia Records to sign with Warner Bros., which offers him a joint record-and-movie deal.
1980	Writes and stars in the film One-Trick Pony, a box-office flop.
1981	Reunites briefly with Garfunkel for a concert in Manhattan's Central Park and a national tour.
1983	Marries Carrie Fisher, actor/writer. Six months later, they divorce.
1985	Goes to Johannesburg to record Graceland, causing an international uproar.
1986	Wins Grammy Award for best album for Graceland.
1987	Wins Grammy for best song for "Graceland." Hits new career high.
1990	Is inducted, with Art Garfunkel, into the Rock and Roll Hall of Fame.
1992	Marries Edie Brickell, singer and songwriter with the New Bohemians; includes Johannesburg as a stop on his "Born at the Right Time" tour, despite threats of violence from the Azanian Youth Organization and the Pan Africanist Congress. (There was one actual grenade attack on the office of the concert's promoters.)
1993	Son Adrian is born.
1995	Daughter, Lulu, is born.
1998	Musical The Capeman is expected to premiere.

Discography

Simon and Garfunkel Albums

1964
Wednesday Morning, 3 A.M. (Columbia PC 9049)

You Can Tell the World
Last Night I Had the Strangest Dream
Bleecker Street
Sparrow
Benedictus
The Sounds of Silence
He Was My Brother
Peggy-O
Go Tell It On the Mountain
The Sun Is Burning
The Times They Are A-Changin'
Wednesday Morning, 3 A.M.

1966
Sounds of Silence (Columbia CS 9269)

The Sounds of Silence
Leaves That Are Green
Blessed
Kathy's Song
Somewhere They Can't Find Me
Anji

Richard Cory
A Most Peculiar Man
April Come She Will
We've Got a Groovy Thing Goin'
I Am a Rock

Simon and Garfunkel (Pickwick SPC 3059)

This album consists of "Tom and Jerry" recordings from the late '50s, including their lone pop hit, "Hey Schoolgirl."

Hey Schoolgirl
Dancin' Wild
Our Song
Teen Age Fool
True or False
Tijuana Blues
Simon Says
Don't Say Goodbye
Two Teen-Agers
That's My Story

Parsley, Sage, Rosemary and Thyme (Columbia SC 9363)

Scarborough Fair/Canticle
Patterns
Cloudy
Homeward Bound
The Big Bright Green Pleasure Machine
The 59th Street Bridge Song (Feelin' Groovy)
The Dangling Conversation
Flowers Never Bend with the Rainfall
A Simple Desultory Philippic (Or How I Was Robert McNamara'd Into Submission)
For Emily, Whenever I May Find Her
A Poem on the Underground Wall
7 O'Clock News/Silent Night

1968

Bookends (Columbia KCS 9529)

Bookends Theme (Instrumental)
Save the Life of My Child
America
Overs
Voices of Old People
Old Friends
Bookends Theme
Fakin' It
Punky's Dilemma
Mrs. Robinson
A Hazy Shade of Winter
At the Zoo

The Graduate (Columbia OS 3180)

The Sounds of Silence
The Singleman Party Foxtrot
Mrs. Robinson
Sunporch Cha-Cha-Cha
Scarborough Fair/Canticle (Interlude)
On the Strip
April Come She Will
The Folks
Scarborough Fair/Canticle
A Great Effect
The Big Bright Green Pleasure Machine
Whew
Mrs. Robinson
The Sounds of Silence

1970

Bridge Over Troubled Water (Columbia KCS 9914)

Bridge Over Troubled Water
El Condor Pasa

Cecilia
Keep the Customer Satisfied
So Long, Frank Lloyd Wright
The Boxer
Baby Driver
The Only Living Boy in New York
Why Don't You Write Me?
Bye Bye Love
Song for the Asking

1972

Simon and Garfunkel's Greatest Hits (Columbia PC 31350)

Bridge Over Troubled Water
Mrs. Robinson
The Sound of Silence
The Boxer
The 59th Street Bridge Song (Feelin' Groovy)
Scarborough Fair/Canticle
I Am a Rock
Kathy's Song
Cecelia
America
Bookends
Homeward Bound
El Condor Pasa (If I Could)
For Emily, Whenever I May Find Her

1981

The Concert in Central Park (Warner Brothers 2 BSK 3654)

Record 1:
Mrs. Robinson
Homeward Bound
America
Me and Julio Down by the Schoolyard
Scarborough Fair/Canticle
April Come She Will
Wake Up Little Suzie

Still Crazy After All These Years
American Tune
Late in the Evening
Record 2:
Slip Slidin' Away
A Heart in New York
Kodachrome
Maybelline
Bridge Over Troubled Water
50 Ways to Leave Your Lover
The Boxer
Old Friends
The 59th Street Bridge Song (Feelin' Groovy)
The Sound of Silence

Paul Simon Solo Albums

1965
The Paul Simon Songbook (London, CBS)

I Am a Rock
Leaves That Are Green
A Church is Burning
April Come She Will
The Sounds of Silence
A Most Peculiar Man
He Was My Brother
Kathy's Song
The Side of a Hill
A Simple Desultory Philippic (Or How I Was Robert McNamara'd into Submission)
Flowers Never Bend with the Rainfall
Patterns

1971
Paul Simon (Columbia KC 30750)

Mother and Child Reunion
Duncan

Everything Put Together Falls Apart
Run That Body Down
Armistice Day
Me and Julio Down by the Schoolyard
Peace Like a River
Papa Hobo
Hobo's Blues
Paranoia Blues
Congratulations

1973

There Goes Rhymin' Simon (Columbia KC 32280)

Kodachrome
Tenderness
Take Me to the Mardi Gras
Something So Right
One Man's Ceiling Is Another Man's Floor
American Tune
Was a Sunny Day
Learn How to Fall
St. Judy's Comet
Loves Me Like a Rock

1974

Live Rhymin' (Columbia PC 32855)

Me and Julio Down by the Schoolyard
Homeward Bound
American Tune
El Condor Pasa (If I Could)
Duncan
The Boxer
Mother and Child Reunion
The Sounds of Silence
Jesus Is the Answer
Bridge Over Troubled Water
Loves Me Like a Rock
America

1975
Paul Simon: Still Crazy After All These Years (Columbia 35032)

Still Crazy After All These Years
My Little Town
I Do It For Your Love
50 Ways to Leave Your Lover
Night Game
Gone at Last
Some Folks Lives Roll Easy
Have a Good Time
Duncan
Me and Julio Down by the Schoolyard
Something So Right

1977
Paul Simon—Greatest Hits, Etc. (Columbia 35032)

Slip Sliding Away
Stranded In a Limousine
Still Crazy After All These Years
Have a Good Time
Duncan
Me and Julio Down by the Schoolyard
Something So Right
Kodachrome
I Do It for Your Love
50 Ways to Leave Your Lover
American Tune
Mother and Child Reunion
Loves Me Like a Rock
Take Me to the Mardi Gras

1980
One-Trick Pony (Warner Brothers HS 3472)

Late in the Evening
That's Why God Made the Movies
One-Trick Pony

How the Heart Approaches What It Yearns
Oh Marion
Ace in the Hole
Nobody
Jonah
God Bless the Absentee
Long, Long Day

1981

Hearts and Bones *(Warner Brothers W1-23942)*

Allergies
Hearts and Bones
When Numbers Get Serious
Think Too Much (b)
Song About the Moon
Think Too Much (a)
Train in the Distance
Rene and Georgette Magritte with Their Dog After the War
Cars Are Cars
The Late Great Johnny Ace

1986

Graceland *(Warner Brothers 25447-2)*

The Boy in the Bubble
Graceland
I Know What I Know
Gumboots
Diamonds on the Soles of Her Shoes
You Can Call Me Al
Under African Skies
Homeless
Crazy Love: Vol. II
That Was Your Mother
All Around the World or the Myth of Fingerprints

1988
Negotiations and Love Songs (Warner Brothers 25789)

Mother and Child Reunion
Me and Julio Down by the Schoolyard
Something So Right
St. Judy's Comet
Loves Me Like a Rock
Kodachrome
Have a Good Time
50 Ways to Leave Your Lover
Still Crazy After All These Years
Late in the Evening
Slip Slidin' Away
Hearts and Bones
Train in the Distance
Rene and Georgette Magritte with Their Dog After the War
Diamonds on the Soles of Her Shoes
You Can Call Me Al

1990
The Rhythm of the Saints (Warner Brothers 122 26098-2)

The Obvious Child
Can't Run, But
The Coast
Proof
Further to Fly
She Moves On
Born at the Right Time
The Cool, Cool River
Spirit Voices
The Rhythm of the Saints

1993
Paul Simon: 1964–1993 (Warner Brothers 9 45394-2)

Disc 1:
Leaves That Are Green

The Sound of Silence
Kathy's Song
America
Cecilia
El Condor Pasa (If I Could)
The Boxer
Mrs. Robinson
Bridge Over Troubled Water (demo)
Bridge Over Troubled Water
The Breakup (dialogue)
Hey, Schoolgirl
My Little Town
Me and Julio Down by the Schoolyard
Peace Like a River
Mother and Child Reunion
Congratulations
Duncan
American Tune
Disc 2:
Loves Me Like a Rock
Tenderness
Kodachrome
Gone at Last
Take Me to the Mardi Gras
St. Judy's Comet
Something So Right
Still Crazy After All These Years
Have a Good Time
Jonah
How the Heart Approaches What It Yearns
50 Ways to Leave Your Lover
Slip Slidin' Away
Late in the Evening
Hearts and Bones
Rene and Georgette Magritte with Their Dog After the War
The Late Great Johnny Ace
Disc 3:
The Boy in the Bubble
Graceland

Under African Skies
That Was Your Mother
Diamonds on the Soles of Her Shoes
You Can Call Me Al
Homeless
Spirit Voices
The Obvious Child
Can't Run But
Thelma
Further to Fly
She Moves On
Born at the Right Time
The Cool, Cool River
The Sound of Silence

Simon and Garfunkel Singles

1966

The Sounds of Silence/We've Got a Groovy Thing Going (Columbia 43396)
Homeward Bound/Leaves That Are Green (Columbia 43511)
Flowers Never Bend With the Rainfall/I Am a Rock (Columbia 43617)
The Dangling Conversation/The Big Bright Green Pleasure Machine (Columbia 43728)
A Hazy Shade of Winter/For Emily, Whenever I May Find Her (Columbia 43873)

1967

At the Zoo/The 59th Street Bridge Song (Feelin' Groovy) (Columbia 44046)

1968

Fakin' It/You Don't Know Where Your Interest Lies (Columbia 44232)
Scarborough Fair/April Come She Will (Columbia 44465)
Mrs. Robinson/ Old Friends/Bookends (Columbia 44511)

1969

The Boxer/Baby Driver (Columbia 44785)

1970

Bridge Over Troubled Water/Keep the Customer Satisfied (Columbia 45079)
Cecilia/The Only Living Boy in New York (Columbia 45133)
El Condor Pasa (If I Could)/Why Don't You Write Me (Columbia 45237)

1972

For Emily, Whenever I May Find Her/America (Columbia 45663)
My Little Town/Rag Doll/P.S. You're So Kind (Columbia 10230)

Simon and Garfunkel Singles Released as "Tom and Jerry"

1957

Hey Schoolgirl/Dancin' Wild (Big 613)

1958

Don't Say Goodbye/That's My Story (Big 618)
Our Song/Two Teenagers (Big 619)
Baby Talk/Two Teenagers (Big 621)

1959

That's My Story/Don't Say Goodbye (Hunt 319)
Baby Talk (Tom and Jerry)/I'm Going to Get Married (Ronnie Lawrence) (Bell 120)

1960

Hey Schoolgirl/Dancin' Wild (King 45-5167)

1962

Surrender, Please Surrender/Fightin' Mad (ABC-Paramount 45-10363)
That's My Story/Tijuana Blues (ABC-Paramount 45-10788)

As "True Taylor"

1958

True or False/Teen Age Fool (Big 614)

As "Tico" of "Tico and the Triumphs"

1960
Motorcycle/I Don't Believe Them (Madison M-169)
Cry Little Boy Cry/Get Up and Do the Wobble (Amy 860)
Express Train/Wildflower (Amy 845)
Motorcycle/I Don't Believe Them (Amy 835)

As "Jerry Landis"

1961
Cards of Love/Noise (Amy 876)
The Lonely Teen Ranger/Lisa (Amy 875)
Cards of Love/Noise (Amy 861)

1962
The Lonely Teen Ranger/Lisa (Jason Scott Records 22)
I'm Lonely/Wish I Weren't in Love (Can-Am 130)
Swanee/Toot, Toot Tootsie, Goodbye (Warwick 522)
Just a Boy/Shy (Warwick 552)
I Want to Be the Lipstick On Your Collar/Just a Boy (Warwick 588)
Play Me a Sad Song/It Means a Lot (Warwick 619)
Anna Belle/Loneliness (MGM K-12822)

As "Paul Kane"

1963

Carlos Dominguez/He Was My Brother (Tribute 1746)

Filmography

1967

The Graduate

An Embassy Production, distributed by United Artists

Filmed in Panavision Technicolor

Starring Dustin Hoffman, Anne Bancroft, Katherine Ross, Murray Hamilton, William Daniels, Elizabeth Wilson

Producer—Lawrence Turman

Director—Mike Nichols

Photographer—Robert Surtees

Songs by Paul Simon: Mrs. Robinson; The Sounds of Silence; April Come She Will; Scarborough Fair/Canticle; The Big Bright Green Pleasure Machine.

Additional music composed and conducted by David Grusin

105 minutes

Shampoo

A Vista Production

Technicolor

Starring: Warren Beatty, Julie Christie, Lee Grant, Goldie Hawn, Jack Warden, Tony Bill

Producer—Warren Beatty

Director—Hal Ashby

Photographer—Laszlo Kovacs

Music by Paul Simon

110 minutes

Annie Hall

United Artists

Color by De Luxe

Starring: Woody Allen, Diane Keaton, Tony Roberts, Carol Kane, Paul Simon, Shelly Duvall

Producer—Jack Rollin/Charles H. Joffee

Director—Woody Allen

Photographer—Gordon Willis

Music: Various

93 minutes

One-Trick Pony

Warner Brothers

Technicolor

Starring: Paul Simon, Blair Brown, Lou Reed, Tiny Tim

Producers—Michael Tannen, Michael Hansman

Director—Robert M. Young

Photographer—Richard Bush

Music by Paul Simon

Songs: Late in the Evening; That's Why God Made the Movies; One-Trick Pony; How the Heart Approaches What it Yearns; Oh, Marion; Ace in the Hole; Jonah; God Bless the Absentee; Long, Long Day

118 minutes

Selected Bibliography

Allen, Jennifer, "The Apostle of Angst," *Esquire*, June 1987.

Alterman, Loraine, "Paul Simon," *Rolling Stone*, May 28, 1970.

———, "There Goes Rhymin' Simon," *New York Times*, May 6, 1973, p. 30.

Ames, Morgan, "Simon & Garfunkel in Action," *High Fidelity*, November 1967, pp. 62–66.

Associated Press, "Paul Simon Removed From U.N. Boycott List," *New York Times*, February 3, 1987.

"AT&T Hangs Up on Simon & Garfunkel," *Rolling Stone*, January 21, 1970.

Bayles, Martha, *Hole In Our Soul: The Loss of Beauty & Meaning in American Popular Music*, Chicago: The University of Chicago Press, 1994.

Christgau, Robert, "South African Romance," *Village Voice*, September 23, 1986.

Cocks, Jay, "Songs of a Thinking Man," *Time*, November 12, 1990, pp. 112–114.

Cohen, Mitchell S., *Simon & Garfunkel: A Biography in Words & Pictures*, Sire Books, Chappell & Co, Inc., 1977.

Contreras, Joseph, "Caught in the Cross-Fire," *Newsweek*, January 20, 1992, pp. 58–59.

Cowan, Paul, "Paul Simon: The Odysseus of Urban Melancholy," *Rolling Stone*, July 1, 1976.

Current Biography Yearbook, 1975, edited by Current Biography staff, New York: H. W. Wilson, 1975.

Dannen, Fredric, *Hit Men,* New York: Vintage Books, 1990.

Davis, Clive, with James Willwerth, *Clive: Inside the Record Business,* New York: William Morrow & Co., 1975, pp. 249–259.

Dwyer, Jim, "Doo-Wop Tells a Story of the '50s," *Newsday,* May 31, 1995, p. A2.

Eldridge, Royston, "What Friendship Means to Simon and Garfunkel," *Melody Maker,* June 7, 1969.

Fong-Torres, Ben, "The *Rolling Stone* Interview with Art Garfunkel," *Rolling Stone,* October 11, 1973.

Fricke, David, "Paul Simon's Amazing Graceland Tour," *Rolling Stone,* July 2, 1987.

Gates, David, "In Praise of Midlife Crisis," *Newsweek,* January 14, 1991.

Glass, Philip, "Graceland and Beyond," liner notes from *Paul Simon: 1964/1993,* Warner Brothers Records.

Gleason, Ralph, "The Artistry of Simon & Garfunkel," *Jazz & Pop,* July 1968.

Green, Jesse, "The Song Is Ended," *New York Times Magazine,* June 2, 1996.

Greenfeld, Josh, "For Simon and Garfunkel," *New York Times Magazine,* October 13, 1968.

Guterman, Jimmy, and Owen O'Donnell, *The Worst Rock 'n' Roll Records of All Time,* New York: Carol Publishing Group, 1991.

Heckman, Don, "View from Simon's Bridge," *New York Times,* February 27, 1972.

Hodenfeld, Jan, "Paul Simon. . . To A Different Drummer," *The New York Post,* May 26, 1973.

Holden, Stephen, "Simon and Garfunkel—A Greatest Hits Album That Lives Up to Its Name," *Rolling Stone,* August 3, 1972.

———, "Class Reunion: It Looks Like a Lasting Thing," *Rolling Stone,* March 18, 1982.

———, "Backbeat: Simon & Garfunkel. Maybe," *High Fidelity,* May 1982, pp. 62–64.

———, "Can a Pop Composer Help Out Broadway?" *New York Times,* September 24, 1995.

Howlett, Kevin, "The Early Years," liner notes from *Paul Simon: 1964/1993,* Warner Brothers Records.

Humphries, Patrick, *Paul Simon: Still Crazy After All These Years*, New York: Doubleday, 1988.

Landau, Jon, "The *Rolling Stone* Interview with Paul Simon," *Rolling Stone*, July 20, 1972.

Maren, Michael, "The Sins of Paul Simon," *Africa Report*, July–August 1987.

Marsh, Dave, "What to Do When You're Not a Kid Anymore and You Still Want to Rock & Roll?" *Rolling Stone*, October 30, 1980.

Matthew-Walker, Robert, *Simon and Garfunkel*, Hippocrene Books, Inc., 1984.

Mgxashe, Mxolisi, "A Conversation with Ray Phiri," *Africa Report*, July–August 1987.

Morella, Joseph, and Patricia Barey, *Simon and Garfunkel: Old Friends, A Dual Biography*, New York: Carol Publishing Group, 1991.

Murphy, Karen, and Gross, Ronald, "'All You Need Is Love. Love Is All You Need,'" *New York Times Magazine*, April 13, 1969.

Novicki, Margaret A., and Akhalwaya, Ameen, "Interview with Hugh Masekela," *Africa Report*, July–August 1987.

Orth, Maureen, "Simon Says," *Newsweek*, December 15, 1975.

Pareles, Jon, "Talkin' 'Bout Two Generations—At Odds," *New York Times*, May 5, 1996.

Pollock, Bruce, "Paul Simon: Survivor from the Sixties," *Stereo Review*, June 12, 1976.

"Pop Think In: Paul Simon," *Melody Maker*, April 30, 1966, p. 7.

Robins, Wayne, "Simon Says: 'The Rhythm of the Saints' Started with the Sound of Brazilian Percussion. Then Came the Music and Last, The Words," *Newsday*, October 14, 1990.

Robinson, Lisa, "Simply Great Simon," *New York Post*, October 4, 1993.

Sandall, Robert, "The Man Who Still Packs A Song In His Art," *The Sunday Times*, October 28, 1990.

Scott, Walter, from "Personality Parade," *Newsday*, July 21, 1996.

Scherman, Tony, "Words and Music by Paul Simon," *Life* Magazine, November 1993.

Schwartz, Tony, "It's Simon and Garfunkel Again," *New York Times*, February 28, 1982.

————, "*Playboy* Interview: Paul Simon," *Playboy*, February 1984.

Sparks, Daniel, "Simon Defends S.A. Trip, New Album," *The Hilltop* (student newspaper of Howard University), vol. 70, no. 4.

Stevenson, James, "Simon and Garfunkel," *The New Yorker*, September 2, 1967.

Steyn, Mark (interviewer), *Paul Simon Solo*, TV Rock Documentary, BBC TV production, 1987.

Swartley, Ariel, "Love Me, Love My Lyrics," *New York Times*, June 14, 1992.

Trow, George W. S. "Growing Up is Hard To Do," *Harper's Magazine*, 1976.

Whitburn, Joel, *The Billboard Book of Top 40 Albums*, 3rd ed., New York: Billboard Books, 1995.

White, Timothy, *Rock Lives*, Henry Holt and Company, Inc., 1990.

Zollo, Paul, "Garfunkel," *SongTalk*, Spring 1990.

————, "Recording with Roy Halee," *SongTalk*, Spring 1990.

————, "Paul Simon; The *SongTalk* Interviews, Parts One and Two," *SongTalk*, Spring 1990, Fall 1990.

————, "The Solo Years," liner notes from *Paul Simon: 1964/1993*, Warner Brothers Records.

Zolotow, Sam, "Dustin Hoffman to Try Broadway," *New York Times*, May 20, 1968, p. 58.

Permissions

Guterman, Jimmy, and Owen O'Donnell, "The Dangling Conversation," excerpt from *The Worst Rock 'n' Roll Records of All Time,* New York: Carol Publishing Group, 1991, pp. 32–33. Copyright © 1991 by Jimmy Guterman and Owen O'Donnell. Published by arrangement with Carol Publishing Group. A Citadel Press Book.

Holden, Stephen, "Simon and Garfunkel—A Greatest Hits Album That Lives Up to Its Name," *Rolling Stone,* August 3, 1972. © by Straight Arrow Publishers, Inc., 1972. All rights reserved. Reprinted by permission.

Landau, Jon, "The Rolling Stone Interview with Paul Simon," *Rolling Stone,* July 20, 1972. © by Straight Arrow Publishers, Inc., 1972. All rights reserved. Reprinted by permission.

Cowan, Paul, "Paul Simon: The Odysseus of Urban Melancholy," *Rolling Stone,* July 1, 1976. © by Straight Arrow Publishers, Inc., 1976. All rights reserved. Reprinted by permission.

Trow, George W. S. "Growing Up is Hard to Do," *Harper's Magazine,* 1976. Copyright © 1976 by *Harper's Magazine.* All rights reserved. Reproduced from the April issue by special permission.

Pollock, Bruce, "Paul Simon: Survivor from the Sixties," *Stereo Review,* June 12, 1976, pp. 43–44, 59. Copyright © 1976 by Hachette Filipacchi Magazines, Inc. All rights reserved. Reprinted from Stereo Review, June 1976, with permission.

Marsh, Dave, "What to Do When You're Not a Kid Anymore and You Still Want to Rock & Roll?" *Rolling Stone,* October 30, 1980. © by Straight Arrow Publishers, Inc., 1980. All rights reserved. Reprinted by permission.

Schwartz, Tony, "It's Simon and Garfunkel Again," *New York Times,* February 28, 1982. Copyright © 1982 by The New York Times Co. Reprinted by permission.

Schwartz, Tony, "Playboy Interview: Paul Simon," *Playboy* magazine, February 1984. Copyright © 1984 by Playboy. All rights reserved. Used with permission.

Fricke, David, "Paul Simon's Amazing Graceland Tour," *Rolling Stone,* July 2, 1987. © by Straight Arrow Publishers, Inc., 1987. All rights reserved. Reprinted by permission.

Maren, Michael, "The Sins of Paul Simon," *Africa Report,* July–August 1987. Reprinted by permission of Africa Report, copyright 1987.

Mgxashe, Mxolisi, "A Conversation with Ray Phiri,"*Africa Report,* July–August 1987. Reprinted by permission of Africa Report, copyright 1987.

Novicki, Margaret A., and Ameen, Akhalwaya, "Interview with Hugh Masekela," *Africa Report,* July–August 1987. Reprinted by permission of Africa Report, copyright 1987.

Allen, Jennifer, "The Apostle of Angst," *Esquire,* June 1987. Reprinted by permission of author.

Christgau, Robert, "South African Romance," *Village Voice,* September 23, 1986. Reprinted by permission of the author and The Village Voice.

Zollo, Paul, "Recording with Roy Halee," *SongTalk,* Spring 1990. © 1990 SongTalk. Reprinted by permission.

Cocks, Jay, "Songs of a Thinking Man," *Time,* November 12, 1990, pp. 112–114. © 1990 Time Inc. Reprinted by permission.

Robins, Wayne, "Simon Says: 'The Rhythm of the Saints' Started with the Sound of Brazilian Percussion. Then Came the Music and Last, The Words," *Newsday,* October 14, 1990, p. 4. Newsday, Inc., Copyright 1990. Reprinted by permission.

Zollo, Paul, "Paul Simon; The *SongTalk* Interviews, Parts One and Two," *SongTalk,* Spring 1990, Fall 1990. © 1990, SongTalk. Reprinted by permission.

Dwyer, Jim, "Doo-Wop Tells a Story of the '50s," *Newsday,* May 31, 1995, p. A2. Newsday, Inc., Copyright 1995. Reprinted by permission.

Index

Dylan, Bob (*cont.*)
    in the seventies, 125
    and Simon, 3, 6, 7, 13, 33, 36, 111,
        215, 234
    style of, 72

"Earth Angel," 242
Earthworks (group), 181
"El Condor Pasa," 65, 73, 79, 83, 86,
    88, 230
"El Watusi" (Barretto), 206
"Eleanor Rigby" (Beatles), 103
election of 1968, 122
elitist rock, 71
Ellington, Duke, 156
encores, 25
Everly Brothers, 3, 7, 34, 39, 145, 182
exiles, South African, 152, 157, 158,
        164, 168, 169–70, 171–72,
        186
Exodus, The (film), 62
Eyerly, Scott, 227

"Fakin' It," 72, 95–96
Falwell, Jerry, 179
Fame (film), 132
Farber, Mr., 114–16, 117
"Feelin' Groovy (Fifty-ninth Street
        Bridge Song)," 7, 68, 72, 103,
        118
fifties music, 3, 20, 124, 129, 145, 222,
        235. *See also* pop music
"Fifty Ways to Leave Your Lover," 120,
        124, 199, 207
*Fifty Worst Rock 'n' Roll Records of All
    Time,* 70–71
"Fifty-ninth Street Bridge Song (Feelin'
        Groovy)," 7, 68, 72,103, 118
Fisher, Carrie (second wife), 132, 140,
        200, 201, 202
Fleetwoods (group), 35
"Flowers Never Bend with the Rainfall,"
        93
folk music, 3, 4, 10, 20, 41
    in Europe, 11
    and folk rock, 71, 72, 122, 131
    influence on Simon, 41–42, 234
    and Jews, 11, 12
    of Simon and Garfunkel, 70, 71, 111,
        144, 145, 201
    traditional artists in, 12
"For Emily, Wherever I May Find Her,"
        54, 68, 72

"For God's Sake Give More Power to
        the People" (Chi-Lites), 101
For the Roses (Mitchell), 123
Forest Hills, 113, 201
Forest Hills High School, 4, 118, 206,
        243
Forest Hills Music Festival perfor-
        mances, 24–25
Frampton, Peter, 132
Frankie Lymon and the Teenagers
        (group), 206
Franklin, Aretha, 25, 28–29, 74, 102,
        215
"Free Nelson Mandela," 153
Freed, Alan, 5, 40, 206
Freewheelin' Bob Dylan, 41, 42
Frost, Robert, 71
fundraising, 97–98
funk, 130, 145, 183, 185

Gabriel, Peter, 230
Garba, Evelyn, 166
Garba, Joseph, 165, 166, 175, 177
Garfunkel, Art, 201
    and acting, 58–59, 81, 105, 136,
        138, 201
    appearance of, 4, 12, 19
    arranging by, 4, 45–46, 53, 82
    in *Bad Timing—A Sensual Obsession,*
        138
    in *Carnal Knowledge,* 36, 80
    in *Catch-22,* 26, 58, 65, 82, 84,
        201
    at Columbia, 5, 6, 41
    contributions to Simon and
        Garfunkel, 23, 145
    and Dylan, 41–42
    early years of, 39–41
    education of, 4–5
    as Art Garr, 12, 41
    income of, 19–20, 65
    and Laurie Bird, 138
    lyric writing by, 53
    musical preferences and styles of,
        136, 139
    and names, 9, 11–12
    and performing, 6
    personality of, 5, 86
    in recording sessions, 27
    relationship with Simon, 14, 15, 23,
        49, 57–60, 62, 79–86, 202
    singing by, 4, 136, 137, 145
    solo acts of, 14, 42

Manhattan School of Music, 156
"La Marseillaise," 101
Martin, Dean, 107
Masekela, Hugh, 149, 150, 151, 152,
    154, 155, 156, 158, 159, 161,
    163, 164, 166, 168, 169–70,
    170–77, 173
Mathis, Johnny, 66
May, Elaine, 68
"Maybelline" (Berry), 134
"Me and Julio Down by the
    Schoolyard," 67, 68, 69,
    91–92, 118, 120, 192, 199
Meat Loaf, 132
melody, 242. *See also* Simon, Paul, on
    melody
MGM, 51
Michaels, Lorne, 199, 202
Midnight Express (film), 132
Miller, Mitch, 62
Mitchell, Joni (singer/songwriter), 120,
    122, 123, 125, 139
Mnumzana, Neo, 167, 185, 186
Montanez, Victor, 192
Morella, Joseph and Patricia Barey,
    *Simon and Garfunkel: Old
    Friends,* xiii, 3
Morrison, Jim, 123
"Most Peculiar Man, A," 94
"Mother and Child Reunion," 67, 68,
    69, 80, 88, 89, 124, 151, 196,
    201, 241
Mothobi, Jeanette, 155, 157
Motloheloa, Forere, 184
"Mr. Tambourine Man" (Dylan), 44,
    73
"Mrs. Robinson," 24, 51, 52, 62, 68,
    73, 93, 103, 122, 207
"Mrs. Roosevelt," 52
Mtshali, Isaac, 158, 183
Murray, Albert, 185
Murray the K (disc jockey), 15
music
    feud, 131–32
    industry, 6, 112. *See also* recording
        industry
    of other cultures, 77, 79, 88–89,
        149–88, 191, 203, 205, 206,
        214, 225, 231, 233–34
    See also individual musical styles
musical theater, xiv, 191, 192, 193, 205,
    236–37, 242–44. *See also*
    Broadway shows

"My Little Town," 78, 124, 137
names
    of Dylan, 3, 5, 11
    of Simon and Garfunkel, 3, 5, 9,
        11–12
NBC, 108, 109
N'Dour, Youssou, 182
Nederlander Theater, 242
Nelson, Ricky, 139
Never on Sunday (film), 6, 381
New Christy Minstrels, 11
new wave avant–gardism, 130, 136
New York Rock and Roll Ensemble, 38
New York Univerisity, 26, 32–35, 177
Newman, Randy, 126, 214, 217
NGOs (non-governmental organiza-
    tions), 167
Nichols, Mike, 15, 36, 37, 51, 59, 50,
    62, 63, 64, 65, 68, 136
Nicholson, Jack, 36
Nixon, Richard, 99
"N'Kosi Sikeleli" ("God Bless Africa"),
    152, 154, 168
Noland, Kenneth, 136
Nylon Curtain, The (Joel), 182
Nyro, Laura, 122, 123, 125

"Obvious Child, The," 199, 206
Ochs, Phil, 122, 123, 125
"Oh Marion," 212
"Old Friends," 50, 51, 137
Olodum (group), 205
"On the Side of a Hill," 42, 47
One Plus One (film), 129
"One Trick Pony," 129
One-Trick Pony (film), 78, 126–34, 138,
    140, 142, 149, 204
One-Trick Pony (soundtrack album), 78,
    133, 140, 211–12, 231–33
"Only Living Boy in New York, The,"
    32, 58, 60, 83, 93, 202
Oppenheimer, Harry, 175
Osborn, Joe, 87

Paley, William, 108
Palmer, Robert, 137
Pan Africanist Congress, 174
"Papa Hobo," 91
Paramount, 51
Parker, Alan, 132–33
Parsley, Sage, Rosemary and Thyme
    (album), 4, 19, 27, 30, 47, 50,
    93, 106, 201

royalties, 20, 64, 112, 157, 170, 171, 178
"Run Your Body Down," 91
Ruskin, Leonard, 25

"St. Louis Blues," 102
Sainte-Marie, Buffy, 122, 123
Salinger, J. D., *The Catcher in the Rye,* 74
salsa sounds, 243
Sanacore, Vicki, 242, 243
Sanchez, Manny, 243
Sanders Recording Studio, 35
"Satisfaction," 36
Saturday Night Live (television show), 108, 109, 129, 133, 181, 199
scalpers, 24
"Scarborough Fair," 36, 42, 47, 48, 51, 62, 103, 104, 120, 207
Schisgal, Murray, 192
Scissors Cut (Garfunkel), 138
Scott, Jack, 130
Sears, Big Al, 206
Sebastian, John, 97, 122, 123, 192
Seeger, Pete, 11
Sellers, Peter, 131
Sgt. Pepper (Beatles, album), 123
session musicians, 136
seventies, 123, 125, 126
Shabalala, Joseph, 149, 159–61, 176, 187, 188
Shabalala, Nellie, 160
Shaka Zulu (Ladysmith Black Mambazo), 152, 159, 162
Shampoo (film), 132
Shanachie label, 162, 181
Sharpeville massacre, 186
"She Moves On," 198, 200
Shelton, Robert, 13
Showtime cable special, 154
Sibeko, Elizabeth, 174
Silber, Irwin, 21
"Silent Night/7 O'Clock News," 47, 120
Simon, Adrian (son), 294
Simon, Belle (mother), 206
Simon, Eddie (brother), 14, 23, 64, 95
Simon and Garfunkel: Old Friends (Morella and Barey), xiii, 3
Simon and Garfunkel, 22–23, 145, 207, 215
    and AT&T television show, 37–83
    breakup of, 58–60, 61, 65–66, 68, 77, 79–86, 103–6, 118, 122, 124, 135–36, 202
    and Clive Davis, 61–70
    critics of, 21, 85–86
    Garfunkel's contributions, 23
    and groupies, 96
    and Halee, 193–95
    harmony of, 46, 53, 93, 105, 136
    message of, 19, 31
    names of, 3, 5, 9, 11–12
    pop music of, 4, 18
    record sales of, 4, 19
    recording "Punky's Dilemma," 14–18
    reunion concert in Central Park, 78, 135–39, 140, 142–44, 202
    Simon's contributions, 23
    sound and style of, 19, 72, 93
    success of, 22
    superstardom of, 64
    touring by, 46, 81, 84, 104, 135, 143, 144, 196
Simon and Garfunkel's Greatest Hits, 71–74
Simon, Harper (son), 79, 109, 117, 134, 198, 202, 229
Simon, John, 15, 16–17
Simon, Louis (father), 24, 64, 206, 216
Simon, Lulu (daughter), 294
Simon, Paul
    and analysts, 26, 113, 140–42
    appearance of, 4, 12, 18–19, 26
    and bands, 127, 138, 129, 142, 206
    "bridge fixation" of, 72
    as businessman, 112
    on chord changes, 216, 229
    contributions to Simon and Garfunkel, 23, 145
    and control, 6, 8, 65, 107, 118, 127, 132–33
    and critics, 13, 106, 124–25, 131, 133, 138, 157, 240
    on death, 90
    depressions of, 77, 78, 108–9, 122, 140–42, 149
    and drugs, 25, 108, 110, 123
    and Dylan, 3, 6, 7, 13, 33, 36, 111, 215, 243
    early years of, 39–41, 206
    education of, 4–5
    experimentation by, 77–79, 136, 182–83

Simon, Paul (*cont.*)
　　on *Graceland* tour, 151–63
　　guitar by, 4
　　on happiness, 37
　　Howard University appearance,
　　　　177–80
　　and humor, 91
　　imagery and symbolism of, 7, 43,
　　　　111, 130, 211, 213, 230
　　on imagination, 216–17
　　income of, 19–20, 21, 112–13,
　　　　131–32
　　on interviews, 6, 26
　　Jewish heritage of, 113–16
　　on lyrics, 22, 31–32, 111, 124, 130,
　　　　217–18, 221, 235
　　and marriage, 22, 23, 122, 124, 140,
　　　　198, 200, 201, 202
　　on melody, 31–32, 221–22, 228, 229,
　　　　230
　　musical influences on, 3, 7, 34, 41,
　　　　47, 128, 129–30, 145, 215–16,
　　　　234–36
　　musical preferences and styles of,
　　　　136, 139, 201
　　and musical theater, xiv, 191, 192,
　　　　193, 205, 236–37, 242–44
　　and names, 3, 5, 9, 11–12
　　nightmare of, 107, 118
　　and performing, 6, 117, 144
　　　　in Europe, 10–11, 13–14, 43,
　　　　　　44–45
　　personal life of, 21–22, 109–10
　　personality of, 5, 8, 37, 49, 54, 79,
　　　　107, 110, 112–13, 122, 203,
　　　　240
　　physical problems of, 110, 142
　　and poetry, 5, 7, 22, 70–71, 73, 111,
　　　　200, 235–36
　　on producing, 27
　　on recording sessions, 27–28, 86
　　relationship with Garfunkel, 14, 15,
　　　　23, 49, 57–60, 62, 79–86, 202
　　screenplay by, 236
　　singing by, 4, 137, 237–38
　　as sixties survivor, 121–26
　　solo albums of, 66–70, 77–79, 120,
　　　　124, 195, 201
　　songwriting by, 4, 5–6, 123–25,
　　　　129–30, 137, 226–27, 230–34
　　　　process of, 7, 10–11, 22, 33, 130,
　　　　　　191–92, 203–7, 208–23, 225,
　　　　　　233

　　study of music by, 110–11, 123, 124,
　　　　130, 238–39
　　style of, 72, 180
　　on subconscious, 219
　　teaching, 26, 32–33
　　on tour, 69–70, 79, 110, 133–34
　　and writer's block, 140–42, 210–11
　　See also music, of other cultures;
　　　　United Nations, boycott
Simon, Peggy Harper (first wife), 79, 81,
　　　　85, 87, 90, 113, 117, 134
"Simple Desultory Phillipic, A," 49
Sinatra, Frank, 25, 99, 139
Singer, Isaac Bashevis, 116
single cuts, 46–47
single recordings, 122
Sivuca (Brazilian musician), 77
sixties, 102, 107, 111, 120, 121, 125,
　　　　126, 222, 234
ska, 90, 123
Sky, Pat, 122, 125
slavery, 223–24
"Slip Slidin' Away," 216
Smile (Nyro, album), 125
Smith, Bessie, 102
SNCC. *See* Student Nonviolent
　　　　Coordinating Committee
Snow, Phoebe, 116
"So Long, Frank Lloyd Wright," 58, 60,
　　　　202
social movements, 11–12. *See also* politi-
　　　　cal movements
"Soft Parachutes," 232
"Somebody to Love," 30
Songwriters on Songwriters (Zollo), xiv,
　　　　208
songwriting
　　political, 153, 157–58, 162, 176–77,
　　　　180, 186–88
　　of the sixties, 121–26
Soukous, 181
soul, 185, 242
Soul Brothers (group), 181
Sound of Silence (album), 27, 47, 62,
　　　　93–94
"Sounds of Silence, The," 6, 10, 36, 43,
　　　　44, 45, 51, 61, 62, 68, 69, 71,
　　　　72–73, 103, 109, 115, 118, 120,
　　　　122, 127, 131, 201, 229, 234
South Africa, 149, 155, 174, 185
　　student union, 179
South American music, 77, 79, 88, 89,
　　　　149–88

About the Editor

Stacey Luftig is a playwright, lyricist, and editor living in New York City. Her work for the stage has been performed off-Broadway and across the U.S., and currently she is writing the book and lyrics for *Hercules,* a children's musical. Luftig is a former award-winning copywriter for Ogilvy & Mather Direct, and has been a guest lecturer at Pace University and New York University.